A GUIDE TO AMERICAN CATHOLIC HISTORY

A
GUIDE TO
AMERICAN CATHOLIC
HISTORY

Second Edition,
Revised and Enlarged

JOHN TRACY ELLIS
and
ROBERT TRISCO

ABC-Clio

Santa Barbara, California   Oxford, England

Library of Congress Cataloging in Publication Data

Ellis, John Tracy, 1905–
   A guide to American Catholic history.

   Includes index: p. 205
   1. Catholic Church—United States—History—Biblio-
graphy.   2. United States—Church history—Bibliography.
I. Trisco, Robert Frederick.   II. Title.
Z7778.U6E38   1981   [BX1406.2]   016.282'73   81–17585
ISBN 0–87436–318–7   AACR2
ISBN 0–87436–315–2 - Paper

ABC-Clio, Inc.
Riviera Campus
2040 Alameda Padre Serra, Box 4397
Santa Barbara, California 93103

Clio Press Ltd.
Woodside House, Hinksey Hill
Oxford, OX1 5BE, England

Manufactured in the United States of America

CONTENTS

Preface to the First Edition

AT THE TIME that I was appointed in July, 1941, to take over the courses in American Catholic history of the late Monsignor Peter Guilday, I was granted a year's leave of absence to familiarize myself with this new field. I spent a good portion of that year at Harvard University where I set about compiling a bibliography for my personal use and the use of my future students. After it had circulated in mimeographed form for several years a publisher who had come on a copy of the work suggested in 1946 that it be put in print. The result was *A Select Bibliography of the History of the Catholic Church in the United States* (New York, 1947). While that work served to acquaint students and other interested persons with the extant literature on American Catholicism, it had several basic defects which could not be eliminated except by a radical revision. One of these defects was including the titles of books in general American history in the mistaken notion that it might facilitate their use as background material for the Catholic history of the nation. Actually there was no such need for there were numerous bibliographies covering every phase of American history, and since that time the *Harvard Guide to American History* (Cambridge, 1954) has provided an amplitude of titles on every aspect of the nation's past and thus serves adequately for the background necessary to a proper understanding of American Catholic history. It has been thought proper, therefore, in the present work to eliminate all items that are not directly related to the field of the Catholic history of the United States.

The general divisions of material will, I think, be self-explanatory, and as an additional aid to those who will use this volume several subdivisions have been provided with further introductory notes concerning the nature and limitations of the items listed under the respective headings. The divisions in themselves reveal both the strength and weakness of the present literature on American Catholicism. For example, there is a relative scarcity of scholarly histories of dioceses and parishes, whereas the number and quality of the items in the category of biographies is correspondingly high. Again there are certain pitfalls that await the student who is in search of histories of religious communities and of books in the history of American Catholic education, and these have been indicated in the introductory notes. In the division entitled "Special Studies," it will be found that works on Nativism in its anti-Catholic phases are fairly numerous and substantial, while those on Catholic colonization, journalism, and the numerous national groups that have gone to make up the American Catholic community are rather few, and some of these are not of a scientific character. In other words, it is hoped that the GUIDE may serve to emphasize in the minds of those who use it the need for further research and writing in certain areas as well as to afford them an introduction to what has already been published.

In the compilation of this work, as was true of the volume *Documents of American Catholic History* (Milwaukee, 1956), I have above all become indebted to the students in my seminar who during the past few years have given me a great deal of assistance in tracking down books and in working up critical comments on them. I am happy to acknowledge my gratitude, therefore, to the Reverends George J. Bryan, C.SS.R., Carl D. Hinrichsen, Oscar H. Lipscomb, Francis G. McManamin, S.J., Claude Seeberger, O.S.B., and Fintan Warren, O.F.M., who as members of the seminar were exceedingly helpful at all times. I am likewise under obligation to the Reverend Robert F. McNamara, professor of church history in St. Bernard's Seminary, for taking the time, when he could ill afford to do so, to go over the entire manuscript and to offer many excellent suggestions and criticisms. For a similar service I wish to thank Mr. Eugene P. Willging, director of libraries of the Catholic University of America. And my good friend, the Very Reverend Louis A. Arand, S.S., of the Catholic University of America went quite beyond the call of duty as ecclesiastical censor in kindly calling to my attention a number of inaccuracies and obscure points. The manuscript was also read in part, especially the section entitled "Manuscript Depositories," by the following to whom I am grateful for their suggesions and corrections: the Reverends Colman J. Barry, O.S.B., of St. John's University, Collegeville; Francis X. Curran, S.J., of Loyola Seminary, Shrub Oak; William L. Davis, S.J., of Gonzaga University; Joseph A. Gorham of the Catholic University of America; Thomas T. McAvoy, C.S.C., of the University of Notre Dame; John B. McGloin, S.J., of the University of San Francisco; William C. Repetti, S.J., of Georgetown University; and James J. Hennesey, S.J., of Woodstock College. While I am anxious to acknowledge my debt to all these kind friends I would not wish to have them held in any way for whatever errors in fact or in judgment may appear in the following pages. For these I am alone responsible. Finally I wish to express my deep appreciation to my secretary, Mrs.

Ruth K. Carney, for the cheerful readiness that she showed at all times in interrupting her numerous office duties to type the manuscript and, too, to Miss Rosabelle A. Kelp for the expert manner in which she compiled the index.

John Tracy Ellis
The Catholic University of America
Washington, D.C.

December 5, 1958

Preface to the Second Edition

THE FIRST EDITION of this guide, published in 1959, was well received and soon sold out. Responding to the requests of many scholars, we have prepared this revised and expanded edition.

While retaining most of the entries contained in the first edition, we have corrected errors in them, brought the comments up to date, inserted cross references to more recent books on the same subjects, and noted subsequently published volumes of multivolume works. Furthermore, we have given the facts of publication for reprints wherever we have been aware of them; this information will be useful to those who wish to purchase books that had previously been out of print.

The section of the first edition entitled "Manuscript Depositories" has been deleted here because this area has become too vast to be covered in a guide that is predominantly bibliographical. In the past decade, especially since the celebration of the Bicentennial of American Independence, Catholic institutions of higher education, dioceses, and religious orders of men and women have professionally organized and materially enlarged their archival holdings and manuscript collections. In particular the Catholic University of America, the University of Notre Dame, and Marquette University have acquired numerous and voluminous bodies of records from important national Catholic organizations. The Center for Migration Studies, Staten Island, New York, and the Immigration History Research Center of the University of Minnesota, St. Paul, have built up extensive collections of papers and serials that are essential for the study of the history of Catholic ethnic groups in the United States. Instead of attempting to suggest the wealth of such storehouses of source materials, we must content ourselves with merely referring researchers to the *Directory of Archives and Manuscript Repositories in the United States* (Washington, D.C.: National Historical Publications and Records Commission, 1978), the second edition of which is to be published in 1981; to *A Guide to Archives and Manuscripts in the United States*, edited by Philip M. Hamer (New Haven: Yale University Press, 1961), and to the *National Union Catalog of Manuscript Collections*, compiled and edited by the Library of Congress and published annually or biennially beginning with the volume for 1959–1961. We also wish to point out two Catholic undertakings. In 1979 the American Catholic Historical Association's Committee on the History of American Catholicism, under the chairmanship of the Reverend Thomas E. Blantz, C.S.C., of the University of Notre Dame, compiled a listing of research materials preserved in 128 American diocesan archives. Copies of this compilation are available at a small charge. Secondly, the Leadership Conference of Women Religious has conducted, under the direction of Sister Evangeline Thomas, C.S.J., of Marymount College, Salina, Kansas, a nationwide survey of documentary materials to be found in approximately 650 congregations of women religious in the United States and intends to publish a guide to these archives in the near future. Although the now outdated descriptions of individual repositories which were included in the first edition have been omitted here, printed guides to archives and manuscript collections are listed in the first section of this edition.

The remaining entries have been arranged in the same order as they were in the first edition with some refinements in the subheadings and with the notable exception of the subdivisions of the section entitled "Special Studies." The proliferation of books on topics that in the past were relatively neglected has necessitated an increase in the number of different categories. Since in many cases the same title could reasonably be placed under two or even three headings, we ask the users of this guide to consult other sections if they do not find what they are seeking where they first look.

To the entries in the first edition 489 new ones have been added here. Of these, 51 are titles published before 1959, and 438 are titles published between 1959 and 1980. Though we do not claim to have fully attained our goal, we have aimed at complete coverage up to the end of 1979. If we have overlooked any substantial work that appeared within that period, we shall be grateful to anyone who will bring such a title to our attention in order that we may include it in a possible third edition of this guide.

As in the first edition, the section entitled "Biographies, Correspondence, and Memoirs" comprises the largest number of entries. We have not thought it desirable, however, to mention works of this nature pertaining to persons who, though Catholic, were not principally active as such. Thus in regard to President John Fitzgerald Kennedy we have listed only the three books that treat his life from a religious point of view.

Those who desire longer evaluations than the descriptive and critical annotations following the titles in this guide are reminded that more of these books have been reviewed in the *Catholic Historical*

Review by specialists in the respective fields than in any other learned journal.

We wish to acknowledge with sincere gratitude the assistance that we have received from others in the preparation of this new edition. Several members of the staff of the John K. Mullen Memorial Library of the Catholic University of America, especially those in the Interlibrary Loan Division, have been most helpful. Miss Rosabelle A. Kelp, who compiled the index of the first edition, has with equal thoroughness and skill performed the same task once again. Mr. Herschel Burleson of Arlington, Virginia, has very accurately and expeditiously typed the entire text. Miss Anne M. Wolf, secretary in the editorial office of the *Catholic Historical Review* and in the executive office of the American Catholic Historical Association, has contributed her efficient services in countless ways throughout the course of our labors. To all of them we offer our heartfelt thanks for their indispensable aid.

John Tracy Ellis
Robert Trisco
The Catholic University of America
Washington, D.C.

I. GUIDES

1.   Beers, Henry Putney. *The French in North America: A Bibliographical Guide to French Archives, Reproductions, and Research Missions.* Baton
Rouge: Louisiana State University Press. 1957. An excellent guide
that includes a considerable amount of ecclesiastical material located
in or reproduced from originals in French archives; relates to Canada
as well as to the United States.

2.   Cadden, John Paul. *The Historiography of the American Catholic
Church: 1785–1943.* Washington, D.C.: Catholic University of
America Press. 1944. Reprint. New York: Arno. 1978. A thesis for
the S.T.D. degree; quite comprehensive in coverage if at times
somewhat weak in critical comment; the chapter on Catholic historical societies offers a handy summary of data on these ephemeral
groups.

3.   *Catholic Periodical Index.* New York, Washington, D.C.: Catholic
Library Association. 1930–1933; 1939. Begun in 1930, this work
covers all American Catholic historical journals.

4.   Chavez, Angelico, O.F.M. *Archives of the Archdiocese of Santa Fe,
1678–1900.* Washington, D.C.: Academy of American Franciscan
History. 1957. A calendar ranging from the oldest extant mission
manuscript to papers dated at the start of this century.

5.   Ciangetti, Paul P. "A Diocesan Chronology of the Catholic
Church in the United States," *Catholic Historical Review,* XXVIII
(April, 1942), 57–70. A list of the ecclesiastical jurisdictions in the
United States down to the establishment of the Diocese of Pueblo
(November 15, 1941), alphabetically arranged with changes of juris-
diction, exact dates, and references to the official documents; a
highly useful item.

6.   Doughty, Arthur G. "Sources for the History of the Catholic
Church in the Public Archives of Canada," *Catholic Historical Review,*
XIX (July, 1933), 148–166. Relates mostly to Canada, but has some
value for colonial American Catholicism.

7.   Ellis, John Tracy. "Old Catholic Newspapers in Some Eastern Catholic Libraries," *Catholic Historical Review*, XXXIII (October, 1947), 302–305. Gives the names, volume numbers, and dates of Catholic newspaper holdings in five eastern libraries.

8.   English, Adrian T., O.P. "The Historiography of American Catholic History, 1785–1884," *Catholic Historical Review*, XI (January, 1926), 561–597. A master's thesis confined to a description and critical analysis of works that treated the American Church as a whole, e.g., the early major reports of bishops to the Congregation de Propaganda Fide such as those of Carroll (1785) and Flaget (1815), and early histories of the Church in the United States, e.g., McGee (1855) and DeCourcy-Shea (1856). Same ground covered in less detail in Chapter I of Cadden (No. 2).

9.   Fish, Carl Russell. *Guide to the Materials for American History in Roman and Other Italian Archives*. Washington, D.C.: Carnegie Institution of Washington. 1911. This old volume has worth by way of indicating the general location of the chief manuscript sources pertaining to American Catholicism, though it is superseded by Kenneally (No. 17) for the Propaganda Fide Archives.

10.   Garraghan, Gilbert J., S.J. *A Guide to Historical Method*. Ed. by Jean Delanglez, S.J. New York: Fordham University Press. 1946. More up to date than Bernheim or Feder; has added feature of some illustrative materials drawn from the history of the Catholic Church and from English and American history.

11.   Geiger, Maynard J., O.F.M. *Calendar of Documents in the Santa Barbara Mission Archives*. Washington, D.C.: Academy of American Franciscan History. 1947. A carefully compiled calendar to one of the most important depositories of manuscript material for early Catholicism in California.

12.   Gorman, Robert. *Catholic Apologetical Literature in the United States, 1784–1858*. Washington, D.C.: Catholic University of America Press. 1939. Reprint. New York: AMS. 1974. A Ph.D. thesis that describes the principal publications written in defense of Catholicism during the period covered; good for indicating one phase of Catholic reaction to the nativists and Know-Nothings.

13.   Guilday, Peter. "Catholic Lay Writers of American Catholic History," *Catholic Historical Review*, XXIII (April, 1927), 52–62. A useful list of names and titles, but comments often lacking in critical approach.

14. _____ . "Guide to the Biographical Sources of the American Hierarchy," *Catholic Historical Review*, V (April, 1919)–VI (January, 1921), 120–128; 290–296; 128–132; 267–271; 548–552. A series of references to printed materials on the lives of individual bishops, accumulated to facilitate a dictionary of the American hierarchy. The series ran alphabetically from Joseph S. Alemany (1814–1888), first Archbishop of San Francisco, to Henry Northrop (1842-1916), fourth Bishop of Charleston, but was then discontinued.

15. _____ . "Recent Studies in American Catholic History," *Ecclesiastical Review*, LXXXIV (May, 1931), 528–546. An over-all classified list of works with some critical comment, although the criticism is quite uneven; "recent" in the title is misleading since books published as early as the middle of the nineteenth century were included.

16. _____ . "The Writing of Parish Histories," *Ecclesiastical Review*, XCIII (September, 1935), 236–257. A useful item for prospective parish historians; on the same subject cf. also Henry J. Browne, "The Priest and Local History," ibid., CXXXIV (April, 1954), 251–254.

17. Kenneally, Finbar, O.F.M. *United States Documents in the Propaganda Fide Archives: A Calendar*. First series. 7 vols. Washington, D.C.: Academy of American Franciscan History. 1966–1977. All documents in the archives of the Congregation de Propaganda Fide which deal in any way with the history of the Catholic Church within the present limits of the United States from the seventeenth century to 1865 are calendared in this first series. They are divided according to archival record groups. Each entry contains an abstract of the document and the names of all persons mentioned in it and cross references link the entries whenever possible. Each volume has an index of persons, and two further volumes of a comprehensive index are planned.

18. Lane, M. Claude, Sister, O.P. *Catholic Archives of Texas: History and Preliminary Inventory*. Houston: Sacred Heart Dominican College. 1961. This mimeographed master's thesis in library science at the University of Texas contains a historical section on the work of those who collected from many depositories and preserved at Austin the records of the Catholic Church in Texas.

19. Louis, William L. *Diocesan Archives*. Washington, D.C.: Catholic University of America Press. 1941. A thesis for the J.C.D. degree that gives a historical survey of the Church's law on ecclesias-

tical archives, the legislation of the Code of Canon Law of 1918, and an accompanying commentary.

20. Lucey, William L., S.J. "Catholic Magazines, 1865–1880," *Records* of the American Catholic Historical Society of Philadelphia, LXIII (March, 1952), 21–36. In this and successive issues (LXIII [June, 1952], 85–109; [September, 1952], 133–156; [December, 1952], 197–223) the late librarian of the College of the Holy Cross assembled a convenient checklist of the most important Catholic magazines and periodicals for the period from 1865 to 1900.

21. Nolan, Charles E. *A Southern Catholic Heritage.* Vol. I: *Colonial Period, 1704–1813.* New Orleans: Archdiocese of New Orleans. 1976. This inventory describes all the records dating from the indicated years which are now located in the chancery, parish, and religious community archives in Louisiana, Alabama, and Mississippi; it is especially useful for research in local history and genealogy.

22. O'Connor, Thomas F. "The Church in Mid-America: A Selective Bibliography," *Historical Bulletin*, XIII (January, 1935), 30–32; (April, 1935), 51–52; (May, 1935), 74–76; XIV (November, 1935), 11–13. A classified list with some critical comment; not intended to be exhaustive but rather to serve as an introduction to the history of the Church in the region covered; "Mid-America" taken as the Bureau of the Census' North Central States plus Kentucky and Tennessee.

23. _____ . "Writings on United States Catholic History, 1944: A Selective Bibliography," *The Americas*, I (April, 1945), 480–485, to VI (April, 1950), 451–466. An annual classified list that ran here through six years and was then taken over by Edward R. Vollmar, S.J. (No. 32).

24. *Official Catholic Directory.* New York: P. J. Kenedy. 1912. Under various titles, editors, and publishers there has been an annual volume of this kind since 1817, with the exception of the years 1818–1821, 1823–1832, and 1863. These directories are an indispensable tool for the research student, although the statistics on population are only approximations and should be used with caution. Complete files available at the Catholic University of America (also on microfilm here) and Georgetown University. See also Joseph H. Meier, "The Official Catholic Directory," *Catholic Historical Review*, I (October, 1915), 299–304.

25. Parsons, Wilfrid, S.J. *Early Catholic Americana*. New York: Macmillan. 1939. The best guide for books written by Catholics before 1831; contains 1,119 titles. See also Forrest B. Bowe, "Some Corrections and Additions to *Early Catholic Americana*," *Catholic Historical Review*, XXVIII (July, 1942), 249–257.

26. Reiter, Ernst A., S.J. *Schematismus der katholischen deutschen Geistlichkeit in den Ver. Staaten Nord-Amerika's*. New York: Frederick Pustet. 1869. The first German Catholic directory for the United States; other volumes appeared in later years under various editors and publishers, e.g., W. Bonenkamp, Joseph Jessing, and J. B. Müller, *Schematismus der deutschen und deutschsprechenden Priester, sowie der deutschen Katholiken-Gemeinden in den Vereinigten Staaten Nord-Amerika's*. St. Louis: Herder. 1882.

27. Romig, Walter. *The Guide to Catholic Literature*. 8 vols. Detroit: Walter Romig. 1940–1968. These volumes give an alphabetical list of books and pamphlets written by Catholics in all fields, and in some instances biographical data on authors, references to book reviews, etc. Cf. the unpublished master's theses of the Department of Library Science of the Catholic University of America, prepared with a view to bridging the gap between Parsons (No. 25) which left off in 1830 and Romig whose listings began with 1888 and end with 1967.

28. Ryan, Joseph Paul, M.M. "Travel Literature as Source Material for American Catholic History," *Illinois Catholic Historical Review*, X (January, 1928), 179–238; (April, 1928), 301–363. A discussion of travelogues from Johan Printz's *Narrative of Early Pennsylvania, West New Jersey and Delaware* (1644) to Charles Dickens' *American Notes* (1842) with brief excerpts, data on the authors, and some comments on their works.

29. Schmandt, Raymond H., comp. "A Check-List of Eighteenth and Nineteenth Century Pamphlets in the Library of the American Catholic Historical Society," *Records* of the American Catholic Historical Society of Philadelphia, LXXXI (June, September, December, 1970), 89–122, 131–175, 214–247; LXXXII (March, December, 1971), 6–46, 195–264. A list of 3,196 titles arranged chronologically by year from 1707 to 1899 and alphabetically under each year, with a complete index of authors and subjects.

30. Steck, Francis Borgia, O.F.M. *A Tentative Guide to Historical Materials on the Spanish Borderlands*. Philadelphia: American Catholic Historical Society. 1943. Includes popular works and lists periodical

literature; some critical notes; a good beginning for students working on a problem in the Spanish borderlands; contains, however, at least as many items in secular history as in ecclesiastical history.

31.   Tomasi, Silvano M., and Edward C. Stibili. *Italian-Americans and Religion: An Annotated Bibliography.* New York: Center for Migration Studies. 1978. The 1,158 entries are divided into repositories of archival materials, bibliographies, serials, theses and dissertations, parish histories, and books and articles; most of them include a descriptive or critical note. There is an index of authors and subjects. The missionary work of Italians among their compatriots in North America and the Italian immigrants' experiences in the Catholic and Protestant churches from the later nineteenth century to the present are covered.

32.   Vollmar, Edward R., S.J. "Bibliography of United States Church History," *The Historical Bulletin,* XXIX–XXX (1951–1952); "Writings in United States Church History," ibid., XXXI–XXXIV (1953–1956); "Writings on the History of Religion in the United States," *Manuscripta,* I–XV (1957–1971). Up to 1956 this annual bibliography was limited to books and articles dealing with the Catholic Church; from 1957 on, works pertaining to all religious bodies were included. This listing is alphabetical by authors and contains almost no annotations.

33.   _____ . *The Catholic Church in America: An Historical Bibliography.* 2nd ed. New York: Scarecrow. 1963. An alphabetical listing by author, subject, or place of 5,919 items (books, pamphlets, periodical articles, unpublished doctoral dissertations and master's theses, etc.) dated between 1850 and 1961, which are not classified in any way, though some are furnished with descriptive notes. The bibliography proper is preceded by a "general survey" of American Catholic historiography and is followed by an ample index. Although the coverage is not complete in certain categories, it includes much widely scattered material which would otherwise be hard to find.

34.   Weber, Francis J. "Printed Guides to Archival Centers for American Catholic History," *The American Archivist,* XXXII (October, 1969), 349–356. A useful compilation of guides published either separately or in periodicals.

35.   _____ . *A Select Bibliographical Guide to California Catholic Periodical Literature, 1844–1973.* Los Angeles: Dawson's Book Shop.

[1973.] The 800 titles listed here in alphabetical order pertain to the Catholic history of California from colonial times on and have appeared in both religious and secular periodicals. Each one is briefly annotated.

36. _____ . *A Select Bibliography: The California Missions, 1765 – 1972.* Los Angeles: Dawson's Book Shop. [1972.] The 500 titles of books and articles are annotated with descriptive or critical comments.

37. _____ , comp. *A Select Bibliography to California Catholic Literature, 1856–1974.* Los Angeles: Dawson's Book Shop. 1974. In this fifth and final volume of the editor's bibliographical series, he lists and succinctly describes or evaluates 500 publications, including parish histories and rare pamphlets.

38. _____ . *A Select Guide to California Catholic History.* Los Angeles: Westernlore. 1966. The entries, annotated where the title does not clearly indicate the nature of the contents or where some special features need to be pointed out, are divided into guides, printed sources, periodical articles, parochial, religious, and institutional publications, unpublished works (especially doctoral dissertations and master's theses), journalism, diocesan and parochial directories, and archival depositories, followed by a complete index.

39. Willging, Eugene Paul, and Herta Hatzfeld. *Catholic Serials of the Nineteenth Century in the United States: A Descriptive Bibliography and Union List.* First series: Part I: Alabama, Arizona, Arkansas, Colorado, Connecticut, Delaware, Florida, Georgia, Idaho, Kansas, Maine, Montana, Nebraska, Nevada, New Hampshire, New Jersey, New Mexico; Part II: North Carolina, Oklahoma, Oregon, Rhode Island, South Carolina, Tennessee, Utah, Vermont, Virginia, Washington, West Virginia, Wyoming. Washington, D.C.: Catholic University of America Press. 1968. Second series: Part I: Minnesota, North Dakota, and South Dakota (1959); Part II: Wisconsin (1960); Part III: Illinois (1961); Part IV: Indiana (1962); Part V: Pennsylvania (1964); Part VI: Iowa (1963); Part VII: Michigan (1964); Part VIII: California (1964); Part IX: Missouri (1965); Part X: Massachusetts (1965); Part XI: Maryland [and] District of Columbia (1965); Part XII: 1. Kentucky, 2. Ohio (1966); Part XIII: Louisiana, Mississippi [and] Texas (1966); Part XIV: New York City and State (1967); Part XV: Statistical Analysis of the First Series, Parts I and II, and of the Second Series, Parts I–XIV (1968). The term "serials" includes newspapers, magazines, periodicals, and annuals. For each

state the compilers give first some historical background, then a description of the serials arranged alphabetically according to place of publication, the sources of information used, the locations of the serials in libraries and other depositories, and finally a special bibliography of sources used, an alphabetical table or chart with a statistical conclusion, and a chronological table or chart showing which serials were still current at the time of publication of this bibliography. Since approximately half of these titles had not been described previously in the standard reference works, this is a very useful tool for researchers.

40. _____ . "Nineteenth Century Polish Catholic Periodical Publications in the United States," *Polish American Studies*, XII (July–December, 1955), 88–100; XIII (January–June, 1956), 19–35; (July–December, 1956), 89–101. Another portion of the Willging-Hatzfeld survey which describes 105 titles, of which eighty-three had not been recorded in previously published lists.

II. GENERAL WORKS

THIS SECTION of the *Guide* is intended to cover not only those works which survey the entire history of the Catholic Church in this country, e.g., McAvoy (No. 67)—or a single phase of that history carried through a particular period, e.g., Ellis (No. 54)—but also general collections of sources not related to any particular geographical area or religious community such as the *Annales* (No. 43). Monographs dealing with a special place or theme will be found under other subdivisions.

41. Alvarez, David J., ed. *An American Church: Essays on the Americanization of the Catholic Church.* Moraga: Saint Mary's College of California. 1979. These seventeen papers, which were originally presented at a conference in 1978, treat a broad variety of topics.

42. *Annalen der Glaubensverbreitung.* Munich: Ludwig-Missionsverein. 1848–1918. This publication, a continuation of the *Annalen* of the Abbey of Einsiedeln in Switzerland, 1832–1847, is an important source for Catholicism among the German communities of the United States; a set of eighty-six volumes of the *Annalen*, containing about 300 letters from this country, was presented to the Catholic University of America by the Ludwig-Missionsverein in 1932.

43. *Annales de l'Association de la Propagation de la Foi.* Paris: L'Oeuvre de la Propagation de la Foi. 1822. Initially published in 1822 in pamphlet form, this rich series of source materials soon grew to an annual volume of letters from missionaries all over the world containing valuable data for the church historian of the respective countries; a series of prime importance for the historian of nineteenth-century American Catholicism. There was also an English edition of the *Annales* which began publication at Paris in 1838 and was later continued from London. For a further description see Hickey (No. 1130), pp. 167–172.

44. Bolts, T. William, S.M. *The Catholic Experience in America: A History of the Catholic Church in the United States.* Encino, Calif.:

Benziger. 1980. A textbook for high schools embodying the inquiry method.

45. Bunson, Maggie. *Founding of Faith: Catholics in the American Revolutionary Era.* Boston: St. Paul Editions. 1977. In this popular book illustrated with numerous drawings, chapters on missions in the future United States and on the Church in each of the English colonies are followed by biographical sketches (in alphabetical order) of Catholics in the American Revolution and in the succeeding decades to the middle of the nineteenth century. Some parts were previously published in *Our Sunday Visitor*'s Bicentennial Series.

46. *The Catholic Church in the United States of America.* 3 vols. New York: Catholic Editing Company. 1912. A popular, cooperative work prepared as a souvenir of St. Pius X's golden jubilee; numerous illustrations.

47. *The Catholic Encyclopedia.* 16 vols. New York: Robert Appleton. 1907–1912. This work, although now badly out of date in many particulars, remains the greatest single monument to scholarship to have appeared under American Catholic auspices before the *New Catholic Encyclopedia* (No. 74); two *Supplements* (1922, 1953) contain some brief items on the American Church; additional fascicles have appeared at irregular intervals.

48. Clarke, Richard H. *History of the Catholic Church in the United States.* Reprint (2 vols. in 1). Philadelphia: Gebbie. 1891. An old and popular work that is still of some value for photographic reproductions of bishops, cathedral churches, etc.

49. Cogley, John. *Catholic America.* New York: Dial. 1973. Paperback edition. Garden City, N.Y.: Doubleday. 1974. This "panoramic view," written by a journalist, undocumented, and based on a limited number of secondary sources, interprets the past in terms of the present and emphasizes contemporary developments with a liberal bias.

50. Curran, Francis X., S.J. *Major Trends in American Church History.* New York: America Press. 1946. A brief survey of the development of churches, sects, and religious thought in the United States with special emphasis on Protestantism; sources mainly secondary.

51. DeCourcy, Henry, and John Gilmary Shea. *The Catholic Church in the United States.* New York: Edward Dunigan. 1856. Long

since outdated, but of some interest as the product of a foreign Catholic observer of the mid-nineteenth century; appendix contains documents on the Bedini mission of 1853–1854.

52. Eberhardt, Newman C., C.M. *A Survey of American Church History*. St. Louis: B. Herder. 1964. This concise introduction to the history of Catholicism in the western hemisphere is an adaptation and expansion of sections of Volume II of *A Summary of Catholic History* by the same author. It provides the necessary background of secular history and emphasizes the achievements more than the struggles of the Church.

53. Ellis, John Tracy. *American Catholicism*. Chicago: University of Chicago Press. 1956. 2nd ed., rev. 1969. This survey of the Church's development from the time of Columbus to the time of publication includes a bibliographical essay with critical comments and a table of important dates. The author was awarded the John Gilmary Shea Prize of the American Catholic Historical Association for the first edition.

54. _____ . *Catholics in Colonial America*. Baltimore: Helicon. 1965. This comprehensive survey includes separate sections on the Spanish, French, and English missions and ends with the return of the newly consecrated first bishop, John Carroll, to Baltimore in 1790.

55. _____ , ed. *Documents of American Catholic History*. Milwaukee: Bruce. 1956. 2nd ed. 1962. 3rd ed. , 2 vols.; Chicago: Henry Regnery. 1967. The first edition contains 163 items of source material—or excerpts therefrom—running from 1493 to 1939. Four documents were added to the second edition, and five more to the third. Each item is preceded by an introductory note.

56. _____ . *Perspectives in American Catholicism*. Baltimore: Helicon. 1963. A collection of essays, sermons, and reprints of previous articles.

57. Gleason, Philip, ed. *Contemporary Catholicism in the United States*. Notre Dame: University of Notre Dame Press. 1969. This collection of fourteen essays by various writers, none of whom except the editor is a historian, covers all important topics except theology and pastoral and liturgical practice.

58. _____ , ed. *Documentary Reports on Early American Catholicism*.

New York: Arno. 1978. These six reports and essays by bishops and priests, dated between 1785 and 1836, are reproduced by the photo-offset process from earlier printed editions with an introduction by the editor and without continuous pagination.

59.   Greeley, Andrew M. *The Catholic Experience: An Interpretation of the History of American Catholicism.* Garden City, N.Y.: Doubleday. 1967. Image Book Edition, 1969. This selective survey, hastily and poorly written by a sociologist of religion, while containing some original insights and provocative observations, suffers from numerous factual errors, unproved assumptions, and unacknowledged borrowings from the works of others.

60.   Guilday, Peter. *National Pastorals of the American Hierarchy, 1792–1919.* Washington, D.C.: National Catholic Welfare Conference. 1923. A convenient collection of thirteen lengthy documents which provide a commentary on the events and influences which have affected Catholic life in the United States; introductory notes offer adequate background. Cf. Nos. 64, 74a.

61.   Halsey, William M. *The Survival of American Innocence: Catholicism in a Era of Disillusionment, 1920–1940.* Notre Dame: University of Notre Dame Press. 1980. In this intellectual and cultural history, remarkable for its originality of conception and acuity of vision, Catholic organizations and individuals are shown to have adopted and preserved much of the optimism and idealism which their Protestant and secular contemporaries were already abandoning in the face of various forms of irrationalism.

62.   Herr, Dan, and Joel Wells, eds. *Through Other Eyes: Some Impressions of American Catholicism by Foreign Visitors from 1777 to the Present.* Westminster, Md.: Newman. 1965. Each of the twenty-nine selections from both Catholic and non-Catholic writers in this anthology has a brief introduction.

63.   Hertling, Ludwig, S.J. *Geschichte der Katholischen Kirche in den Vereinigten Staaten.* Berlin: Morus-Verlag. 1954. Written for Europeans, this popular work offers nothing new to informed American readers. Inaccuracies are indicated in a critical review in the *Catholic Historical Review*, XLII (July, 1956), 210–213.

64.   Huber, Raphael, O.F.M. Conv. *Our Bishops Speak.* Milwaukee: Bruce. 1951. A collection of eighty-two statements of Catholic teach-

ing and policy issued by American bishops between 1919 and 1951; a continuation of No. 60. Cf. No. 74a.

65. Lally, Francis J. *The Catholic Church in a Changing America.* Boston: Little, Brown. 1962. A journalist analyzes the effects that the election of John F. Kennedy to the presidency of the United States in 1960 had on the attitudes of most Americans toward the Catholic Church and on the role of the Church in American society.

66. Leckie, Robert. *American and Catholic.* Garden City, N.Y.: Doubleday. 1970. This popularized treatment of the historical development of the Church in the United States from the days of the early explorers and missionaries to the period following the Second Vatican Council lacks precision of detail, citation of sources, and a bibliography, while it abounds in careless use of the literature, unsupported generalizations, and factual errors.

67. McAvoy, Thomas T., C.S.C. *A History of the Catholic Church in the United States.* Notre Dame: University of Notre Dame Press. 1969. In this sizable survey extending from 1634 to 1968, the author relates many facts and narrates events in strictly chronological order and with general accuracy, but repeats certain points needlessly and omits many important topics altogether. He tries to study the history of the Church in terms of a minority's reaction and adaptation to a dominant culture.

68. _____ , ed. *Roman Catholicism and the American Way of Life.* Notre Dame: University of Notre Dame Press. 1960. Eighteen brief essays on various phases of twentieth-century Catholicism in the United States; originally the essays were presented as papers at two symposia at Notre Dame.

69. McGuire, Constantine E. *Catholic Builders of the Nation.* 5 vols. Boston: Continental. 1923. A collection of 121 popular essays by different authors on a variety of topics which aim to show the contributions of Catholics to American life; not of scientific value.

70. Marino, Anthony I. *The Catholics in America.* New York: Vantage. 1960. A popular, unreliable survey of the contributions of Catholics to education, politics, warfare, literature, entertainment, art, science, business, sports, etc., mainly from 1880 to 1960.

71. Maynard, Theodore. *The Catholic Church and the American Idea.*

New York: Appleton-Century-Crofts. 1953. A popular effort to relate the Church to the American scene in terms of its history in the United States.

72. _____ . *The Story of American Catholicism*. New York: Macmillan. 1941. An eminently readable popular work with emphasis on the reciprocal influences of the Catholic community and American national life; its value lessened by considerable oversimplification, conjecture, and inaccuracy. See critical review in the *Catholic Historical Review*, XXVIII (April, 1942), 94–103.

73. Nevins, Albert J., M.M. *Our American Catholic Heritage*. Huntington, Ind.: Our Sunday Visitor. 1972. This attractive pictorial history may provide uninformed readers with an initial knowledge of the Church in the United States from colonial times to the present.

74. *New Catholic Encyclopedia*. 15 vols. New York: McGraw-Hill. 1967. Vol. XVI: *Supplement 1967–1974*. Washington, D.C.: Publishers Guild. 1974. Vol. XVII: *Supplement 1974–1979*. Publishers Guild. 1979. This basic reference work, truly a storehouse filled with information, contains a separate article on each state, diocese, Catholic university, college, and religious order and on every important (deceased) person, nationality, organization, movement, and event, as well as general articles on such topics as the Catholic press, Church and State in the United States, and missions in colonial America.

74a. Nolan, Hugh, ed. *Pastoral Letters of the American Hierarchy, 1792–1970*. Huntington, Ind.: Our Sunday Visitor. 1971. The letters of John Carroll, of the first seven Provincial and the three Plenary Councils of Baltimore, and of certain annual meetings of the bishops from 1919 on, as well as statements of the National Catholic Welfare Conference and of the National Conference of Catholic Bishops, are divided chronologically into seven sections, each of which has its own historical introduction. This collection renders Guilday and Huber (Nos. 60, 64) obsolete.

75. O'Gorman, Thomas. *A History of the Roman Catholic Church in the United States*. New York: Charles Scribner's. 1907. For the most part a condensation of Shea (No. 85) up to 1866 and thereafter hardly more than an outline; now of little use; Volume IX of the American Church History Series.

76. O'Neill, James M. *Catholicism and American Freedom*. New

York: Harper and Bros. 1952. Written in reply to Paul Blanshard's attacks on the Church; primarily a popular work, although supplied with notes, bibliography, and index; first eleven chapters summarize Catholic support of American freedom and certain Catholic teachings and practices that touch closely on public affairs.

77.   Ong, Walter J., S.J. *Frontiers in American Catholicism: Essays on Ideology and Culture.* New York: Macmillan. 1957. Six brief essays which attempt to reinterpret the American Catholic community vis-à-vis the national ethos; contains fresh insights and challenging approaches, but likewise some questionable interpretations.

78.   Pattee, Richard. *El Catolicismo en Estados Unidos.* Mexico City: Editorial Jus. 1945. A popular and interpretative survey intended to make Catholicism in the United States better known to Spanish and Latin American readers; of no scientific value.

79.   Phelan, Thomas P. *Catholics in Colonial Days.* New York: P. J. Kenedy. 1935. Of no scientific value; based in part on dubious sources and including questionable interpretations and unverifiable claims; superseded by Ellis (No. 54).

80.   Putz, Louis J., C.S.C. *The Catholic Church, U.S.A.* Chicago: Fides. 1956. Twenty-three essays by as many authors ranging from several of an historical nature to those on current religious sociology; the quality of the essays varies greatly.

81.   Rahill, Peter J. *The Catholic Church in America, from Colonial Times to the Present Day.* Chicago: Franciscan Herald Press. 1961. A simple, brief survey that emphasizes the recurrent bigotry against Catholics.

82.   Roemer, Theodore, O.F.M.Cap. *The Catholic Church in the United States.* St. Louis: B. Herder. 1951. In general, a factually accurate work, although unbalanced due to avoidance of controversial issues; intended as a seminary textbook. See the review in the *Catholic Historical Review*, XXXVI (January, 1951), 467–470.

83.   Sargent, Daniel. *Our Land and Our Lady.* New York: Longmans, Green. 1939. A brief, popular work, showing aspects of the American cult of the Blessed Virgin from colonial times.

84.   Shaughnessy, Gerald, S.M. *Has the Immigrant Kept the Faith?* New York: Macmillan. 1925. Reprint. New York: Arno and the New

York Times. 1969. A statistical analysis of Catholic population trends in the United States to 1920; although it remains the only general treatment of the subject, its methodology is of dubious validity and its conclusions are questionable.

85.   Shea, John Gilmary. *The History of the Catholic Church in the United States.* 4 vols. New York: John G. Shea. 1886–1892. Reprint. New York: Arno. 1978. Unexcelled as a general history down to 1866, although poorly arranged and now out of date in view of later research.

86.   Shearer,   Donald   C.,   O.M.Cap.   *Pontificia   Americana: A Documentary History of the Catholic Church in the United States, 1784– 1884.* Washington, D.C.: Catholic University of America Press. 1933. A Ph.D. thesis giving the texts of 159 documents from the Holy See in original languages—with English summaries—from January 15, 1783, to October 25, 1884.

87.   Shields, Currin V. *Democracy and Catholicism in America.* New York: McGraw-Hill. 1958. An able discussion by a non-Catholic scholar of the interrelationship of the principal tenets of Catholicism, democracy, and liberalism in the field of politics.

88.   Shuster, George N. *The Catholic Spirit in America.* New York: Dial. 1927. Reprint. New York: Arno. 1978. An essay in intellectual history that attempts an interpretation from the literary viewpoint.

89.   Stokes, Anson Phelps. *Church and State in the United States.* 3 vols. New York: Harper and Bros. 1950. A monumental work by a canon of the Protestant Episcopal Church; admirably thorough in coverage and objective in tone. For certain reservations see "Church and State in the United States: A Critical Appraisal," *Catholic Historical Review,* XXXVIII (October, 1952), 285–316. A revised one-volume edition, edited by Leo Pfeffer, was published in 1964.

90.   Tavard, Georges. *Catholicism in U.S.A.* Trans. Theodore Du Bois. New York: Newman. 1969. Originally published as *Les catholiques américains: Nouvelles frontières* (Paris: Editions du Centurion. 1966). This interpretative essay by a French priest who has lived in the United States since 1952 draws on historical, sociological, and theological sources.

91.   Timpe, Georg. *Katholisches Deutschtum in den Vereinigten Staaten von Amerika. Ein Querschnitt.* Freiburg im Breisgau: Herder and Co.

97. Ahern, Patrick H., ed. *Catholic Heritage in Minnesota, North Dakota, South Dakota.* Published by the Most Reverend Archbishop and Bishops of the Province of St. Paul. 1964. This folio-sized, copiously illustrated, popular book contains a separate chapter by a different writer on each of the ten dioceses of the ecclesiastical province. It commemorates the seventy-fifth anniversary of the erection of the province and of five of the dioceses.

98. Alerding, Herman J. *A History of the Catholic Church in the Diocese of Vincennes.* Indianapolis: Carlon and Hollenbeck. 1883. Although this popular compilation contains a good deal of material, it is poorly organized and has many inaccuracies; now superseded by McAvoy, McNamara, and Schroeder (Nos. 200, 204, 242) for the years 1789–1877.

99. _____ . *The Diocese of Fort Wayne, 1857–September 22–1907.* Fort Wayne: Archer. 1907. A collection of varied content, including biographical sketches of bishops and priests, several topical essays, and chapters on the religious congregations and diocesan institutions by the fourth Bishop of Fort Wayne; indexed but lacking in critical approach and apparatus.

100. Archibald, Robert. *The Economic Aspects of the California Missions.* Washington, D.C.: Academy of American Franciscan History. 1978. Working from primary sources, the author studies the missions as frontier institutions engaged in pastoral, agricultural, mercantile, and financial operations; he investigates in particular price regulation, the connection with the port of San Blas, mission reports and accounts, economic relationships with civilian, military, and government, trade with the outside world, and mission labor and agriculture.

101. Bagley, Clarence B. *Early Catholic Missions in Old Oregon.* 2 vols. Seattle: Lowman and Hanford. 1932. Volume I reprints a series of sketches from the *Catholic Sentinel* of Portland (February 7–September 12, 1878) written by Francis Norbert Blanchet (1795–1883), first Archbishop of Oregon City, who was a participant in many of the events described; also an account of the celebrated murder of Dr. Marcus Whitman (1802–1847) by the Cayuse Indians written by Jean B. A. Brouillet (1813–1884), a Catholic missionary who reached the Oregon Country a few months before the massacre. Volume II contains a narrative of the early Catholic missions in Oregon compiled from reports to the Society for the Propagation of the Faith, along with ten letters written by the Sisters of Notre Dame

at St. Paul on the Willamette to their community in Belgium and dated between April, 1844, and July, 1846. Cf. No. 503.

102.   Bailey, James Henry, II. *A History of the Diocese of Richmond: The Formative Years.* Richmond: Chancery Office. 1956. Originally a Ph.D. thesis, this work carries the story down to 1872; its scientific value is lessened by a pietistic tone and a tendency to exaggerate.

103.   Balcom, Mary G. *The Catholic Church in Alaska.* Chicago: Adams. 1970. A popular, undocumented sketch of the development of the Church from the nineteenth-century missions to the time of writing.

104.   Baudier, Roger. *The Catholic Church in Louisiana.* New Orleans: Chancery Office. 1939. A vast amount of useful data has been assembled here by a nonprofessional with references to the sources employed, although the work is poorly organized and unattractively produced.

105.   Bayard, Ralph, C.M. *Lone-Star Vanguard: The Catholic Re-Occupation of Texas, 1838–1848.* St. Louis: Vincentian. 1945. A competent treatment of a critical decade done from archival sources; the narrative is built around the Vincentian missionaries, and especially John Timon, C.M. (1797–1867).

106.   Bayley, James Roosevelt. *A Brief Sketch of the History of the Catholic Church on the Island of New York.* 2nd rev. ed. New York: Catholic Publication Society. 1870. Reprint. New York: United States Catholic Historical Society. 1973. This old work—originally published in 1853—is now of little value save for the later prominence of its convert author, a native of the city; it deals with the first half of the nineteenth century.

107.   Becker, Martin Joseph. *A History of Catholic Life in the Diocese of Albany, 1609–1864.* New York: United States Catholic Historical Society. 1975. An attempt to study the Church in the area comprising the diocese founded in 1847 "from the viewpoint of the laity and their missionary priests." There are chapters on early Indian history, natural features, economic activity, apostasy, immigration, ethnic numbers, lay trusteeism, and Catholic revivalism. Originally a doctoral dissertation at Fordham University.

108.   Beckman, Peter, O.S.B. *The Catholic Church on the Kansas Frontier, 1850–1877.* Washington, D.C.: Catholic University of

America Press. 1943. One of a series of doctoral theses on the Church and the frontier; makes use of manuscript sources and is helpful for insights on the problems of personnel, equipment, and finance among these rural immigrant communities.

109. Beitzell, Edwin Warfield. *The Jesuit Missions of St. Mary's County, Maryland*. 2nd ed. Abell, Md.: The Author. 1976. The first edition appeared in 1960. Now revised and expanded and published under the sponsorship of the St. Mary's County Bicentennial Commission, this book contains detailed information on each of the missions and churches in the county in seven time periods from 1634 to 1975. It is large in format, rich in genealogical data, abundantly illustrated, and reproduced from a typescript.

110. Bennett, William Harper. *Catholic Footsteps in Old New York: A Chronicle of Catholicity in the City of New York, 1524–1808*. New York: Schwartz, Kirwin, and Fauss. 1909. Reprint. New York: United States Catholic Historical Society. 1973. An outdated popular treatment whose extensive quoting without reference to the sources used leaves an unsatisfactory impression. Isaac Jogues, S.J., Thomas Dongan, and Bishop John Carroll are among those treated; the manner of Catholic life in the colonial and early federal periods is described.

111. Berger, John A. *The Franciscan Missions of California*. New York: G. P. Putnam's. 1941. A general work for the popular reader that depends on the standard scholarly treatments; beautifully illustrated.

112. Bischoff, William N., S.J. *The Jesuits in Old Oregon*. Caldwell, Idaho: Caxton Printers. 1945. The author describes this work as "a sketch of Jesuit activities in the Pacific Northwest," embracing the area from South Dakota to the Pacific; carries the customary critical apparatus, although one reviewer took exception to many statements and interpretations (*Catholic Historical Review*, XXXII [April, 1946], 76–78); an appendix gives a series of helpful biographical sketches of forty Jesuits who worked on these missions.

113. *The Bishops of Newark, 1853–1978*. South Orange, N.J.: Seton Hall University Press. 1978. This illustrated volume consists of brief, popular, undocumented essays by six different writers illuminating the history of the archdiocese through the lives of its seven ordinaries. Prepared under the direction of the New Jersey Catholic Historical Records Commission.

114.   Blanchard, Charles. *History of the Catholic Church in Indiana*. 2 vols. Logansport: A. W. Bowen. 1898. A popular and cooperative work that contributes little that is new; now superseded for most of the period covered by more recent research, e.g., McAvoy, Schauinger, and Schroeder (Nos. 200, 562, 242).

115.   Bonta, Robert Eugene. *The Cross in the Valley: The History of the Establishment of the Catholic Church in the Northern San Joaquin Valley of California up to 1863*. Fresno: Academy of California Church History. 1963. A carefully researched and documented monograph centering on the area that became in 1962 the Diocese of Stockton.

116.   Boyd, Mark F., Hales T. Smith, and John W. Griffin. *Here They Once Stood: The Tragic End of the Apalachee Missions*. Gainesville: University of Florida Press. 1951. An edition of forty-five documents dated November 4, 1693, to April 16, 1704, from the Archives of the Indies with maps, charts, and illustrations; the area once had fourteen mission stations which were wiped out by the British-Creek raiders in 1704.

117.   Bradley, Cyprian, O.S.B., and Edward J. Kelly. *History of the Diocese of Boise, 1863–1953*. Vol. I. Boise: Chancery Office. 1953. This volume by the late pastor of Buhl, Idaho, and the late Bishop of Boise gives a documented account with bibliography and index; clarifies a long-standing confusion over jurisdictional boundaries in the early and mid-nineteenth century.

118.   Bringas de Manzaneda y Encinas, Diego Miguel, O.F.M. *Friar Bringas Reports to the King: Methods of Indoctrination on the Frontier of New Spain, 1796–1797*. Trans. and ed. Daniel S. Matson and Bernard L. Fontana. Tucson: University of Arizona Press. 1977. The Franciscan reported to King Charles III what he had learned about the vast area during an official visit of the missions and proposed specific reforms to expedite the work of civilization and conversion of the Indians.

119.   Brown, Thomas Elton. *Bible Belt Catholicism: A History of the Roman Catholic Church in Oklahoma, 1905–1945*. New York: United States Catholic Historical Society. 1977. Reproduced by the photo-offset process from a typescript, this doctoral dissertation written at Oklahoma State University treats various problems, in part unique to that state, faced by the Catholic clergy and laity, especially the multiform bigotry of the overwhelming conservative, Protestant, rural majority, from the erection of the Diocese of Oklahoma to the end of World War II.

120.   Bunson, Maggie. *Faith in Paradise: A Century and a Half of the Roman Catholic Church in Hawaii.* Boston: St. Paul Editions. 1977. This copiously illustrated but undocumented survey from the arrival of the first French missionaries (Picpus Fathers) in the Sandwich Islands to the administration of Bishop John J. Scanlan is intended for the general reader.

121.   Byrne, William. *History of the Catholic Church in the New England States.* 2 vols. Boston: Hurd and Everts. 1899. A large cooperative work done on a diocesan basis; now superseded by Riley and Lord-Sexton-Harrington (Nos. 232, 197).

122.   Casper, Henry W., S.J. *History of the Catholic Church in Nebraska.* Vol. I: *The Church on the Northern Plains, 1838–1874.* Milwaukee: Bruce. 1960. Beginning with the Jesuits' short-lived St. Joseph's Mission to the Potawatomi in Council Bluffs, this well-documented work covers the vast area included in the Vicariate Apostolic which was erected in 1859 and administered by Bishop James M. O'Gorman. Vol. II: *The Church on the Fading Frontier, 1864–1910.* Milwaukee: Bruce. 1966. This volume deals mainly with the institutional progress during the episcopate of James O'Connor (vicar apostolic, 1876–1885, and first Bishop of Omaha, 1885–1890), with additional chapters on education, parishes, and religious orders of women. Vol. III: *Catholic Chapters in Nebraska Immigration, 1870–1900.* Milwaukee: Bruce. 1966. Only the organized programs of Irish colonization, Bohemian immigration, and Polish colonies are studied.

123.   Castañeda, Carlos E. *Our Catholic Heritage in Texas.* 7 vols. Austin: Von Boeckmann-Jones. 1936–1958. Reprint. New York: Arno. 1976. The first six volumes, based upon a vast amount of unpublished sources and carrying the story from 1519 to 1936, constitute a work of genuine scholarship. The seventh contains a supplement to 1950.

124.   Chavez, Angelico, Fray. *My Penitente Land: Reflections on Spanish New Mexico.* Albuquerque: University of New Mexico Press. 1974. Intertwining personal views with historical facts, and representing the mentality of his people, a descendant of the old settlers who is a Franciscan priest and well-known writer has presented the Hispanic uniqueness of the region mainly in terms of race and environment.

125.   Conley, Patrick T., and Mathew J. Smith. *Catholicism in Rhode Island: The Formative Era.* Providence: Rhode Island Bicentennial

Foundation. 1976. Although intended for the general reader and lacking footnotes, this copiously illustrated history, which extends from the colonial period to the establishment of the Diocese of Providence in 1872, contains an extensive bibliographical essay; it gives ample attention to the several immigrant groups, especially the Irish.

126.   Connelly, James F., ed. *The History of the Archdiocese of Philadelphia*. Philadelphia: Archdiocese of Philadelphia. 1976. Nine professional historians have contributed chronologically distinct chapters (except the last one, which treats intellectual history) to this large volume covering eastern Pennsylvania from the early eighteenth century to the Forty-first International Eucharistic Congress in 1976, although some precision and detail have been lost through revision and shortening by a literary editor. This history supersedes Kirlin (No. 186).

127.   Cook, Sherburne Friend. *The Conflict between the California Indian and White Civilization*. Berkeley and Los Angeles: University of California Press. 1943. (Ibero-Americana, No. XXI–XXIV.) Reprint. Berkeley: University of California Press. 1976. (With both the original pagination of the four volumes and new consecutive pagination.) These pioneering six studies in ethnohistory and anthropology were written by a biologist and (especially the first and longest, "The Indian Versus the Spanish Mission") contain much information on the impact of the Catholic religion and European culture on the aborigines; not all the conclusions, however, can be accepted without question. See Francis F. Guest, O.F.M., "An Examination of the Thesis of S. F. Cook on the Forced Conversion of Indians in the California Missions," *Southern California Quarterly*, LXI (Spring, 1979), 1–77.

128.   Cullen, Thomas F. *The Catholic Church in Rhode Island*. North Providence: Franciscan Missionaries of Mary. 1936. A popular compilation published to commemorate the 300th anniversary of the founding of the city of Providence. Cf. Conley-Smith (No. 125).

129.   Curley, Michael J., C.SS.R. *Church and State in the Spanish Floridas, 1783–1822*. Washington, D.C.: Catholic University of America Press. 1940. Reprint. New York: AMS. 1974. This large Ph.D. thesis exploits a great amount of archival material and is noteworthy as a study of Church-State relations in an area of frequently conflicting national claims.

130. Defouri, James H. *Historical Sketch of the Catholic Church in New Mexico.* San Francisco: McCormick. 1887. A brief popular treatment by a missionary of the area.

131. Delanglez, Jean, S.J. *The French Jesuits in Lower Louisiana, 1700–1763.* Washington, D.C.: Catholic University of America Press. 1935. Reprint. New York: AMS. 1974. A Ph.D. thesis based in the main on unpublished sources, but somewhat marred by a polemical tone.

132. *Diamond Jubilee, 1847–1922, of the Diocese of Galveston and St. Mary's Cathedral.* La Porte, Tex.: [St. Mary's Seminary]. 1922. A popular and illustrated booklet compiled by a number of authors with some correspondence included, but not of scientific value.

133. Donohue, John Augustine, S.J. *After Kino: Jesuit Missions in Northwestern New Spain, 1711–1767.* Rome and St. Louis: Jesuit Historical Institute. 1969. In this carefully researched history of the missions to the Indians from the death of Eusebio Kino to the expulsion of the Jesuits in an area that included part of the present-day state of Arizona (Pimería Alta), the author presents the dialectic between the desire for expansion and the threat of secularization.

134. Doyon, Bernard, O.M.I. *The Cavalry of Christ on the Rio Grande, 1849–1883.* Milwaukee: Bruce. 1956. The history of the missions of the Oblates of Mary Immaculate along the border of Mexico and eastern Texas done largely from manuscripts in both European and American archives; maps, illustrations, and a classified bibliography.

135. Duggan, Thomas C. *The Catholic Church in Connecticut.* New York: State History. 1930. A popular compilation, two-thirds of which is devoted to a survey of individual parishes on a county basis; no evidence of sources used.

136. Duratschek, Mary Claudia, Sister, O.S.B. *Crusading Along Sioux Trails: A History of the Catholic Indian Missions of South Dakota.* Yankton: Benedictine Convent of the Sacred Heart. 1947. A fully documented account—with illustrations— that summarizes the period covered by the following entry and brings the story down to date.

137. _____ . *The Beginnings of Catholicism in South Dakota.* Wash-

ington, D.C.: Catholic University of America Press. 1943. This Ph.D. thesis is especially helpful for the Indian missions of the area down to about 1890.

138.   Engelhardt, Zephyrin, O.F.M. *The Franciscans in Arizona.* Harbor Springs, Mich.: Holy Childhood Indian School. 1899. The period beginning in 1767, when fourteen friars from the College of Santa Cruz at Querétaro arrived in the Primería Alta to take the place of the expelled Jesuits, continuing with the establishment of the Custody of San Carlos in 1783, and ending with its dissolution in 1791, is here studied.

139.   _____ . *The Franciscans in California.* Harbor Springs, Mich.: Holy Childhood Indian School. 1897. A survey of the friars' work from the founding of the first mission in 1769 to the 1890's. Now superseded by Geiger, Guest, and Geary (Nos. 378, 383, 156).

140.   _____ . *The Missions and Missionaries of California.* 4 vols. San Francisco: James H. Barry. 1908–1915. Although now superseded by more recent research in special aspects of early Franciscan California history, this work of a pioneer historian is still of value for the immense amount of data assembled; a second and revised edition of Volume I was published at the Old Mission, Santa Barbara, in 1929.

141.   Espinosa, José E. *Saints in the Valley: Christian Folk Art of Spanish New Mexico.* Albuquerque: University of New Mexico Press. 1960. A scholarly volume with illustrations.

142.   Faherty, William Barnaby, S.J. *Dream by the River: Two Centuries of Saint Louis Catholicism, 1766–1967.* St. Louis: Piraeus. 1973. Resting on archival and other research and giving references to sources, this well-balanced presentation is divided (after Part I) by episcopates from Louis W. V. Du Bourg to Joseph E. Ritter and covers every aspect of the topic (prominent clergymen and laymen, institutions and movements). The book is of folio size and is illustrated copiously with pictures, drawings, and maps. It is more readable, less detailed, and farther extended than Rothensteiner (No. 233).

143.   Fecher, Vincent J., S.V.D. *A Study of the Movement for German National Parishes in Philadelphia and Baltimore, 1787–1802.* Rome: Apud Aedes Universitatis Gregorianae. 1955. A thesis for the doctorate in church history that draws heavily on manuscript sources in the archives of the Congregation de Propaganda Fide; good for the

problem of nationalism and its relation to lay trusteeism in the early American Church.

144.   Fenwick, Benedict Joseph, S.J. *Memoirs to Serve for the Future Ecclesiastical History of the Diocess [sic] of Boston*. Ed. Joseph M. McCarthy. Yonkers, N.Y.: United States Catholic Historical Society. 1978. The Second Bishop of Boston, who compiled this account with the intention of publishing it, begins with the later part of the eighteenth century, devotes much attention to John Thayer, and concludes with his own attendance at the First Provincial Council of Baltimore in October, 1829; it is of meager historical value.

144a.   Fink, Leo Gregory. *Old Jesuit Trails in Penn's Forest*. New York: Paulist. 1936. The theme of these semipopular and illustrated essays is the activities of the Jesuits in Pennsylvania from 1741 to date; done from printed sources and secondary works.

145.   Fisher, Gerald Edward. *Dusk Is My Dawn: The First Hundred Years: Diocese of La Crosse, 1868–1968*. La Crosse: Diocese of La Crosse. 1969. After sketching the history of the Church in the west central part of Wisconsin before the founding of the diocese, the author with considerable, but not exhaustive, documentation recounts the main events in the episcopates of Michael Heiss and his five successors.

146.   Fitton, James. *Sketches of the Establishment of the Church in New England*. Boston: P. Donahoe. 1872. Although now superseded by Lord-Sexton-Harrington and Riley (Nos. 197, 232), this old account by one of the most famous missionary priests of New England (1805–1881) is still of interest; from the time of his ordination in 1827 to the beginning of his permanent Boston pastorate in 1855, Fitton traversed a good portion of New England and was an eyewitness to some of the events he describes.

147.   Fitzgerald, Mary Paul, Sister, S.C.L. *Beacon on the Plains*. Leavenworth, Kans.: Saint Mary College. 1939. Originally a Ph.D. thesis, this work treats the missions among the Osage Indians from the 1820's to near the end of the century; extensive use of manuscript materials, a map, lists of personnel, and an index.

148.   Fitzmorris, Mary Angela, Sister. *Four Decades of Catholicism in Texas, 1820–1860*. Washington, D.C.: Catholic University of America Press. 1926. A Ph.D. thesis that is now largely superseded by Volumes VI and VII of Castañeda (No. 123).

149.   Flanigen, George J. *Catholicity in Tennessee: A Sketch of Catholic Activities in the State, 1541–1937*. Nashville: Ambrose. 1937. A popular brochure that gives the only consecutive outline in print of Catholicism in Tennessee from colonial times to the present.

150.   Flynn, Joseph M. *The Catholic Church in New Jersey*. Morristown: The Author. 1904. A popular book containing a large body of data arranged by parishes; now superseded by Yeager (No. 594) for the years 1853–1872.

151.   Gallagher, John P. *A Century of History: The Diocese of Scranton, 1868–1968*. Scranton: Diocese of Scranton. 1968. A trained historian has written a reliable and critical account of the growth and impact of Catholicism in northeastern Pennsylvania, beginning a half-century before the founding of the diocese. The narrative of the schisms of the Polish and Lithuanian national churches that arose there makes the book useful for American ethnic religious history.

152.   Gannon, Michael V. *The Cross in the Sand: The Early Catholic Church in Florida, 1513–1870*. Gainesville: University of Florida Press. 1965. Although it is written for the general public and lacks footnotes, this survey of religious life under Spanish, British, and American rule culminating in the establishment of the Diocese of St. Augustine is based on solid research and contains an essay on the sources.

153.   Garraghan, Gilbert J., S.J. *Catholic Beginnings in Kansas City, Missouri*. Chicago: Loyola University Press. 1920. A brief documented treatment which concentrates on the period from the 1820's to 1848; lacking an index.

154.   _____ . *The Catholic Church in Chicago, 1673–1871: An Historical Sketch*. Chicago: Loyola University Press. 1921. Reprint. Ann Arbor, Mich.: University Microfilms. 1968. The best work so far published on the early history of Catholicism in Chicago; embodies considerable correspondence, is carefully documented, and well illustrated.

155.   _____ . *Chapters in Frontier History: Research Studies in the Making of the West*. Milwaukee: Bruce. 1934. These nine brief essays are well described in the subtitle; like all the works of this historian, they are well done.

156.   Geary, Gerald J. *The Secularization of the California Missions, 1810–1846*. Washington, D.C.: Catholic University of America

Press. 1934. Reprint. New York: AMS. 1974. Both manuscript and printed sources were employed in this Ph.D. thesis to help unravel an involved chapter in California's Catholic history.

157.   Geiger, Maynard, O.F.M., and Clement W. Meighan. *As the Padres Saw Them: California Indian Life and Customs as Reported by the Franciscan Missionaries, 1813–1815.* Santa Barbara: Santa Barbara Mission Archive Library. 1976. These replies from the individual missions to a questionnaire sent out by the Spanish government not only provide abundant data for anthropologists and ethnographers interested in the aborigines of Upper California, but also reflect the attitudes of the friars toward their charges.

158.   _____ . *The Franciscan Conquest of Florida, 1573–1618.* Washington, D.C.: Catholic University of America Press. 1937. A wide coverage of manuscript material makes this Ph.D. thesis a solid contribution to the history of the Florida missions up to the eve of the so-called "golden age" of the Franciscans in the colony.

159.   _____ . *Franciscan Missionaries in Hispanic California, 1769–1848: A Biographical Dictionary.* San Marino, Calif.: Huntington Library. 1969. This collection of concise, candid biographies of 142 friars, based on data drawn from sources widely scattered in Spain and North America, is a useful reference tool.

160.   Gerow, Richard O. *Catholicity in Mississippi.* Natchez: The Author. 1939. A large centennial volume by the late Bishop of Natchez-Jackson that contains a great deal of authenticated data on bishops, priests, religious communities, parishes, and diocesan institutions.

161.   Gleeson, William. *History of the Catholic Church in California.* 2 vols. San Francisco: A. L. Bancroft. 1872. Semipopular in nature, this work is especially full for the colonial period, although now superseded by more recent research, e.g., Engelhardt, Geiger, Guest (Nos. 139, 378, 383), etc.

162.   Guilday, Peter. *The Catholic Church in Virginia, 1815–1822.* New York: United States Catholic Historical Society. 1924. A monograph that embodies a good number of documents—many *in extenso*—on one of the worst cases of rebellious lay trustees in American Catholic history.

163.   Hanley, Thomas O'Brien, S.J. *Their Rights and Liberties: The Beginnings of Religious and Political Freedom in Maryland.* Westminster,

Md.: Newman. 1959. A reworking of the traditional account of Church-State relations in colonial Maryland from the broader background of English Catholic theory and practice.

164.   Harris, William R. *The Catholic Church in Utah*. Salt Lake City: Intermountain Catholic Press. 1909. A popular account that traces the story from the earliest Spanish explorers in the region to date; now superseded by Bolton (No. 358) for the Escalante expedition.

165.   Hartley, James J. *Diocese of Columbus: The History of Fifty Years, 1868–1918*. Columbus: Chancery Office. 1918. A popular chronicle done on a parish basis by the fourth Bishop of Columbus; no references to sources, bibliography, or index.

166.   Heming, Harry H. *The Catholic Church in Wisconsin*. Milwaukee: Catholic Historical Publishing Company. 1895–1898. A large volume, popular in character, that surveys the colonial and early national periods and then discusses the Church by dioceses; table of important dates, illustrations, and index; appeared in a German edition from the same publisher (Milwaukee, 1899).

167.   Hewett, Edgar L., and Reginald G. Fisher. *Mission Monuments of New Mexico*. Albuquerque: University of New Mexico Press. 1943. A handsomely-illustrated volume that gives a careful account of the Franciscans in New Mexico with data on the old missions, their restoration and repair, and appendices containing useful lists of the friars in the area.

168.   Hewitt, William P. H. *History of the Diocese of Syracuse*. Syracuse: Catholic Sun. 1909. A popular work done on a parish-by-parish basis.

169.   Hoffmann, Mathias M. *Centennial History of the Archdiocese of Dubuque*. Dubuque: Columbia College Press. 1938. A popular, illustrated volume with no references to sources or bibliography, although it has an index.

170.   Houck, George F. *A History of Catholicity in Northern Ohio and in the Diocese of Cleveland*. Cleveland: J. B. Savage. 1903. A large volume, popular in character, now superseded for the most part by Hynes (No. 171).

171.   Hynes, Michael J. *History of the Diocese of Cleveland: Origin and*

Growth, 1847–1952. Cleveland: Chancery Office. 1953. This handsomely produced and documented work by a trained historian is one of the better and more up-to-date diocesan histories, although scholars would have appreciated more information on controversial issues; nearly 500 illustrations, a bibliography, and index.

172. Ives, J. Moss. *The Ark and the Dove: The Beginning of Civil and Religious Liberties in America*. New York: Longmans, Green. 1936. A semipopular treatment by a lawyer with reference to the printed sources used, a bibliography, and an index.

173. James, George Wharton. *The Old Franciscan Missions of California*. Boston: Little, Brown. 1913. Reprint. Boston: Longwood. 1977. This early history of the mission system and of each establishment lacks documentary references but contains numerous illustrations.

174. Johnson, Bradley T. *The Foundation of Maryland and the Origin of the Act concerning Religion of April 21, 1649*. Baltimore: Maryland Historical Society. 1883. One of a number of studies treating the early years of the Maryland colony; references given to archival and printed sources, but now superseded by more recent works, e.g., Ives and Russell (Nos. 172, 235).

175. Johnson, Kenneth M. *The Pious Fund*. Los Angeles: Dawson's Book Shop. 1963. This third volume in the series Famous California Trials is a brief account of the protracted legal dispute between the United States and Mexico which was settled by the Permanent Court of Arbitration at The Hague in 1902 in favor of the claims of the Church in California.

176. Johnson, Peter Leo. *Centennial Essays for the Milwaukee Archdiocese, 1843–1943*. Milwaukee: The Author. 1943. These fourteen brief essays, extending in time from the early seventeenth century to date, treat most of the leading personalities and institutions of Milwaukee's Catholic history; notes, illustrations, and index.

177. Keegan, Gregory Joseph, M.M., and Leandro Tormo Sanz. *Experiencia misionera en la Florida (siglos XVI y XVII)*. Madrid: Consejo Superior de Investigaciones Científicas, Instituto Santo Toribio de Mongrovejo. 1957. This scholarly study of the evangelization of the aborigines in the southeastern part of the present-day United States consists of (1) an exposition of the facts reconstructed through a critical analysis of the sources and (2) an evaluation of the missionary

methods used by the religious orders (Dominicans, Jesuits, and Franciscans) and others, and of their success or failure in the "spiritual conquest."

178.   Keffer, John Poist. *Catholic Colonial Conewago*. York, Pa.: York Composition. 1965. Reprint. Westminster, Md.: Christian Classics. 1974. In this carefully compiled study (mostly from secondary sources) of the settlement in southern Pennsylvania which was served by resident Jesuit missionaries from 1741 on, the Sulpician preparatory seminary at Pigeon Hill, the old families of the area, and the clergy up to 1963 are given separate chapters. The author, a descendant of Matthias Keffer who came from the Rhineland to Pennsylvania in 1740, published *The Keffers of the Conewago Valley* in 1960.

179.   Kelly, Henry Warren. *Franciscan Missions of New Mexico, 1740–1760*. Albuquerque: University of New Mexico Press. 1941. Both the friars' ministry to the converted and heathen Indians and their conflict with the secular authorities during a period of "mellow decline" and of attack by predatory nomads are presented on the basis of some manuscript sources in this thesis submitted for honors at Harvard University. It is Volume X of the Historical Society of New Mexico's Publications in History series.

180.   Kennedy, John H. *Jesuit and Savage in New France*. New Haven: Yale University Press. 1950. A monograph that brings a fresh approach to an old theme through a reworking of the standard printed sources with a view to showing the "debt of Bourbon France to Indian America and of free thinking reformers to men of orthodoxy" (p. vii); originally a Ph.D. thesis; awarded the John Gilmary Shea Prize of the American Catholic Historical Association in 1950.

181.   Kenny, Michael, S.J. *The Romance of the Floridas*. Milwaukee: Bruce. 1934. A semipopular account of the Jesuit missions from 1565 to 1574 with introductory chapters on the period 1512–1565.

182.   Kessell, John L. *Friars, Soldiers, and Reformers: Hispanic Arizona and the Sonora Mission Frontier, 1767–1856*. Tucson: University of Arizona Press. 1976. Built on extensive research in manuscript as well as published sources, and beautifully illustrated, this history extending from the expulsion of the Jesuits through Mexican independence to the coming of the United States Army is focused on the

leading personalities among the Franciscans and their difficulties with the civil and military authorities, the colonists, the Indians, the Bishop of Sonora, and some of their own confreres.

183. _____ . *Kiva, Cross, and Crown: The Pecos Indians and New Mexico, 1540–1840.* Washington, D.C.: National Park Service, U.S. Department of the Interior. 1979. Based on primary sources and richly illustrated, this history uses the village of Cicuye on the Pecos River as a lens to project a broad picture of the missions, including the protracted conflicts between the Franciscans and the government authorities.

184. _____ . *Mission of Sorrows: Jesuit Guevavi and the Pimas, 1691–1767.* Tucson: University of Arizona Press. 1970. This first study in depth of a single missionary center, that of Los Santos Ángeles de Guevavi (located in what is now southern Arizona), is woven around the lives of the sixteen resident or itinerant Jesuits who served it in spite of the indifference or hostility of the local Indians, the attacks of marauding savages, and the greed and arrogance of the colonists.

185. Kinsella, Thomas A. *A Centenary of Catholicity in Kansas, 1822–1922.* Kansas City: Casey. 1921. Popular sketches and notes on priests, religious, and parishes; an appendix carries a translation of the diary of Christian Hoecken, S.J. (1808–1851), a Belgian-born missionary who labored among the Potawatomi Indians from 1838 to 1847.

186. Kirlin, Joseph L. J. *Catholicity in Philadelphia.* Philadelphia: John J. McVey. 1909. A large semipopular work based on printed sources; lists of priests ordained for the Archdiocese of Philadelphia from 1832 to date; now superseded by Connelly (No. 126).

187. Kocher, Paul H. *California's Old Missions: The Story of the Founding of the Twenty-one Franciscan Missions in Spanish Alta California, 1769–1823.* Chicago: Franciscan Herald Press. 1976. A brief chronological account with references to sources is followed by an appendix on the development of each mission after its establishment and its subsequent history up to the present day.

188. Labbé, Dolores Egger. *Jim Crow Comes to Church: The Establishment of Segregated Catholic Parishes in South Louisiana.* 2nd ed. Lafayette: University of Southwestern Louisiana. 1971. Reprint.

New York: Arno. 1978. This master's thesis, reproduced from a typescript, studies the introduction of separate parishes for blacks between 1895 and 1918 and their becoming permanent and normal.

189.   Lambing, Andrew A. *A History of the Catholic Church in the Dioceses of Pittsburgh and Allegheny.* New York: Benziger. 1880. A semipopular work done by counties, religious communities, parishes, etc.

190.   Lamott, John H. *History of the Archdiocese of Cincinnati, 1821–1921.* New York: Frederick Pustet. 1921. A centennial work by a trained historian that provides one of the best accounts of an American diocese; fully documented, an ample index, and a lengthy appendix that contains useful additional data.

191.   Landerholm, Carl. *Notices and Voyages of the Famed Quebec Mission to the Pacific Northwest.* Portland: Oregon Historical Society. 1958. A competent translation and edition of letters and missionary reports sent from the Oregon Country to ecclesiastical superiors in Quebec for the years 1838–1847; an introduction, contemporary maps, and a good index.

192.   Lanning, John Tate. *The Spanish Missions of Georgia.* Chapel Hill: University of North Carolina Press. 1935. A work of thorough scholarship on these seventeenth-century missions; equipped with notes, bibliography, maps, etc.

193.   Leahy, Walter T. *The Catholic Church of the Diocese of Trenton.* Princeton: The Author. 1907. A popular compilation containing biographical sketches, pastoral letters, and data on religious communities.

194.   Leger, Mary Celeste, Sister. *The Catholic Indian Missions in Maine, 1611–1820.* Washington, D.C.: Catholic University of America Press. 1929. Reprint. New York: AMS. 1974. A slender but competent Ph.D. thesis based upon manuscript materials and printed sources with accompanying maps.

195.   Lemarié, Charles. *Les missionnaires bretons de l'Indiana au XIXe siècle.* Angers: The Author. 1973. A sequel to the life of Bishop Bruté of Vincennes (No. 510), this well-documented volume, reproduced from a typescript, treats the episcopate of Célestine de la Hailandière (1839–1847), the founding and trials of the Sisters of Providence at

Saint Mary-of-the-Woods, and the lives of the priests from Brittany who labored in Indiana. It is the third volume of the author's trilogy Etudes sur les missionnaires bretons dans le Middle West Américain.

196.   Lewis, Clifford M., S.J., and Albert J. Loomie, S.J. *The Spanish Jesuit Mission in Virginia, 1570–1572.* Chapel Hill: University of North Carolina Press. 1953. A thorough and scholarly monograph that makes full use of all available sources on the brief and fatal mission; besides the narrative there are tables, maps, charts, a bibliography, and a section on anthropological data; a further lengthy section includes documents in the original Spanish with accompanying translations, which run from the letter of the mission leaders on September 12, 1570, to documents as late as 1609 that deal with the sequel to the mission.

197.   Lord, Robert H., John E. Sexton, and Edward T. Harrington. *History of the Archdiocese of Boston in the Various Stages of Its Development, 1604–1943.* 3 vols. New York: Sheed and Ward. 1944. This work took rank at once as the best history of an American diocese so far published; a work of thorough scholarship for the first two and a half volumes, the last half of the final volume being too recent for definitive treatment; see the review in the *Catholic Historical Review*, XXX (January, 1945), 427–429.

198.   Lucey, William Leo, S.J. *The Catholic Church in Maine.* Francetown, N.H.: Marshall Jones. 1957. A general account written to commemorate the centennial of the Diocese of Portland; the bibliographical notes (pp. 351–355) discuss the sources used.

199.   Lyons, Letitia Mary, Sister. *Francis Norbert Blanchet and the Founding of the Oregon Missions, 1838–1848.* Washington, D.C.: Catholic University of America Press. 1940. Reprint. New York: AMS. 1974. An able Ph.D. thesis that makes good use of manuscript sources in Quebec archives for a critical decade in the Oregon Country.

200.   McAvoy, Thomas T., C.S.C. *The Catholic Church in Indiana, 1780–1834.* New York: Columbia University Press. 1940. Reprint. New York: AMS. 1967. This able Ph.D. thesis is particularly notable for the amount of unpublished material brought to light from widely scattered ecclesiastical archives.

201.   McGee, John W. *The Catholic Church in the Grand River Valley,*

1833–1950. Grand Rapids: The Author. 1950. A semipopular work which is more in the nature of a chronicle of Catholicism in Grand Rapids and its environs than a history of the diocese.

202. McGovern, Patrick A. *History of the Diocese of Cheyenne.* Cheyenne: Chancery Office. 1941. A series of brief popular sketches on a parish basis by the fourth Bishop of Cheyenne; based on data submitted in questionnaires by pastors; not a scientific work.

203. McNamara, Robert F. *The Diocese of Rochester, 1868–1968.* Rochester: Diocese of Rochester. 1968. This well-written history of the Church in twelve counties of western New York begins with the early seventeenth century and concludes with the first half-year of Bishop Fulton J. Sheen's administration. It includes the social concerns of the Catholics and relates the growth and struggle of the Church to contemporary secular events and developments.

204. McNamara, William, C.S.C. *The Catholic Church on the Northern Indiana Frontier, 1789–1844.* Washington, D.C.: Catholic University of America Press. 1931. Reprint. New York: AMS. 1974. A Ph.D. thesis that is now largely superseded by McAvoy (No. 200).

205. Magri, F. Joseph. *The Catholic Church in the City and Diocese of Richmond.* Richmond: Whittet and Shepperson. 1906. A brief popular and illustrated account by episcopal administrations; no indication of sources, although there is an index; now superseded in part by Bailey (No. 102).

206. Martin, M. Aquinata, Sister, O.P. *The Catholic Church on the Nebraska Frontier, 1854–1885.* Washington, D.C.: Catholic University of America Press. 1937. Reprint. New York: AMS. 1974. The place that the Church occupied as a social institution among the early settlers is elucidated from a variety of sources.

207. Mattingly, Mary Ramona, Sister. *The Catholic Church on the Kentucky Frontier, 1785–1812.* Washington, D.C.: Catholic University of America Press. 1936. Reprint. New York: AMS. 1974. This and the above item belong to a series of Ph.D. theses which offer good accounts of the effect of the frontier in shaping the history of the Church in these western outposts.

208. Member of the Order of Mercy [Mary Teresa Austin Carroll]. *A Catholic History of Alabama and the Floridas.* New York: P. J.

Kenedy. 1908. Reprint. Freeport, N.Y.: Books for Libraries. 1970. A popular compilation with emphasis on the colonial period.

209. Merwick, Donna. *Boston Priests, 1848–1910: A Study of Social and Intellectual Change.* Cambridge, Mass.: Harvard University Press. 1973. This revised doctoral dissertation from the University of Wisconsin reveals how the lives and attitudes of Catholic clergymen, of whom many prominent ones were not Irish immigrants, were influenced by the surrounding Yankee culture; it centers on the long episcopate of Archbishop John J. Williams, whose laissez-faire policy fostered diversity and pluralism within the archdiocese; it is reliable in its main conclusions in spite of some factual inaccuracies.

210. Miller, Robert R. *That All May Be One: A History of the Rockford Diocese.* Rockford, Ill.: Diocese of Rockford. 1976. Organized in imitation of the Second Vatican Council's constitution *Lumen Gentium* but supported by insufficient research, this popular, profusely illustrated book gives the background to the erection of the diocese in 1908, biographical sketches of the bishops, historical profiles of the individual parishes, institutions, and agencies, and brief accounts of the religious congregations of men and women.

211. Moeder, John W. *Early Catholicity in Kansas and History of the Diocese of Wichita.* Wichita: Chancery Office. 1937. A series of popular sketches and notes on bishops, priests, religious, and parishes.

212. Mulrenan, Patrick. *A Brief Historical Sketch of the Catholic Church on Long Island.* New York: P. O'Shea. 1871. A popular work now superseded by Sharp (No. 243).

213. Noll, John F. *The Diocese of Fort Wayne: Fragments of History.* Vol. II. Fort Wayne: The Author. 1941. A popular account that takes up where Alerding (No. 99) left off in 1907; compiled by the fifth Bishop of Fort Wayne.

214. Norton, Mary Aquinas, Sister. *Catholic Missionary Activities in the Northwest, 1818–1864.* Washington, D.C.: Catholic University of America Press. 1930. A Ph.D. thesis that employs a considerable amount of material from Canadian as well as American archives.

215. Nute, Grace Lee. *Documents relating to the Northwest Missions, 1815–1827.* St. Paul: Minnesota Historical Society. 1942. An excellent edition of letters and reports—with translations—from the

Indian missions in the Red River area; although dealing mostly with Canadian efforts, the boundaries at the time were not clear and later missionaries in this region came from the United States.

216.   O'Connell, Jeremiah J. *Catholicity in the Carolinas and Georgia, 1820–1878*. New York: D. and J. Sadlier. 1879. Facsimile reprint: Westminster, Md.: Ars Sacra. 1964. Reprint. Spartanburg, S.C.: Reprint Company. 1972. Although based on consultation of many historical records and documents, this book is essentially written from the personal recollections of the author, a priest, and from eyewitness accounts of contemporary people. It relates the establishment of missions, churches, and institutions, and describes the work of the early clergy.

217.   O'Connor, Dominic, O.F.M.Cap. (Vol. I), and Patrick J. Gaire (Vol. II). *A Brief History of the Diocese of Baker*. Reprint (2 vols. in 1). St. Benedict, Ore.: Benedictine Press. 1966. This inspirational survey of the diocese founded in 1903 for a sparsely populated part of Oregon emphasizes topics that interested the authors and lacks references to the diocesan archives and other source materials that have been used.

218.   O'Donnell, James H. *History of the Diocese of Hartford*. Boston: D. H. Hurd. 1900. A series of disparate chapters focused on the colonial period and the years preceding the establishment of the diocese in 1843 is followed by biographical sketches of the bishops and an account of the founding of each parish and mission church.

219.   O'Hara, Edwin V. *Pioneer Catholic History of Oregon*. 3rd ed. Paterson: St. Anthony Guild. 1939. A brief popular account, now superseded by later research, e.g., Lyons (No. 199); written by the late Bishop of Kansas City and originally published in 1911, when he was a priest of the Archdiocese of Oregon City.

220.   O'Neill, Charles Edwards. *Church and State in French Colonial Louisiana: Policy and Politics to 1732*. New Haven: Yale University Press. 1966. The fruit of extensive research which is evidenced both in the footnotes and in the bibliography, this pioneering study of the religious policy of the French monarchy in the colonization of the lower Mississippi Valley treats theory and practice through successive regimes from the founding of the colony in 1699 to its retrocession to the king by the Company of the Indies. It focuses on the interrelated attitudes and activities of ecclesiastical and civil officials in Louisiana, Canada, and France, places these relationships in the

context of European national rivalries, and includes not only missionary work among the Indians and interracial problems, but also conflicts among the churchmen themselves.

221. O'Rourke, Alice, O.P. *The Good Work Begun: Centennial History of Peoria Diocese.* N.p. [1977]. This brief history treats chiefly the persons and events that have affected the development of the Church in north central Illinois, beginning with the missionary work and early settlement that preceded the appointment of the first bishop, John Lancaster Spalding, in 1877.

222. O'Rourke, Thomas P., C.S.B. *The Franciscan Missions in Texas, 1690–1793.* Washington, D.C.: Catholic University of America Press. 1927. Reprint. New York: AMS. 1974. A Ph.D. thesis done entirely from printed sources and secondary works and now superseded by Castañeda (No. 123).

223. Owens, M. Lilliana, Sister. *Jesuit Beginnings in New Mexico, 1867–1885.* El Paso: Revista Católica. 1950. A brief documented treatment followed by a reprint of the New Mexico mission diary of Livio Vigilante, S.J. (1818–1895), from May 27, 1867, to October 18, 1874; one of several works on the missions of the Neapolitan Jesuits in the Southwest.

224. Palladino, Lawrence B., S.J. *Indian and White in the Northwest: A History of Catholicity in Montana, 1831–1891.* Rev. ed. Lancaster, Pa.: Wickersham. 1922. A full account by a missionary who spent nearly forty years in Montana; contains a good deal of information with quotations from various sources, although the latter are not systematically indicated.

225. Palm, Mary Borgias, Sister. *The Jesuit Missions of the Illinois Country, 1673–1763.* N.p. 1933. A Ph.D. dissertation done at St. Louis University under the direction of Gilbert J. Garraghan, S.J. The account extends from the voyage of Jacques Marquette to the banishment of the French Jesuits.

226. Paré, George. *The Catholic Church in Detroit, 1701–1888.* Detroit: Gabriel Richard. 1951. A work of solid scholarship that treats the story from the founding of Detroit to the advent of John S. Foley (1833–1918), the fourth bishop to govern the See of Detroit; awarded the John Gilmary Shea Prize of the American Catholic Historical Association in 1951.

227. Pillar, James J., O.M.I. *The Catholic Church in Mississippi, 1837–1865*. New Orleans: Hauser. 1964. Based on extensive archival research in Europe and the United States, this history of the Diocese of Natchez from its establishment to the end of the Civil War was originally written as a doctoral dissertation at the Pontifical Gregorian University.

228. Prince, Le Baron Bradford. *Spanish Mission Churches of New Mexico*. Cedar Rapids, Iowa: Torch. 1915. Reprint. Glorietta, N. Mex.: Rio Grande. 1977. The history of each church is given, along with a description of the building or the ruins.

229. Purcell, William P. *Catholic Pittsburgh's One Hundred Years*. Chicago: Loyola University Press. 1943. A series of eighteen popular essays by various authors written in commemoration of the establishment of the Diocese of Pittsburgh in August, 1843; not, however, a history of the diocese.

230. Reardon, James Michael. *The Catholic Church in the Diocese of St. Paul*. St. Paul: North Central. 1952. Intended as a commemoration of the diocesan centennial (July 19, 1850), this large volume treats the subject under the heading of the various episcopal administrations; parish and institutional sketches are sensibly placed at the back of the book; about one-third of the volume is devoted to the regime of John Ireland (1838–1918).

231. Rezek, Antoine Ivan. *History of the Diocese of Sault Ste. Marie and Marquette*. 2 vols. Houghton, Mich.: The Author. 1906–1907. A popular and illustrated compilation.

232. Riley, Arthur J. *Catholicism in New England to 1788*. Washington, D.C.: Catholic University of America Press. 1936. This large and competent Ph.D. thesis is more a study of anti-Catholicism in the area than the title would indicate.

233. Rothensteiner, John. *History of the Archdiocese of St. Louis*. 2 vols. St. Louis: The Author. 1928. One of the better diocesan histories, although not a readable work; makes ample use of both unpublished and printed materials. For the period subsequent to the year of publication see Faherty (No. 142).

234. Rummel, Leo, O.Praem. *History of the Catholic Church in Wisconsin*. Madison: Wisconsin State Council, Knights of Columbus. 1976. This bicentennial publication is not a chronologically arranged account but rather consists of two introductory chapters on the white

man's entrance into the area and the early organization of the Church, sketches of each immigrant group, religious order, seminary, university, and college, a list of parishes by diocese, and a series of biographical profiles of the bishops in the state since 1844.

235. Russell, William T. *Maryland: The Land of Sanctuary*. Baltimore: J. H. Furst. 1907. An old but still useful book by the fifth Bishop of Charleston which carefully documents the story from the founding of the colony to the American Revolution.

236. Ryan, Paul E. *History of the Diocese of Covington, Kentucky*. Covington: Chancery Office. 1954. A large volume to commemorate the diocesan centennial (July 29, 1853) treated on the basis of episcopal administrations with sketches of the parishes, diocesan institutions, and priests serving the diocese at time of publication; citation of sources with notes (pp. 947–1028).

237. Salpointe, Jean Baptiste. *Soldiers of the Cross: Notes on the Ecclesiastical History of New Mexico, Arizona, and Colorado*. Banning, Calif.: St. Boniface's Industrial School. 1898. Reprint. Albuquerque: Calvin Horn. 1967. Well described in the subtitle, this old work has value for the last third of the volume where the author, a missionary priest and bishop for nearly forty years (1859–1898) in the Southwest, gives firsthand descriptions of many of the events and persons he had experienced and known.

238. Schiwetz, Edward Muegge. *Six Spanish Missions in Texas: A Portfolio of Paintings*. Austin: University of Texas Press. 1968. Six large reproductions in full color with brief accounts of the founding and building of the eighteenth-century missions by Robert S. Weddle.

239. Schoenberg, Wilfred P., S.J. *A Chronicle of Catholic History of the Pacific Northwest, 1743–1960*. Spokane: Gonzaga Preparatory School. 1962. A lengthy listing of events in Catholic history of the region with references to further reading, sources, etc.

240. Scholes, France V. *Church and State in New Mexico, 1616–1650*. Albuquerque: University of New Mexico Press. 1937. A scholarly monograph that appeared originally as a series of articles in the *New Mexico Historical Review;* extensive quotations from manuscript sources in the numerous notes.

241. _____ . *Troublesome Times in New Mexico, 1659–1670*. Albuquerque: University of New Mexico Press. 1942. A continuation

of the above, this work is especially enlightening for the role played by the Holy Office in New Mexico's colonial history.

242.   Schroeder, Mary Carol, Sister, O.S.F. *The Catholic Church in the Diocese of Vincennes, 1847–1877.* Washington, D.C.: Catholic University of America Press. 1946. A Ph.D. thesis that puts the history of a troubled generation in Indiana Catholicism on a solid basis with the use of much archival material.

243.   Sharp, John K. *History of the Diocese of Brooklyn, 1853–1953.* 2 vols. New York: Fordham University Press. 1954. This attractively produced centennial work embodies a large amount of data, although the value to scholars is lessened by an uncritical approach.

244.   Smith, John Talbot. *The Catholic Church in New York.* 2 vols. New York: Hall and Locke. 1908. These two large and well-written volumes were published as a commemoration of New York's diocesan centennial (April 8, 1808); they lack the critical attitude of the trained historian and are out of date in many particulars; a new history of the Archdiocese of New York is badly needed.

245.   _____ . *A History of the Diocese of Ogdensburg.* New York: John W. Lovell. 1885. An old and popular work done on a town-by-town basis. Now superseded by Taylor (No. 249).

246.   Sorrentino, Giuseppe M., S.J. *Dalle Montagne Rocciose al Rio Bravo: Brevi appunti storici circa la missione gesuitica del Nuovo Messico e Colorado negli Stati Uniti di America.* Naples: Casa Editrice Federico e Ardia. 1948. An account of the Neapolitan Jesuits' missions in the United States from 1867 to 1919 by one of the missionaries; a list of the archives consulted given at the end of the book.

247.   Spalding, Martin J. *Sketches of the Early Catholic Missions of Kentucky from their Commencement in 1787 to the Jubilee in 1826.* Louisville: B. J. Webb. 1844. Reprint. New York: Arno. 1970. An important source for Kentucky Catholicism in the years covered by an eyewitness to some of the events described, a member of one of Kentucky's leading Catholic families who served in the state as priest and bishop (1834–1864) and died as seventh Archbishop of Baltimore. With the aid of an early missionary, Spalding compiled this important account of Catholic life on the western frontier. Since much of the material on which these sketches are based is now lost, the value of this unique history is greatly enhanced.

248. Stanton, Thomas J. *A Century of Growth, Or the History of the Church in Western Maryland.* 2 vols. Baltimore: John Murphy. 1900. A popular and illustrated account of the parishes and institutions treated by county.

249. Taylor, Mary Christine, Sister, S.S.J. *A History of the Foundations of Catholicism in Northern New York.* New York: United States Catholic Historical Society. 1976. Beginning with the French missionary activity of the seventeenth century, the author traces the development of the Church in the eight counties which were to comprise the Diocese of Ogdensburg in 1872 and concludes with the death of the first bishop, Edgar P. Wadhams, in 1891. She presents a documented chronology of the establishment of institutions, but also describes the poor immigrant laity and the national friction between the Irish and the French-Canadians. This volume is a reproduction of the typescript of a doctoral dissertation done at Saint Louis University in 1968. Cf. No. 245.

250. Thompson, Joseph J. *The Diocese of Springfield in Illinois.* Springfield: Hartman. 1928. A diamond jubilee production, popular in character.

251. Timon, John, C.M. *Missions in Western New York and Church History of the Diocese of Buffalo.* Buffalo: Catholic Sentinel Print. 1862. A brief sketch by the first Bishop of Buffalo; more apologetic than historical in character; most of the volume deals with the colonial period; this part is now out of date and contains numerous inaccuracies; the account is carried down to 1847, the year of the establishment of the See of Buffalo; the latter part has more value, since the author himself was then on the scene.

252. Trisco, Robert Frederick. *The Holy See and the Nascent Church in the Middle Western United States, 1826–1850.* Rome: Gregorian University Press. 1962. This doctoral dissertation, based mainly on research in the Propaganda Fide Archives, studies Rome's contribution to the growth of Catholicism through the establishment of dioceses, the appointment of bishops, the obtaining and training of clergy, the provision of material aid, the governance of religious orders, and the maintenance of discipline.

253. Vogel, Claude L., O.M.Cap. *The Capuchins in French Louisiana, 1722–1766.* Washington, D.C.: Catholic University of America Press. 1928. Reprint. New York: AMS. 1974. A Ph.D.

thesis done largely from manuscript materials; informative on the Capuchin-Jesuit controversy, but at times lacking in an objective tone and approach.

254.   Walker, Fintan G. *The Catholic Church in the Meeting of Two Frontiers: The Southern Illinois Country, 1763–1793*. Washington, D.C.: Catholic University of America Press. 1935. Reprint. New York: AMS. 1974. The printed sources for this Ph.D. thesis have been supplemented by research in the Quebec archives.

255.   Walsh, Henry L., S.J. *Hallowed Were the Gold Dust Trails: The Story of the Pioneer Priests of Northern California*. Santa Clara: University of Santa Clara. 1946. A semipopular treatment done by sections of what is today the Diocese of Sacramento; considerable correspondence printed along with notes and index.

256.   Webb, Ben J. *The Centenary of Catholicity in Kentucky*. Louisville: Charles A. Rogers. 1884. This old but informative work by a nonprofessional is now superseded in many particulars by more recent research, e.g., Schauinger, Mattingly, McGann (Nos. 562, 207, 1174).

257.   Weber, Francis J. *California Catholicism: A Holy Year Tribute*. Los Angeles: The Author. 1975. The 120 vignettes contained in this volume, each less than two pages long, were in large part previously published in unidentified newspapers and magazines but have been revised to some extent; they are divided into seven sections: "Episcopal Trailblazers," "Sacerdotal Pioneers," "Franciscan Giants," "People of God," "Missionary Enterprises," "Pastoral Scene," and "The Church in Action."

258.   _____ . *California Catholicity*. Los Angeles: Dawson's Book Shop. 1979. This sixth volume of brief articles (120 in number) that originally appeared in *The Tidings* and are here augmented and corrected is divided into six sections dealing with individual lay men and women, friars and priests, bishops, the missions, "Reminiscences," and "Pastoral Life."

259.   _____ . *The California Missions as Others Saw Them, 1786–1842*. Los Angeles: Dawson's Book Shop. 1972. In this small book the author critically assesses in chronological order the historical credibility and literary skill of twenty-four visitors who recorded observations of the Franciscans and their Indian charges.

260. _____ . *California's Catholic Heritage*. Los Angeles: Dawson's Book Shop. 1974. The 125 brief articles collected in this fourth volume of the writer's weekly column in *The Tidings* treat a wide variety of topics in popular fashion.

261. _____ . *Catholic Footprints in California*. Newhall, Calif.: Hogarth Press. 1970. This collection of 125 brief essays previously published as newspaper articles dealing with missionary days, prelates, priests and nuns, lay people, organizations and institutions, and miscellaneous topics, and based on much original research, can be useful for local history.

262. _____ , ed. *Documents of California Catholic History, 1784– 1963*. Los Angeles: Dawson's Book Shop. 1965. This collection of sixty-five documents, taken in large measure from the archives of the Archdiocese of Los Angeles, includes not only papal bulls, government decrees, and official reports but also pastoral letters, newspaper accounts, memoirs, and addresses; each document has a brief introduction.

263. _____ , ed. *The Observations of Benjamin Cummings Truman on El Camino Real*. Los Angeles: Dawson's Book Shop. 1978. This series of nineteen articles on the California missions was probably published in the Los Angeles *Star* around 1870. The editor has given identifications and bibliographical references in the footnotes. Thirty-two photographs of some of the missions, taken in 1897, are reproduced here as illustrations.

264. _____ . *The Pilgrim Church in California*. Los Angeles: Dawson's Book Shop. 1973. In this third volume of the series, 150 brief articles that were originally published in the author's weekly column in *The Tidings* have been gathered, in somewhat revised form, for the sake of more convenient and permanent availability.

265. _____ . *Readings in California Catholic History*. Los Angeles: Westernlore. 1967. This collection of 132 brief essays which were originally published in the author's syndicated newspaper column, covers a great variety of topics pertaining to the missions, the bishops, the priests and laymen, the institutions, and local events and buildings of California.

266. _____ , ed. *Some California Catholic Reminiscences for the United States Bicentennial*. Los Angeles: Dawson's Book Shop. 1976.

Twelve papers which were originally presented at three seminars by various scholars treat topics ranging from the colonial to the early American period.

267.   Weibel, John Eugene. *The Catholic Missions of North-East Arkansas, 1867–1893.* Trans. Sister M. Agnes Voth, O.S.B. Ed. Lee A. Dew. State University: Arkansas State University Press. 1967. Originally published in German in 1893, this brief work includes the early history of the first convent of Benedictine nuns in Arkansas, Maria Stein at Pocahontas. The author, a Swiss priest who entered the area in 1879, was one of the itinerant clergy who established churches and schools in the isolated communities.

268.   Yzermans, Vincent A., ed. *Catholic Origins of Minnesota.* St. Cloud: Fourth Degree Knights of Columbus. 1961. This collection of ten brief, popular essays by different writers such as James P. Shannon and Colman J. Barry, O.S.B., is lavishly illustrated.

269.   Zubillaga, Felix, S.J. *La Florida, la Misión Jesuítica 1566–1572, y la Colonización española.* Rome: Institutum Historicum Societatis Jesu. 1941. This doctoral dissertation, written at the Pontifical Gregorian University and based on all the available sources which the author collected through exhaustive research, especially in archives, is a full history of the Spanish ventures in what is now the southeastern United States from 1513 to the death of Menéndez de Avilés.

270.   _____ , ed. *Monumenta antiquae Floridae, 1566–1572.* Rome: Monumenta Historica Societatis Jesu. 1946. Most of the documents pertaining to the ill-fated Jesuit mission in the present-day southeastern United States are published with copious annotations and a long introduction in Latin.

B. PARISH AND MISSION HISTORIES

Among the 18,794 parishes of the Catholic Church in the United States in 1980 several hundred issued publications to commemorate their jubilees. Only a very small portion of these numerous books and brochures, however, have made any contribution to history in the true sense. More frequently than not they have been hurried compilations containing pictures, lists of the pastors, teachers in the parish school, and the names of parishioners who became priests and religious. No effort has been made, therefore, to include them here. The following list represents only a small selection of some of the better works in this category.

271. Bezou, Henry C. *Metairie: A Tongue of Land to Pasture: An Account of the Development of the Faith Community in East Jefferson Deanery Commemorating the Fiftieth Anniversary of St. Francis Xavier Parish, Metairie, Louisiana.* Gretna, La.: Pelican. 1973. Though it lacks references to sources, this is a reliable history not merely of the ecclesiastical parish but of Catholicity in the eastern part of Jefferson Parish from the early eighteenth century to the present.

272. Browne, Henry J. *St. Ann's on East Twelfth Street, New York City, 1852–1952.* New York: Roman Catholic Church of St. Ann. 1952. A scholarly brochure that makes good use of both archival sources and the reminiscences of old parishioners; notable also for the manner in which the record of the parish is woven into the city's history.

273. _____ . *The Parish of St. Michael, 1857–1957: A Century of Grace on the West Side.* New York: Church of St. Michael. 1957. Another centennial brochure that embodies the features mentioned in the above item as well as illustrations and lists of the parish personnel.

274. Burton, Katherine. *The Dream Lives Forever: The Story of St. Patrick's Cathedral.* New York: Longmans, Green. 1960. A popular, undocumented history of the construction and embellishment of the cathedral of New York from the laying of the cornerstone by Archbishop John Hughes in 1858 is combined with a chronicle of the noteworthy religious ceremonies held in it to 1960.

275. Carthy, Mary Peter, Mother, O.S.U. *Old St. Patrick's : New York's First Cathedral.* New York: United States Catholic Historical Society. 1947. Originally a thesis for the A.M. degree, this documented monograph gives an able account of one of the historic parishes of the East.

276. Colley, Van Buren. *History of the Diocesan Shrine of the Immaculate Conception.* Atlanta: Diocesan Shrine of the Immaculate Conception. 1955. This volume tells the story of Catholicism in Atlanta, Georgia, since the 1840's with excellent contemporary photographs; scarcity of parochial records is made up in part by close coverage of the secular press such as the old Atlanta *Daily New Era* and the Atlanta *Constitution.*

277. Culleton, James. *Indians and Pioneers of Old Monterey.* Fresno: Academy of California Church History. 1950. An annotated chroni-

cle of the Mission of San Carlos Borromeo from its founding by
Junípero Serra at Carmel in June, 1770, down to 1819.

278.   Davis, William L., S.J. *A History of St. Ignatius Mission: An
Outpost of Catholic Culture on the Montana Frontier*. Spokane: Gonzaga
University. 1954. A scholarly treatment for the centennial of a
mission established by Pierre-Jean De Smet, S.J. (1801–1873),
northwest of Missoula, Montana; useful for the Indian mission history of the area.

279.   Doll, Louis William. *The History of Saint Thomas Parish, Ann
Arbor*. Ann Arbor: Ann Arbor Press. 1941. A superior study on a
Michigan parish that began in 1840 as an indirect result of the
Michigan Central Railroad.

280.   Dufour, Charles L. *1833 . . . St. Patrick's of New Orleans . . .
1958*. New Orleans: St. Patrick's Parish. 1958. An attractively illustrated work by twelve different authors whose popular essays man-
age to weave a good deal of the history of the city into the story of St.
Patrick's 125 years.

281.   Garraghan, Gilbert J., S.J. *St. Ferdinand de Florissant: The
Story of an Ancient Parish*. Chicago: Loyola University Press. 1923. A
serious monograph on a parish dating from 1789 that was taken over
by the Jesuits in 1823; notable as well for the history of the surrounding Indian missions.

282.   Geiger, Maynard J., O.F.M. *Mission Santa Barbara, 1782–
1965*. Santa Barbara: [Franciscan Fathers of California.] 1965. This
thorough account of the institution that has served as an Indian
mission, episcopal residence, apostolic college, boarding school,
seminary, parish, and archive (as well as tourist attraction) is a useful
contribution to the religious history of California.

283.   _____ . *A Pictorial History of the Physical Development of
Mission Santa Barbara: From Brush Hut to Institutional Greatness,
1786–1963*. Oakland: Franciscan Fathers of California. 1963. The
changes in structure are traced from sketches, paintings, photographs, plats, and blueprints or, where such original materials were
lacking, from drawings based on contemporary documents; each
illustration is accompanied by a descriptive text.

284.   Gerow, Richard O. *Cradle Days of St. Mary's at Natchez*.
Natchez, Miss.: The Author. 1941. In this volume the late Bishop of

Natchez-Jackson traces the story from 1798 to date with numerous documents, in whole or in part from the diocesan archives.

285. Gleeson, Charles J. *Outpost on Poverty Flat*. Central Valley, Calif.: Books. 1978. This brief but well documented and illustrated history of the Church in the Shasta area of California from the coming of the first priest in 1853 to the present contains much information about events and persons not directly related to Catholicism.

286. Greer, Edward C. *Cork Hill Cathedral: The Chronicle of St. Margaret's and Sacred Heart Parish, Davenport, Iowa, 1856–1956*. Davenport: Gordon. 1956. A substantial, if not critical, account of the parish as well as of the cathedral erected in 1890–1891.

287. Habig, Marion A., O.F.M. *The Alamo Chain of Missions: A History of San Antonio's Five Old Missions*. Chicago: Franciscan Herald Press. 1968. In this popular history prepared for the 250th anniversary of the founding of the city each mission is treated separately from its establishment to its secularization and, where verified, to its restoration in the twentieth century.

288. _____ . *San Antonio's Mission San José: State and National Historic Site, 1720–1968*. San Antonio: Naylor. 1968. Simply written for the general reader, lacking references to the primary sources employed, but containing all kinds of disparate data, this book commemorating the bicentennial of the beginning of the existing church narrates the history of the huge mission from its founding down to its twentieth-century restoration.

289. Kelly, George Anthony. *The Parish as Seen from the Church of St. John the Evangelist, New York City, 1840–1973*. New York: St. John's University. 1973. This substantial history of the parish founded for Irish Catholics in midtown Manhattan focuses attention on the pastors while neglecting the parishioners and contains some unsubstantiated generalizations.

290. _____ . *The Story of St. Monica's Parish, New York City, 1879–1954*. New York: Monica. 1954. A diamond jubilee book that makes use of archival materials and incorporates a notable amount of demographic data.

291. Kleber, Albert, O.S.B. *St. Joseph Parish, Jasper, Indiana*. St. Meinrad: St. Meinrad Abbey. 1937. This and the author's similar brochures on St. Ferdinand Parish, Ferdinand, Indiana (1940), and

St. Pius Parish, Troy, Indiana (1947), are of particular interest as studies of German immigrant communities.

292.   McCarthy, Francis Florence. *The History of Mission San Jose, California, 1797–1835*. Fresno: Academy Library Guild. 1958. This work, based on research in the archives of the Archdiocese of San Francisco, Santa Barbara Mission, and the Bancroft Library, was originally written in 1948; the editor, Raymond F. Wood, supplies an epilogue covering the years 1835–1855.

293.   McDermott, John Francis. *Old Cahokia: A Narrative and Documents Illustrating the First Century of Its History*. St. Louis: St. Louis Historical Documents Foundation. 1949. A cooperative work of eight essays by different authors on the old French settlement founded in 1699 and its Holy Family Parish.

294.   McNamara, Robert F. *A Century of Grace: The History of St. Mary's Roman Catholic Church, Corning, New York, 1848–1948*. Corning: St. Mary's Church. 1948. 2nd edition. 1979. A first-class centennial story of a northern New York parish.

295.   Philibert, Helene, Estelle Philibert, and Imogene Philibert. *Saint Matthew's of Washington, 1840–1940*. Baltimore: A. Hoen. 1940. A centennial volume on the cathedral parish of the Archdiocese of Washington that combines accuracy of facts with a well-written narrative, splendid illustrations, and an attractive format; many names of national prominence appear in its pages.

296.   Porter, Jack W., and William F. Stineman. *The Catholic Church in Greencastle, Putnam County, Indiana, 1848–1978*. Greencastle, Ind.: St. Paul the Apostle Church. 1979. This well-documented and -illustrated study adopts a social and cultural approach to local religious history.

297.   Reilly, George L. A. *A Century of Catholicism: History of the Church of the Immaculate Conception, Montclair, New Jersey*. Newark: Washington Irving. 1957. An able work that employs interviews with old parishioners to supplement the meager records; the hand of the trained historian is evident in this and the following item.

298.   ———— . *Sacred Heart in Bloomfield*. Bloomfield, N.J.: Sacred Heart Rectory. 1953. A diamond jubilee book that, like the preceding item, gives more than ordinary attention to the secular background of the area and its relation to parochial developments.

299. Riordan, Michael J. *Cathedral Records from the Beginning of Catholicism in Baltimore to the Present Time*. Baltimore: Catholic Mirror. 1906. Strictly speaking, this is not a parish history, but in lieu of an up-to-date and scholarly treatment of the first American Catholic cathedral parish it is useful as containing a considerable amount of data on the Cathedral of the Assumption.

300. Ryan, Leo Raymond. *Old St. Peter's: The Mother Church of Catholic New York, 1785–1935*. New York: United States Catholic Historical Society. 1935. A century and a half of the history of a parish that played a leading role in the lay trustee troubles of the early nineteenth century; done originally as a Ph.D. thesis.

301. Schulte, Paul C. *The Catholic Heritage of St. Louis: A History of the Old Cathedral Parish, St. Louis, Missouri*. St. Louis: Catholic Herald. 1934. A serious treatment of a parish whose records date from 1766, by a former pastor who became Archbishop of Indianapolis; although there are no footnotes, the work has been done from early parish records and is intended as "a readable though authentic story rather than a book of reference" (p. vi).

302. Sharp, John K. *Priests and Parishes of the Diocese of Brooklyn, 1820–1944*. Manhasset, N.Y.: The Author. 1944. Lists of parishes and the names of the priests who served in them; now supplemented by the author's later work (No. 243).

303. Simpson, Lesley Byrd, ed. *The San Sabá Papers: A Documentary Account of the Founding and Destruction of San Sabá Mission*. Trans. Paul D. Nathan. San Francisco: John Howell. 1959. Most of the fifty-two documents selected from the contents of a manuscript volume composed as a permanent record for the archives of the Captaincy General of New Spain and translated here are depositions taken in the interest of the commandant of the presidio who was responsible for the protection of the mission (near the site of present-day Menard, Texas) when it was attacked by Comanche and other Indians in 1758. Cf. No. 317.

304. Temple, Sydney. *The Carmel Mission from Founding to Rebuilding*. Fresno, Calif.: Valley. 1980. A popular account of Mission San Carlos Borromeo.

305. Tourscher, Francis E., O.S.A. *The Hogan Schism and Trustee Troubles in St. Mary's Church, Philadelphia, 1820–1829*. Philadelphia: Peter Reilly. 1930. The best study so far made of one of the stormiest

episodes in American Catholic parochial history; done from documentary evidence.

306.   *Two Hundred Years, 1773–1973: History of the Catholic Church in St. Thomas.* St. Thomas, U.S. Virgin Islands: Redemptorist Fathers. 1973. This commemorative booklet on Saints Peter and Paul Church is composed of essays by three writers who treat also the broader topics of the Church in the Caribbean and specifically in the Virgin Islands prior to the arrival of the Redemptorists in 1858.

307.   Weber, Francis J. *A History of San Buenaventura Mission.* San Buenaventura, Calif.: San Buenaventura Mission Gift Shop. 1977. This small book consists of a series of popular vignettes on various topics related to the mission which was founded in 1782 and today is a parish whose church was built in 1809 and consecrated in 1976.

308.   ———— , comp. *The Jewel of the Missions: A Documentary History of San Juan Capistrano.* N.p. 1976. A collection of sixty-one items, both narrative and descriptive (documents dating from 1775 on, excerpts from books, newspaper reports, etc.) related to the California mission which was founded in the year of American Independence.

309.   ———— , comp. *The Mission by the Sea: A Documentary History of San Buenaventura Mission.* Los Angeles: Dawson's Book Shop. 1978. Seventy-three items—original documents (translated where necessary) and previously published essays by the editor and other writers—spanning two centuries are collected with introductory notes in this volume, which lacks an index.

310.   ———— , comp. *Mission Dolores: A Documentary History of San Francisco Mission.* Los Angeles: Dawson's Book Shop. 1979. Another in the series of compilations on the individual missions, this volume deals with the sixth in chronological order, which was founded in 1776.

311.   ———— , comp. *The Mission in the Valley: A Documentary History of San Fernando, Rey de España.* Los Angeles: Dawson's Book Shop. 1975. The fifty-five excerpts, articles, notes, essays, and observations by many writers (from the founder, Fray Fermín de Lasuén, to the compiler) of which this volume consists are arranged in chronological order.

312.   ———— . *Mission San Fernando.* Los Angeles: Westernlore.

1968. This small book contains an account of the founding in 1797, the daily life of the Indians, agricultural production, architecture and art, decline, and restoration of the mission located in the San Fernando Valley.

313. _____ , comp. *The Pride of the Missions: A Documentary History of San Gabriel Mission.* Los Angeles: Dawson's Book Shop. [1979.] Seventy-one items of primary and secondary source material have been collected in this volume to illuminate the history of the mission located near the site of the future pueblo of Los Angeles from its founding in 1771, through its years of prosperity, decay, and restoration, to the present.

314. _____ , comp. *Queen of the Missions: A Documentary History of Santa Barbara.* Los Angeles: Dawson's Book Shop. 1979. The sixty-five essays by various writers that are collected in this anthology were previously published in widely scattered books and journals and are here arranged in the chronological order of the subjects treated.

315. _____ . *St. Vibiana's Cathedral: A Centennial History.* Los Angeles: N.p. 1976. This brief account of the original construction, subsequent remodelings, and ultimate retention of the principal church of the Archdiocese of Los Angeles and of the main events that have occurred in it, along with biographical data on its rectors and pastors, is beautifully illustrated.

316. Weddle, Robert S. *San Juan Bautista: Gateway to Spanish Texas.* Austin: University of Texas Press. 1968. This detailed history of the mission along with the civilian settlement and the presidio on the Río Grande (now in the village of Guerrero, Coahuila) from 1700 to the early nineteenth century includes the numerous other undertakings to the north begun from that center. The source material has been used carefully, methodically, and objectively.

317. _____ . *The San Sabá Mission: Spanish Pivot in Texas.* Austin: University of Texas Press. 1964. A well-documented history of Mission Santa Cruz de San Sabá, located on the extreme frontier of New Spain, which was founded by Franciscans in 1757 and destroyed by savages less than a year later, and of the effects of this disaster on Spanish missionary and military policy until the end of the century. Cf. No. 303.

318. Werling, Norman G., O.Carm. *The First Catholic Church in*

Joliet, Illinois. Chicago: Carmelite. 1960. A brief historical sketch of St. Patrick's Parish, founded in 1838, with preliminary chapters on Catholic life in Will County from the earliest days.

319.   Whitehead, Richard S., ed. *An Archeological and Restoration Study of Mission la Purísima Concepción*. Reports Written for the National Park Service by Fred C. Hageman and Russell C. Ewing. Santa Barbara: Santa Barbara Trust for Historic Preservation. 1980. The shorter report, written by Ewing in 1937, deals mostly with the main events in the history of the mission; Hageman's report (1938) is a comprehensive study of the physical aspects of restoring the buildings through the Civilian Conservation Corps.

IV. BIOGRAPHIES, CORRESPONDENCE, AND MEMOIRS

BESIDES THE GENERAL WORKS listed below, attention should be called to the biographical dictionaries of members of a number of American religious communities, which will be found under that heading, as well as to several hundred biographies of American Catholics contained in the *Dictionary of American Biography* (New York: Charles Scribner's. 1926–   ).

A. GENERAL

320.   *American Catholic Who's Who.* Grosse Pointe, Mich.: Walter Romig. 1934/35–1970/71. Washington, D.C.: N. C. Publications. 1972/73–   . After an initial volume compiled in 1911 by Georgina Pell Curtis (St. Louis: B. Herder), this standard reference work, containing thumbnail sketches of prominent American Catholics, has appeared biennially since 1934.

321.   Blied, Benjamin J. *Three Archbishops of Milwaukee.* Milwaukee: The Author. 1955. Brief essays on Michael Heiss, Frederick X. Katzer, and Sebastian Messmer who ruled the See of Milwaukee between 1881 and 1930.

322.   Burton, Katherine. *Three Generations: Maria Boyle Ewing, 1801–1864; Ellen Ewing Sherman, 1824–1888; Minnie Sherman Fitch, 1851–1913.* New York: Longmans, Green. 1947. Popular biographical sketches of three members of the Ewing-Sherman families.

323.   *The Catholic Encyclopedia and Its Makers.* New York: Encyclopedia Press. 1917. A biographical dictionary of the 1,452 contributors representing forty-three countries and listing under the names the titles of articles contributed; practically a "who's who" of the Catholic scholarly world of the early twentieth century.

324.   Carr, Michael W. *A History of Catholicity in Northern Ohio and in the Diocese of Cleveland.* Vol. II. *Biographical.* Cleveland: J. B. Savage.

1903. A series of popular sketches of bishops, priests, and religious; a companion volume to Houck (No. 170).

325.   Cicognani, Amleto G. *Sanctity in America*, 3rd rev. ed. Paterson: St. Anthony Guild. 1945. The author of these seventeen brief sketches of American men and women noted for outstanding holiness of life, with eleven accounts of individuals and groups who "died a martyr's death or in the odor of sanctity," was the apostolic delegate in the United States.

326.   Clarke, Richard H. *Lives of the Deceased Bishops of the Catholic Church in the United States*. 3 vols. rev. ed. New York: Richard H. Clarke. 1872–1888. A popular compilation with photographs accompanying the text; contains a number of inaccuracies and is now out of date.

327.   Code, Joseph Bernard. *Dictionary of the American Hierarchy, 1789–1964*. New York: Joseph F. Wagner. 1964. For each bishop the facts regarding his birth, education, priestly ordination, episcopal consecration, and, when applicable, transfer, promotion, resignation, and death are given, along with bibliographical references, if any exist, and the titles of his publications. Many of the thirty-three appendices also contain valuable information tabulated in various ways. This is a generally reliable and extremely useful reference work. The same author subsequently published a brief supplement in pamphlet form: "American Bishops, 1964–1970" (St. Louis: Wexford. 1970).

328.   Deedy, John. *Seven American Catholics*. Chicago: Thomas More Association. 1978. These superficial essays on Alfred E. Smith, William Henry O'Connell, Francis Joseph Spellman, Leonard Feeney, John Courtney Murray, Dorothy Day, and Tom Dooley, three of which were originally published in *The Critic* in slightly different form, are written by a journalist.

329.   Dolores, M., Sister [Marie Elisabeth Letterhouse]. *The Francis A. Drexel Family*. Cornwells Heights, Pa.: Sisters of the Blessed Sacrament. 1939. Character sketches and reminiscences of the family of Mother Katharine Drexel based on family diaries and correspondence.

330.   Egan, Maurice Francis. *The Hierarchy of the Roman Catholic Church in the United States*. 2 vols. Philadelphia: George Barrie. 1888. Popular illustrated sketches of the bishops with a brief account of

their dioceses; appeared serially but is now outdated and of no scientific value.

331. Finn, Brendan A. *Twenty-four American Cardinals*. Boston: Bruce Humphries. 1947. A popular filiopietistic work; for a detailed criticism and correction of errors see *American Ecclesiastical Review*, CXIX (September, 1948), 231–237.

332. Foley, Albert S., S.J. *God's Men of Color: The Colored Catholic Priests of the United States, 1854–1954*. New York: Farrar, Straus and Company. 1955. Reprint. New York: Arno. 1969. Popular essays on approximately fifty colored priests who have exercised their ministry in this country.

333. Gannon, John Mark. *The Martyrs of the United States of America*. Erie, Pa.: Chancery Office. 1957. Brief accounts of 116 clerics and laymen who suffered violent deaths for their faith within the present territories of the United States; additional material includes a report on the causes for beatification of thirteen Americans for whom diocesan processes had been begun.

334. Germain, Aidan H., O.S.B. *Catholic Military and Naval Chaplains, 1776–1917*. Washington, D.C.: Catholic University of America Press. 1929. A Ph.D. thesis which gives hardly more than a listing of names of many of these chaplains, although some biographical data are supplied in the case of others.

335. Gibson, Laurita, Sister. *Some Anglo-American Converts to Catholicism Prior to 1829*. Washington, D.C.: Catholic University of America Press. 1943. A Ph.D. thesis that treats in narrative form the approximately 250 converts from the seventeenth and eighteenth centuries, most of whom were captives taken to Canada during the Anglo-French wars, ending with the Barber family of New Hampshire in the 1820's.

336. Hackett, James Dominick. *Bishops of the United States of Irish Birth or Descent*. New York: Irish American Historical Society. 1936. A slender volume that traces Irish origins of 268 bishops between 1789 and 1935; few other data supplied; corrects some errors in the dictionaries of Clarke, Egan, O'Donnell, Reuss, and Shea (Nos. 326, 330, 343, 344, 348).

337. Hoehn, Matthew, O.S.B. *Catholic Authors: Contemporary Biographical Sketches, 1930–1947*. Newark: St. Mary's Abbey. 1948.

Brief biographies of 620 American and foreign authors who were either living at time of publication or had died since 1930; see also second volume of same compiler (1952) which contains 374 additional sketches.

338.   Kervick, Francis W. *Architects in America of Catholic Tradition.* Rutland, Vt.: Charles E. Tuttle. 1962. A series of biographical sketches in alphabetical order with sixty-one full-page plates of the more outstanding buildings that certain of the biographees designed. Not all of them created Catholic churches or institutions.

339.   Lambing, Andrew A. *Foundation Stones of a Great Diocese: Brief Biographical Sketches of the Deceased Bishops and Priests Who Labored in the Diocese of Pittsburgh from the Earliest Times to the Present with an Historical Introduction.* Vol. I, *1749–1860.* Pittsburgh: The Author. 1914. A general assortment of biographical sketches, accounts of religious communities and their institutions, as well as of towns and counties that figure in Pittsburgh's Catholic history; not a scientific work.

340.   [Martin], David, Brother, C.S.C. *American Catholic Convert Authors: A Bio-Bibliography.* Detroit: Walter Romig. 1944. Thumbnail accounts of 259 authors who converted to Catholicism between John Thayer (1783) and Helene Magaret (1942).

341.   Maynard, Theodore. *Great Catholics in American History.* New York: Doubleday. 1957. Twenty-one popular biographical sketches from Saint Isaac Jogues to Alfred E. Smith

342.   Mulvey, Mary Doris, Sister, O.P. *French Catholic Missionaries in the Present United States, 1604–1791.* Washington, D.C.: Catholic University of America Press. 1936. Reprint. New York: AMS. 1974. A Ph.D. thesis that contains sketches of the careers of these missionaries by sections, e.g., New England, the Old Northwest, and Louisiana.

343.   O'Donnell, J. Hugh, C.S.C. *The Catholic Hierarchy of the United States, 1790–1922.* Washington, D.C.: Catholic University of America Press. 1922. Reprint. New York: AMS. 1974. A Ph.D. thesis now superseded by Code (No. 327).

344.   Reuss, Francis X. *Biographical Cyclopaedia of the Catholic Hierarchy of the United States, 1784–1898.* Milwaukee: M. H. Wiltzius. 1898. Another dictionary of the American hierarchy; contains numerous errors and is now outdated.

345.   Ruskowski, Leo F., S.S. *French Emigré Priests in the United States, 1791–1815.* Washington, D.C.: Catholic University of America Press. 1940. Reprint. New York: AMS. 1974. A Ph.D. thesis which gives biographical data on these priests with an account of their ministry in both the East and West and their role as members of religious communities, preachers, educators, and ecclesiastical administrators; a continuation of Mulvey (No. 342).

346.   Scannell-O'Neill, D. J. *Distinguished Converts to Rome in America.* St. Louis: B. Herder. 1907. An alphabetically arranged list of some 3,000 nineteenth-century converts. Although conversion date is given in only about 20 percent of the entries, brief biographical information about each convert offers leads for more complete knowledge. A statistical table is included which breaks down the converts according to profession. On the topic see also Richard Clarke, "Our Converts," *American Catholic Quarterly Review*, XVIII (July, 1893), 539–561; XIX (January, 1894), 112–138. Clarke gives an unclassified list of more than 700 prominent nineteenth-century converts, brief biographies of the most notable, and a bibliography of some of the convert authors.

347.   Schauinger, J. Herman. *Profiles in Action: American Catholics in Public Life.* Milwaukee: Bruce. 1966. Thirty-three brief popular sketches of prominent Catholic figures from Columbus to John F. Kennedy.

348.   Shea, John Gilmary. *The Hierarchy of the Catholic Church in the United States.* New York: Office of Catholic Publications. 1886. As in the case of most of these dictionaries of the hierarchy, this work contains inaccuracies, but it was in many ways the best of the earlier compilations.

349.   Spalding, Hughes. *The Spalding Family of Maryland, Kentucky, and Georgia, 1658–1963.* Atlanta: The Author. 1963. A genealogical study of a Catholic family that was founded in Maryland in 1658 by Thomas Spalding from Suffolk County, England. A descendant, Benedict Spalding, migrated to Kentucky in 1791.

350.   Walsh, James J. *Our American Cardinals.* New York: D. Appleton. 1926. Reprint. Freeport, N.Y.: Books for Librarians. 1969. Popular brief biographies of Cardinals McCloskey, Gibbons, Farley, O'Connell, Dougherty, Mundelein, and Hayes.

351.   Waring, George J. *United States Catholic Chaplains in the World*

War. New York: Ordinariate. Army and Navy Chaplains. 1924. At the time of the armistice in November, 1918, there were 1,023 Catholic chaplains in active service with the army, navy, and Knights of Columbus units; this volume gives thumbnail sketches of these men, although admittedly the data are not complete in the case of some of these chaplains.

B. 1492–1790

352.   Baegert, Johann Jakob, S.J. *Observations in Lower California*. Trans. M. M. Brandenburg and Carl L. Baumann. Berkeley: University of California Press. 1952. A factual and candid account by a German Jesuit who spent seventeen years (1751–1768) at San Luís Gonzaga Mission; the work ends with the arrival of the Franciscans who took over the Jesuit missions which they used as supply bases for their exploration and colonization of Alta California, beginning in 1769 under Junípero Serra's (1713–1784) direction.

353.   Bolton, Herbert Eugene. *Anza's California Expeditions*. 5 vols. Berkeley: University of California Press. 1930. Volume I is devoted to Bolton's narrative on the founding of San Francisco which is followed by four volumes of source materials in translation with editorial notes, e.g., the diaries of Anza, Diaz, Garcés, Palóu, and Font, narratives by Palóu and Moraga, and a volume of contemporary correspondence.

354.   _____ . *Coronado on the Turquoise Trail: Knight of Pueblos and Plains*. Albuquerque: University of New Mexico Press. 1949. Contains an account of Fray Marcos de Niza's journey for background; also treats the role of the three Franciscans who remained behind after Coronado had turned back to Mexico.

355.   _____ , ed. *Fray Francisco Palóu, O.F.M.: Historical Memoirs of New California*. 4 vols. Berkeley: University of California Press. 1926. A critical edition of the *Noticias de la Nueva California* by the companion and successor (c. 1722–c. 1790) of Serra as superior of the Franciscan missions in California with twenty-eight letters to and from Palóu; Bolton states that the *Noticias* was "sounder history than the same author's better known *Vida del Padre Serra*" (p. vii).

356.   _____ . *Fray Juan Crespi: Missionary Explorer on the Pacific Coast, 1769–1774*. Berkeley: University of California Press. 1927. Reprint. New York: AMS. 1971. Crespí's diaries and letters relating

the Portolá expedition of 1769, the Fages expedition of 1772, and the Pérez expedition of 1774 are reprinted from Bolton's English edition of Palóu's *New California* with the addition of several important documents, a special introduction, and editorial notes.

357. _____ , ed. *Kino's Historical Memoir of Pimería Alta: A Contemporary Account of the Beginnings of California, Sonora, and Arizona by Father Eusebio Francisco Kino, S.J., Pioneer Missionary, Explorer, Cartographer, and Ranchman, 1683–1711.* 2 vols. Cleveland: Arthur H. Clark. 1919. Reprint. New York: AMS. 1976. A translation and critical edition of the leading source for the greatest Jesuit missionary in the colonial Southwest.

358. _____ . *Pageant in the Wilderness.* Salt Lake City: Utah Historical Society. 1950. An account of the 1776 expedition of Silvestre Escalante, O.F.M. into the interior basin beyond the Rocky Mountains, with a translation and annotated edition of Escalante's diary and itinerary. Cf. No. 423.

359. _____ . *Rim of Christendom: A Biography of Eusebio Francisco Kino.* New York: Macmillan. 1936. Reprint. New York: Russell and Russell. 1960. A first-class life of one of the most famous of colonial missionaries.

360. Burrus, Ernest J., S.J., ed. *Kino Writes to the Duchess: Letters of Eusebio Francisco Kino, S.J., to the Duchess of Aveiro.* Rome: Jesuit Historical Institute; St. Louis: St. Louis University. 1965. This collection of thirty-seven letters, most of which the famous Jesuit missionary wrote to the generous Portuguese benefactress residing in Madrid between 1680 and 1687, is critically edited and is preceded by a lengthy introduction in which approximately 200 letters of other correspondence are briefly summarized. The original Spanish texts of the letters are available in the *Correspondencia del P. Eusebio Francisco Kino con la Duquesa de Aveiro.* [Colección Chimalistac, No. 18] Madrid: Ediciones José Porrúa Turanzas. Rome: Istituto Storico della Compagnia de Gesù. 1964.

361. _____ . *Kino and Manje: Explorers of Sonora and Arizona: Their Vision of the Future: A Study of Their Expeditions and Plans.* Rome and St. Louis: Jesuit Historical Institute. 1971. This huge volume (X in the series Sources and Studies for the History of the Americas) is based on all the pertinent, important records of the expeditions and journeys made by Eusebio Kino and Juan Mateo Manje from 1694 to

1701 and Kino's proposals regarding the Pimería Alta from 1695/96 to 1708–1710; it has an appendix of thirty well-edited documents in Spanish.

362. _____ . *Kino Reports to Headquarters*. Rome: Institutum Historicum Societatis Jesu. 1954. Correspondence of Kino from New Spain with his Roman superiors; original Spanish text of fourteen letters and reports written between February 14, 1682, and February 2, 1702, with English translations and notes.

363. Butler, Ruth Lapham, trans. *Journal of Paul du Ru [February 1–May 8, 1700]*. *Missionary Priest to Louisiana*. Chicago: Caxton Club. 1934. A description of the Jesuit's voyage up the Mississippi from Biloxi Bay with Iberville; Father du Ru (1666–1741) was a member of Iberville's expedition of 1699 and remained in Louisiana until 1702 when he was recalled as a result of the jurisdictional feud with the priests of the Seminary of Quebec; based on a manuscript in the Newberry Library.

364. Chavez, Angelico, O.F.M. *Coronado's Friars*. Washington, D.C.: Academy of American Franciscan History. 1968. This meticulous investigation of the scattered and sometimes contradictory evidence answers as definitely as is possible the centuries-old questions regarding the number, identity, and fate of the Franciscans (aside from Fray Marcos de Niza) who accompanied the expedition of Francisco Vásquez Coronado to New Mexico in 1540.

365. Clark, William Bell. *Gallant John Barry, 1745–1803: The Story of a Naval Hero of Two Wars*. New York: Macmillan. 1938. The best biography of the Irish-born naval officer of American Revolutionary War fame.

366. Coues, Elliott. *On the Trail of a Spanish Pioneer: The Diary and Itinerary of Francisco Garcés in His Travels through Sonora, Arizona, and California, 1775–1776*. New York: Francis P. Harper. 1900. Besides translation and edition of Garcés' final expedition, these volumes include a brief biography of the friar (1738–1781) and an edition of his diary kept on four previous expeditions beginning in 1768. Now superseded by Galvin's edition (No. 377).

367. Dalrymple, E. A. *Relatio Itineris in Marylandiam*. Baltimore: Maryland Historical Society. 1874. An account by Andrew White, S.J. (1579–1656), of his voyage to Maryland in 1633–1634 and of his early days in the new colony; Latin and English texts on facing pages

with brief excerpts from the Jesuits' annual letters from Maryland for the years 1635–1677.

368.   Defouri, James H. *The Martyrs of New Mexico: A Brief Account of the Lives and Deaths of the Earliest Missionaries in the Territory.* Las Vegas, N. Mex.: "Revista Católica" Printing Office. 1893. These popular sketches of forty Franciscan priests and brothers slain between the sixteenth and the nineteenth century are based on secondary sources and are devoid of scholarly merit.

369.   Donnelly, Joseph P., S.J. *Jacques Marquette, S.J., 1637–1675.* Chicago: Loyola University Press. 1968. A needlessly wordy, often pietistic, and sometimes sentimental biography of the French missionary and explorer, in which the author compensates for the sparsity of documentation by inventing incidents, conjectures, and arguments *ex convenientia*, especially for the earlier part of his subject's life. In the appendices he treats in a more scholarly fashion the question of Marquette's ordination, the authorship of his journal, the place of his death, and the site of his grave.

370.   _____ . *Pierre Gibault, Missionary, 1737–1802.* Chicago: Loyola University Press. 1971. The fruit of careful research, this biography of the French-Canadian priest at Kaskaskia in the Illinois country who aided George Rogers Clark in winning the support of the inhabitants of Vincennes during the American Revolution paints an accurate picture of life on both sides of the Mississippi during the last third of the eighteenth century.

371.   _____ . *Thwaites' Jesuit Relations: Errata and Addenda.* Chicago: Loyola University Press. 1967. Mistakes, mistranslations, errors of fact and judgment regarding Catholic practice, misinterpretations of the internal workings of the government of the Society of Jesus, and the like are corrected, and the Biblical quotations in Latin are translated and identified page by page through the seventy-one volumes of the *Jesuit Relations* (No. 420); an extensive bibliography of titles published between 1906 and 1966 continues that of Thwaites.

372.   Dunne, Peter Masten, S.J. *Jacobo Sedelmayr: Missionary, Frontiersman, Explorer in Arizona and Sonora: Four Original Manuscript Narratives, 1744–1751.* Tucson: Arizona Pioneers' Historical Society. 1955. A scholarly edition of Sedelmayr's (1703–1779) descriptions of his work in the Pima country which he reached about thirty-five years after the death of Kino.

373.   Englebert, Omer. *The Last of the Conquistadores, Junípero Serra, 1713–1784*. Trans. Katherine Woods. New York: Harcourt, Brace. 1956. Originally written in French and in a lively narrative style, this biography may be recommended for the general or younger reader.

374.   Field, Thomas Meagher. *Unpublished Letters of Charles Carroll of Carrollton, and of His Father, Charles Carroll of Doughoregan*. New York: United States Catholic Historical Society. 1902. Contains seventy-two letters, starting in 1754 when Carroll was a student in France and ending with a letter of October 30, 1832, written to his daughter two weeks before his death; also contains other pertinent documents and choice portrait reproductions of the Carroll family.

375.   Forrestal, Peter P., C.S.C., and Cyprian Lynch, O.F.M. *Alonso de Benavides: Memorial of 1630*. Washington, D.C.: Academy of American Franciscan History. 1954. A report addressed to Philip IV of Spain; the editor states that this report gives a "more vivid picture of mission life" than the later memorial of Benavides (No. 391).

376.   Galvin, John, ed. *A Journal of Explorations Northward Along the Coast from Monterey in the Year 1775*. San Francisco: John Howell. 1964. This diary, here beautifully printed in translation, was kept by Fray Miguel de la Campa, O.F.M., one of the chaplains of the expedition made by two ships up the Pacific coast.

377.   _____ , ed. *A Record of Travels in Arizona and California, 1775–1776: Fr. Francisco Garcés*. San Francisco: John Howell. 1965. The purpose of the Franciscan missionary's eleven-month, 2,000-mile journey was to determine which Indian tribes were ready for evangelization and to discover an overland route linking the Colorado River country with Monterey and San Francisco. The folio volume is embellished with illustrations and maps.

378.   Geiger, Maynard, O.F.M. *The Life and Times of Fray Junípero Serra, O.F.M., Or, The Man Who Never Turned Back, 1713–1784: A Biography*. 2 vols. Washington, D.C.: Academy of American Franciscan History. 1959. This thoroughly researched work is the definitive life of the great missionary from Majorca who founded the first nine missions in Upper California, beginning with San Diego in 1769. It won the John Gilmary Shea Prize in 1960.

379.   _____ . *Palóu's Life of Fray Junípero Serra*. Washington, D.C.: Academy of American Franciscan History. 1955. A translation and scholarly edition with nearly 1,700 notes.

380. Geiger, Mary Virginia, Sister, S.S.N.D. *Daniel Carroll: A Framer of the Constitution.* Washington, D.C.: Catholic University of America Press. 1943. A Ph.D. thesis on the life of the brother of Archbishop John Carroll.

381. Griffin, Martin I. J. *Commodore John Barry.* Philadelphia: The Author. 1908.

382. _____ . *Stephen Moylan, Muster-Master General, Secretary, and Aide-de-Camp to Washington.* Philadelphia: The Author. 1909. These two items by Griffin are among the leading works of a self-trained historian; while defective in form, they incorporate a good deal of material not readily found elsewhere.

383. Guest, Francis F., O.F.M. *Fermín Francisco de Lasuén, 1736– 1803: A Biography.* Washington, D.C.: Academy of American Franciscan History. 1973. This thoroughly documented and well-written life of the Basque Franciscan who succeeded Junípero Serra as president of the missions of Upper California in 1785 is also a history of the province.

384. Gurn, Joseph. *Charles Carroll of Carrollton, 1737–1832.* New York: P. J. Kenedy. 1932. A popular work now superseded by Smith (No. 412).

385. _____ . *Commander John Barry: Father of the American Navy.* New York: P. J. Kenedy. 1933. A popular biography that adds nothing to Griffin's earlier work (No. 381).

386. Habig, Marion A., O.F.M., ed. *Nothingness Itself: Selected Writings of Ven. Fr. Antonio Margil, 1690–1724.* Trans. Benedict Leutenegger, O.F.M. Chicago: Franciscan Herald Press. 1976. This collection consists mainly of letters written by the famous missionary at various places from Central America to Texas.

387. Hallenbeck, Cleve. *The Journey of Fray Marcos de Niza.* Dallas: Southern Methodist University Press. 1949. 2nd ed. Westport, Conn.: Greenwood. 1973. After sketching the historical background, the author presents an annotated English translation of the friar's narrative of his travels in 1539 and adds a detailed analysis of the narrative, rejecting as fraudulent the friar's claim to have seen the city of Cíbola.

388. Hamer, Pierre. *Raphaël de Luxembourg: Une contribution luxem-*

bourgeoise à la colonisation de la Louisiane. Luxembourg: Imprimerie St.-Paul. 1966. This laudatory biography of the Capuchin missionary who arrived in New Orleans in 1723, founded the first college for boys in the colony, and struggled successfully against the governor Bienville and his Jesuit supporter Beaubois, contains long extracts from his letters.

389.   Hamilton, Raphael N., S.J. *Marquette's Explorations: The Narratives Reexamined.* Madison: University of Wisconsin Press. 1970. Through a rigorous scrutiny of the original manuscripts Father Hamilton has laid to rest the doubts raised by Steck (Nos. 414, 415) and others, and has established that Jacques Marquette was an ordained priest, that he did accompany Jolliet down the Mississippi, and that his superior, Father Claude Dablon, was not guilty of deception in his editing of the *Relation* recounting the voyage.

390.   Hanley, Thomas O'Brien, S.J. *Charles Carroll of Carrollton: The Making of a Revolutionary Gentleman.* Washington, D.C.: Catholic University of America Press. 1970. The formative years of this Maryland Catholic leader up to his emergence into public view in 1773 are studied from his papers, mainly in terms of his social status and political thought. The author's characterizations and interpretations have been challenged as unsupported by his evidence.

391.   Hodge, Frederick Webb, George P. Hammond, and Agapito Rey. *Fray Alonso de Benavides' Revised Memorial of 1634.* Albuquerque: University of New Mexico Press. 1945. A scholarly edition of the Franciscan custos' memorial, addressed to Pope Urban VIII on the New Mexico missions as he found them in 1623–1629, with twenty-five additional documents as appendices.

392.   Holland, Robert E., S.J. *The Positio of the Historical Section of the Sacred Congregation of Rites on the Introduction of the Cause for Beatification and Canonization and on the Virtues of the Servant of God Katharine Tekakwitha, the Lily of the Mohawks.* New York: Fordham University Press. 1940. A collection of documents relating to the cause of the Mohawk Indian maiden (1656–1680) who was declared "Blessed" in 1980.

393.   Kenneally, Finbar, O.F.M., ed. and trans. *Writings of Fermin Francisco de Lasuén.* 2 vols. Washington, D.C.: Academy of American Franciscan History. 1965. A collection of approximately 480 letters and thirty-six reports dated between 1767 and 1803, most of which the Basque Franciscan wrote as a missionary and as president of the

missions of Upper California. The translation is smooth, free, and faithful to the sense of the original Spanish, but the annotation is inadequate.

394.   Kennedy, John H., O.M.I. *Thomas Dongan, Governor of New York, 1682–1688.* Washington, D.C.: Catholic University of America Press. 1930. A biography done as a Ph.D. thesis on one of the few colonial Catholics of prominence.

395.   Kenton, Edna. *The Jesuit Relations and Allied Documents.* New York: Vanguard. 1954. A convenient selection of some of the most important documents contained in the collection edited by Thwaites (No. 420).

396.   King, Kenneth M. *Mission to Paradise: The Story of Junipero Serra and the Missions of California.* Chicago: Franciscan Herald Press. 1956. A popular biography which makes no pretension to scholarship.

397.   Kip, William Ingraham. *The Early Jesuits in North America.* New York: Wiley and Putnam. 1846. An English translation of the documents pertaining to America in Martin (No. 401).

398.   Kittler, Glenn D. *Saint in the Wilderness: The Story of St. Isaac Jogues and the Jesuit Adventure in the New World.* Garden City, N.Y.: Doubleday. 1964. A popular, dramatized biography of no value to historians.

399.   Lockwood, Francis C. *With Padre Kino on the Trail.* Tucson: University of Arizona. 1934. A popular work superseded by Bolton (No. 359).

400.   Martin, Felix, S.J. *The Life of Father Isaac Jogues, Missionary Priest of the Society of Jesus, Slain by the Mohawk Iroquois, in the present State of New York, October 18, 1646, with Father Jogues' Account of the Captivity and Death of His Companion, René Goupil, Slain September 29, 1642.* Trans. John Gilmary Shea. New York, etc.: Benziger. 1885. An edifying life of the first apostle to the Iroquois written by a French Canadian historian in 1873 with a view to the martyr's beatification. Now superseded by Talbot's biography (No. 418).

401.   Martin, Louis Aimé, ed. *Lettres édifiantes et curieuses écrites des Missions Etrangères.* 4 vols. Paris: A. Desrez. 1838–1843. Only Volumes I and II have material on North America, Volume I containing thirteen letters dating from 1715 to 1750, to and from Jesuit mis-

sionaries; Volume II's only American document is a lengthy memoir of François-Marie Picolo, S.J., to one of the founders of the mission at Guadalaxara, Mexico, February 10, 1702 (II, 62–68).

402.   Maynard, Theodore. *The Long Road of Father Serra.* New York: Appleton-Century-Crofts. 1954. A readable book, although not one of the author's most successful popular biographies; in his effort to fill in the background and make up for the scarcity of published sources, he too often loses Serra. It is now superseded by Geiger (No. 378).

403.   Morison, Samuel Eliot. *Admiral of the Ocean Sea.* 2 vols. Boston: Little, Brown. 1942. The definitive life of Christopher Columbus; a work of superb scholarship.

404.   Oberste, William Herman. *The Restless Friar: Venerable Fray Antonio Margil de Jesús, Missionary to the Americas, Apostle of Texas.* Austin, Tex.: Von Boeckmann-Jones. 1971. Intended for the general reader, this biography of Margil (1684–1726) is based mainly on secondary sources. Cf. Rios (No. 409).

405.   Phelan, Thomas P. *Thomas Dongan, Colonial Governor of New York, 1683–1688.* New York: P. J. Kenedy. 1933. A popular work that adds nothing to Kennedy (No. 394).

406.   Piette, Charles J.-G. Maximim, O.F.M. *Evocation de Junipero Serra: Fondateur de la Californie.* Washington, D.C.: Academy of American Franciscan History. 1946. This carefully documented work assembles a good deal of material that illuminates the life of Serra.

407.   Repplier, Agnes. *Père Marquette.* Garden City, N.Y.: Doubleday, Doran. 1929. A well-written popular life, although for the scholar, Thwaites (No. 419) is still more satisfactory and Donnelly (No. 369) more accessible.

408.   _____ . *Junipero Serra, Pioneer Colonist of California.* Garden City, N.Y.: Doubleday, Doran. 1933. A highly readable biography, although not a work of scholarship.

409.   Rios, Eduardo Enrique. *Life of Fray Antonio Margil, O.F.M.* Trans. and rev. Benedict Leutenegger, O.F.M. Washington, D.C.: Academy of American Franciscan History. 1959. The best scholarly

work in English on the famous missionary of Texas who was born in Spain in 1657 and died at Mexico City in 1726.

410.   Rowland, Kate Mason. *Life and Correspondence of Charles Carroll of Carrollton, 1737–1832, with His Correspondence and Public Papers.* 2 vols. New York: G. P. Putnam's. 1898. Although as a biography this work has been superseded by Smith (No. 412), it is still useful for the large number of documents included by the author.

411.   Shea, John Gilmary. *Discovery and Exploration of the Mississippi Valley.* 2nd ed. Albany: Joseph McDonough. 1903. A translation and edition of the original narratives of five leading missionaries— Marquette, Allouez, Membré, Hennepin, and Anastase Douay— who figured prominently in the West in the seventeenth century.

412.   Smith, Ellen Hart. *Charles Carroll of Carrollton.* Cambridge, Mass.: Harvard University Press. 1942. Reprint. New York: Russell and Russell. 1971. The most recent, and the best, life of the Catholic statesman; a work of genuine scholarship that is charmingly written.

413.   Smith, Fay Jackson, John L. Kessell, and Francis J. Fox. *Father Kino in Arizona.* Phoenix: Arizona Historical Foundation. 1966. A series of essays on Kino with an appendix of some documents.

414.   Steck, Francis Borgia, O.F.M. *The Jolliet-Marquette Expedition, 1673.* Washington, D.C.: Catholic University of America Press. 1927. This doctoral dissertation places the event in the context of relations between Church and State in France and New France and concludes that the undertaking cannot be called the "discovery" of the Mississippi River, that the leader was the layman, not the Jesuit, and that the "Narrative" was not written by Marquette.

415.   _____ . *Marquette Legends.* New York: Pageant. 1960. Father Steck denies or calls into question that Jacques Marquette was ever ordained a priest, that he was the author of the "Narrative" of the Mississippi voyage with Louis Jolliet attributed to him, that he even participated in the 1673 expedition, and that he founded the Kaskaskia Mission; the Franciscan writer also discourses on the extant manuscripts and maps. Regarding both of Steck's books see Hamilton (No. 389).

416.   Stratemeier, George B., O.P. *Thomas Cornwaleys: Commissioner*

and Counselor of Maryland. Washington, D.C.: Catholic University of America Press. 1922. A slender book done as a Ph.D. thesis on the life of one of Maryland's founders who remained in the colony until 1659.

417. Talbot, Francis Xavier, S.J. *Saint among the Hurons: The Life of Jean de Brébeuf.* New York: Harper and Bros. 1949.

418. _____ . *Saint among Savages: The Life of Isaac Jogues.* New York: Harper and Bros. 1935. Two able biographies that make intelligent use of the *Jesuit Relations* (No. 420).

419. Thwaites, Reuben Gold. *Father Marquette.* New York: D. Appleton. 1902. Although now very old, this volume is still probably the best life of the Jesuit missionary.

420. _____ . *Jesuit Relations and Allied Documents.* Cleveland: Burrows. 1896–1901. Reprint. (73 vols. in 36). New York: Pageant. 1959. The standard edition of source materials for the Indian missions of these French religious in North America; sixty-six volumes are devoted to the period 1632–1702; five to the subsequent years; and two to the index. For corrections and additions see Donnelly (No. 371).

421. Tibesar, Antonine, O.F.M. *Writings of Junipero Serra.* 4 vols. Washington, D.C.: Academy of American Franciscan History. 1955–1958. An admirably complete and scholarly edition of all the extant writings of Serra with original Spanish and English translations on facing pages; includes a lengthy introduction and a brief biography of Serra (I, xiii–xlv).

422. Treutlein, Theodore E., ed. *Missionary in Sonora: The Travel Reports of Joseph Och, S.J.* San Francisco: California Historical Society. 1964. This German Jesuit was on the missions in Pimería Alta from 1756 to 1765 when illness forced his retirement to Mexico, where he learned of the decree expelling the Jesuits from New Spain. His labors were chiefly in the present Mexican state of Sonora rather than in what is today the United States (Arizona).

423. Warner, Ted J., ed. *The Domínguez-Escalante Journal: Their Expedition through Colorado, Utah, Arizona, and New Mexico in 1776.* Trans. Fray Angelico Chavez. Provo: Brigham Young University Press. 1976. This complete Spanish transcription and new English translation of the journal kept by the two Franciscan explorers,

Fray Francisco Atanasio Domínguez and Fray Silvestre Vélez de Escalante, who completed a 1,700-mile circuit from Santa Fe, is accompanied in the footnotes by modern geographical bearings provided by seven teams of "trail researchers."

424.   Woodgate, Mildred Violet. *Junipero Serra: Apostle of California*. Westminster, Md.: Newman. 1966. Though based on primary sources, this simple, brief biography is devoid of scholarly apparatus and adds nothing to earlier publications.

C. 1790–1866

425.   Andrews, Rena M. *Archbishop Hughes and the Civil War*. Chicago: University of Chicago Libraries. 1935. A sixteen-page abstract of a Ph.D. thesis on Hughes' commission to France in behalf of the Lincoln government.

426.   Armato, Maria Michele, Sister, O.P., and Sister Mary Jeremy Finnegan, O.P., trans. *The Memoirs of Father Samuel Mazzuchelli, O.P.* Chicago: Priory. 1967. These memoirs recount the first years of the Milanese missionary's labors, from 1830 to 1843, among various Indian tribes and the Canadians in Wisconsin and Michigan and among the Catholics and Protestants in Iowa, Wisconsin, and Illinois, and contain his observations on "Protestantism and the Catholic Church in the United States." This excellent translation supersedes that of Kennedy (No. 499).

427.   Athearn, Robert G. *Thomas Francis Meagher: An Irish Revolutionary in America*. Boulder: University of Colorado Press. 1949. Reprint. New York: Arno. 1976. A scholarly biography of an Irish-born soldier, journalist, and politician who came to the United States in 1852, figured prominently in the Civil War, and died in 1867 as acting governor of Montana Territory; emphasis on Meagher's career as an Irish nationalist; a very scanty index.

428.   Bailly de Barberey, Helen. *Elizabeth Seton*. Trans. Joseph B. Code. New York: Macmillan. 1927. An old work that contains some useful correspondence, but now superseded by Dirvin and Melville (Nos. 458, 530).

429.   Barker, Burt Brown. *The McLoughlin Empire and Its Rulers*. Glendale, Calif.: Arthur H. Clark. 1959. An account of the lives of John McLoughlin, famous factor of the Hudson's Bay Company, of his brother, Dr. David McLoughlin, and his sister, Sister St. Henry

of the Quebec Ursulines. The major portion of this volume (pp. 141–346) is given over to the appendices which contain numerous letters and other family records of the McLoughlins; illustrations and good index; this work will be very helpful to future biographers of members of the McLoughlin family since the volume is more a source book than a biography proper.

430.   Bayley, James Roosevelt. *Memoirs of the Right Reverend Simon Wm. Gabriel Bruté, First Bishop of Vincennes*. Rev. ed. New York: Catholic Publishing Society. 1876. The earliest biography of Bruté done largely from his original notes, which were acquired in 1847 by Bishop Hughes of New York; more than half the volume devoted to Bruté's account of victims of the persecution of the Church in France after 1793; superseded by Godecker and Lemarié (Nos. 473, 510).

431.   Bea, Fernando. *Una sola cosa è necessaria*. Turin: Editrice Marietti. 1965. This popular biography of Frederick Baraga, written in the hagiographical style, adds nothing of importance to earlier studies.

432.   Berger, John N., C.SS.R. *Life of the Right Rev. John N. Neumann*. New York: Benziger. 1884. A translation from the German original by Eugene Grimm, C.SS.R.; now superseded as a biography of the fourth Bishop of Philadelphia by Curley (No. 455).

433.   [Bisgood], Marie Thérèse, Mother, S.H.C.J. *Cornelia Connelly: A Study in Fidelity*. Westminster, Md.: Newman. 1963. This sympathetic biography of the American foundress of the Society of the Holy Child Jesus, written by an English member with literary grace, benefits from the previously unused primary source material which was collected by the historical commission appointed to prepare for her beatification. It is the best work on Cornelia Connelly (1809–1879) published thus far.

433a.   Bolduc, Jean Baptiste Zacharie. *Mission of the Columbia*. Ed. and trans. Edward T. Kowrach. Fairfield, Wash.: Ye Galleon. 1979. These journals and letters of a French Canadian priest (1818–1889) who sailed around Cape Horn and undertook work among the Indians of the Oregon Territory in 1842 were originally published in Quebec in 1843 and are here presented in English with annotations and a bibliography in a folio-sized and elegantly designed volume.

434.   Brady, Alexander. *Thomas D'Arcy McGee*. Toronto: Macmillan. 1925. A brief popular account by a lecturer in political science at the University of Toronto; superseded by Skelton (No. 568).

435.   Brann, Henry A. *Most Reverend John Hughes, First Archbishop of New York*. New York: Dodd, Mead. 1892. A brief appreciation by a New York priest; not a real biography.

436.   Brislen, M. Bernetta, Sister, O.S.F. "The Episcopacy of Leonard Neale: Second Archbishop of Baltimore," *Historical Records and Studies*, XXXIV (1945), 20–111. This able A.M. thesis contains a carefully documented treatment of Neale's early years as well as an adequate account of his brief tenure of the See of Baltimore (December, 1815–June, 1817).

437.   Browne, Patrick W. *Etat de l'Eglise Catholique ou Diocèse des Etats-Unis de l'Amérique Septentrionale*. Par Jean Dilhet. Washington, D.C.: Catholic University of America Press. 1922. A Ph.D. thesis that provides a translation and annotated edition of the impressions of American Catholicism by a French Sulpician, Jean Dilhet (1753–1811), who was in this country from 1798 to 1807; done from an original manuscript in the Sulpician archives of Baltimore.

438.   Brownson, Henry F. *Orestes A. Brownson*. 3 vols. Detroit: The Author. 1898–1900. This work by Brownson's son is very detailed but as a biography is superseded by Ryan (No. 559).

439.   _____ . *The Works of Orestes A. Brownson*. 20 vols. Detroit: T. Nourse. 1882–1907. The standard edition of Brownson's writings, edited by his son.

440.   Brownson, Sarah M. *Life of Demetrius Augustine Gallitzin, Prince and Priest*. New York: Frederick Pustet. 1873. A popular account long since superseded by Lemcke (No. 512) et al.

441.   Burnett, Peter Hardeman. *Recollections and Opinions of an Old Pioneer*. New York: D. Appleton. 1880. Memoirs of the first governor of California who became a convert in 1846 in Oregon City and who died in 1895 after serving on Oregon Territory's Supreme Court; he was converted through reading himself into the Church after being stimulated by an account of the Purcell-Campbell debates in Cincinnati. See also Burnett's *The Path Which Led a Protestant Lawyer to the Catholic Church*.

442.   Burton, Katherine. *Celestial Homespun: The Life of Isaac Thomas Hecker*. New York: Longmans, Green. 1943. A popular biography containing numerous inaccuracies; superseded by Holden (No. 485).

443.   _____ . *Faith Is the Substance: The Life of Mother Theodore*

Guerin. St. Louis: B. Herder. 1959. A popular biography of the foundress of the Sisters of Providence of Terre Haute, Indiana; of no scientific value, lacking references, bibliography, and index.

444.   Cailly, Louis de. *Memoirs of Bishop Loras: First Bishop of Dubuque, Iowa, and of Members of His Family, 1792–1858.* New York: Christian Press. 1897. Popular reminiscences of the Loras family by a nephew of the first Bishop of Dubuque who was pastor of St. Joseph's Church, Fort Madison, Iowa, from 1839 to his death in 1897.

445.   Callan, Louise, R.S.C.J. *Philippine Duchesne: Frontier Missionary of the Sacred Heart, 1769–1852.* Westminster, Md.: Newman. 1957. Abridged ed. Newman. 1965. A full and detailed biography of the American foundress of the Religious of the Sacred Heart; notable for the numerous documents which touch upon frontier problems in the Mississippi Valley.

446.   Carey, Mathew. *Autobiography.* Brooklyn: Eugene L. Schwab. 1942. This small volume contains considerable original material on the Philadelphia Catholic publicist, but it is disappointing from the view of his role in ecclesiastical affairs; appeared originally as a series of letters in the *New England Magazine* (July, 1833–December, 1834).

447.   Cavanagh, Michael. *Memoirs of Gen. Thomas Francis Meagher.* Worcester, Mass.: Messenger. 1892. A varied assortment of materials with a strong Irish nationalist emphasis; now superseded by Athearn (No. 427).

448.   Cestello, Bosco D., O.S.B. "James Whitfield, Fourth Archbishop of Baltimore: The Early Years, 1770–1828," *Historical Records and Studies,* XLV (1957), 32–78. A thoroughly documented account that carries Whitfield to his consecration on May 25, 1828; done originally as a thesis for the A.M. degree.

449.   Chittenden, Hiram M., and Albert T. Richardson. *Life, Letters, and Travels of Father Pierre-Jean DeSmet, S.J., 1801–1873.* 4 vols. New York: Harper and Bros. 1905. Reprint. New York: Arno. 1969. The standard source collection for the great promoter of the Jesuit Indian missions of the West, peacemaker between the Sioux and the federal government, and discriminating observer and skillful writer.

450.   Cochran, Alice Lida. *The Saga of an Irish Immigrant Family: The*

Descendants of John Mullanphy. New York: Arno. 1976. The original doctoral dissertation, presented to Saint Louis University in 1958, is reproduced by the photo-offset process. Relying heavily on correspondence, family lore, and reminiscences, the author studies a prominent Catholic family of Saint Louis from 1804 to the 1950's. On the basis of their experience she concludes that the Irish immigrants in the Middle West were more successful than those in the East.

451.   Connelly, James F. *The Visit of Archbishop Gaetano Bedini to the United States of America, June, 1853–February, 1854.* Rome: Librería Editrice dell'Università Gregoriana. 1960. This doctoral dissertation in ecclesiastical history consists of two parts: (1) a detailed narrative of the official visitor's troubled tour, which is uncritical in the use of sources, weak in American materials and background, and deficient in interpretation; and (2) an annotated translation of his lengthy report to the Holy See, which is a document of prime value to historians.

452.   Conroy, Joseph P., S.J. *Arnold Damen, S.J.: A Chapter in the Making of Chicago.* New York: Benziger. 1930. A semipopular account of the founder of Holy Family Parish (1857) and of St. Ignatius College (1870).

453.   Crépeau, Rosemary, Soeur, O.P. *Un Apôtre dominicain aux Etats-Unis: Le Père Samuel-Charles-Gaétan Mazzuchelli.* Paris: J. de Gigord. 1933. A doctoral thesis done at the University of Fribourg in Switzerland on the Italian-born missionary of the Middle West.

454.   Curley, Michael J., C.SS.R. *Cheerful Ascetic: The Life of Francis Xavier Seelos, C.SS.R.* New Orleans: Redemptorist Fathers, New Orleans Vice Province. 1969. This detailed biography of the Bavarian Redemptorist who came to the United States in 1843, exercised the sacred ministry in Pittsburgh, Baltimore, and Cumberland, and died in New Orleans in 1867 studies his reputation for sanctity; it also sheds light on the history of his congregation and the spiritual care of German Catholics in America.

455.   _____ . *Venerable John Neumann, C.SS.R.: Fourth Bishop of Philadelphia.* Washington, D.C.: Catholic University of America Press. 1952. A scholarly biography of the Bohemia-born prelate who has been canonized.

456.   de Goesbriand, Louis. *Catholic Memoirs of Vermont and New Hampshire.* Burlington, Vt.: The Author. 1886. Brief biographical

sketches by the first Bishop of Burlington of early converts such as William Henry Hoyt (1813–1883), Fanny Allen (1784–1819), and the Barber family.

457.   Deuther, Charles G. *The Life and Times of the Rt. Rev. John Timon*. Buffalo: The Author. 1870. A fairly full account of the first Bishop of Buffalo for so early a date; not a scientific work but has merit in narration and arrangement of material; for earlier years of Timon, superseded by Bayard (No. 105).

458.   Dirvin, Joseph I., C.M. *Mrs. Seton: Foundress of the American Sisters of Charity*. New York: Farrar, Straus and Cudahy. 1962. Father Dirvin has used the manuscripts preserved in St. Joseph's Central House, Emmitsburg, Maryland, thoroughly and intelligently to portray in abundant detail both the development of Elizabeth Bayley Seton's spiritual life and the difficulties she faced in caring for her personal family and her religious community.

459.   Doubourg, J. Heun [André J. M. Hamon]. *Life of the Cardinal de Cheverus: Archbishop of Bordeaux*. Trans. E. Stewart. Boston: J. Munroe. 1839. The earlier biography of the first Bishop of Boston; of more value than the translation of Robert M. Walsh (Philadelphia: Hooker and Claxton. 1839) because of its appendices; superseded by Melville (No. 531).

460.   Durkin, Joseph T., S.J., ed. *Confederate Chaplain: A War Journal of Rev. James B. Sheeran, C.SS.R., 14th Louisiana, C.S.A*. Milwaukee: Bruce. 1960. The Irish-born Sheeran (1819–1881) kept a diary from his entrance into the war on August 2, 1862, to May 7, 1865.

461.   _____ . *William Matthews: Priest and Citizen*. New York: Benziger. 1964. A documented account of a pastor of St. Patrick's Church, Washington, D.C., who figured prominently in both Church and State in the first half of the nineteenth century.

462.   Easterly, Frederick J., C.M. *The Life of the Rt. Rev. Joseph Rosati, First Bishop of St. Louis, 1789–1843*. Washington, D.C.: Catholic University of America Press. 1942. Reprint. New York: AMS. 1974. A Ph.D. thesis that employs a considerable amount of manuscript material.

463.   Elliott, Walter. *The Life of Father Hecker*. New York: Columbus. 1891. Reprint. New York: Arno. 1972. This biography of one of

the most important converts to the Catholic Church in the nineteenth century and founder of the Paulists (1819–1888) was written in haste by a devoted confrère and furnished with an introduction by Archbishop John Ireland; in its French translation and adaptation it caused a flurry, especially in Europe, and led to the controversy over Americanism. It is defective in many particulars and now superseded for Hecker's early life by Holden (No. 486).

464.   Erskine, Marjory. *Mother Philippine Duchesne*. New York: Longmans, Green. 1926. A popular account now superseded by Callan (No. 445).

465.   Feeney, Leonard, S.J. *Elizabeth Seton: An American Woman.* New York: America Press. 1938. *Mother Seton: An American Woman.* New York: Dodd, Mead. 1947. *Mother Seton: Saint Elizabeth of New York, 1774–1821.* Cambridge, Mass.: Ravengate. 1975. This popular life has long been superseded by Dirvin's and Melville's scholarly biographies (Nos. 458, 530).

466.   Fox, Columba, Sister. *The Life of the Right Reverend John Baptist Mary David, 1761–1841: Bishop of Bardstown and Founder of the Sisters of Charity of Nazareth.* New York: United States Catholic Historical Society. 1925. A lengthy and illustrated biography that incorporates a good deal of original correspondence; done originally as a thesis for the A.M. degree. See also Lemarié (No. 511).

467.   Frean, W., C.SS.R. *Blessed John Neumann: The Helper of the Afflicted.* Ballarat, Victoria, Australia: Majellan. 1963. Though lacking references to the sources, bibliography, and index, this sizable biography is the fruit of considerable research. Its hagiographical and uncritical style betrays its primary purpose: to promote the cause of canonization.

468.   Furlan, William P. *In Charity Unfeigned: The Life of Father Francis Xavier Pierz.* St. Cloud, Minn.: Chancery Office. 1952. A documented work on the remarkable missionary from Slovenia who labored in the Indian missions of Wisconsin and Minnesota for nearly forty years; Pierz arrived in the United States in 1835 and remained until 1873.

469.   Galvin, James J., C.SS.R. *Blessed John Neumann: Bishop of Philadelphia.* Baltimore: Helicon. 1964. A partly fictionalized biography which has no value for historians.

470.   Gannon, Michael V. *Rebel Bishop: The Life and Era of Augustin Verot*. Milwaukee: Bruce. 1964. Originally presented as a doctoral dissertation at the University of Florida, this well-written and thoroughly documented biography of Verot (1805–1876), who was Vicar Apostolic of Florida, Bishop of Savannah, and first Bishop of St. Augustine, emphasizes his contributions to the Negro question, Civil War politics, the common school crisis, and the First Vatican Council.

471.   Garin, J. *Notices Biographiques sur Mgr. J-B. Miége: Premier Vicaire Apostolique du Kansas et sur les Prêtres de la Paroisse de Chevron (Savoie)*. Moûtiers: Cane Soeurs. 1886. This is primarily a collection of the prelate's letters to his brother et al.; an important source for the French-born Jesuit who ruled the Church in Kansas from 1851 to 1874 and who later (1877) founded what was to become the University of Detroit.

472.   Gilhooley, Leonard. *Contradiction and Dilemma: Orestes Brownson and the American Idea*. New York: Fordham University Press. 1972. This well-researched work, which is both descriptive and analytical, shows how the creative political philosopher at times accepted, modified, and rejected the complex of ideals and aims of the young nation, especially in his *Boston Quarterly Review* (1838–1842) and *Brownson's Quarterly Review* (1845–1859), and critically compares his views with those of his contemporaries.

473.   Godecker, Mary Salesia, Sister, O.S.B. *Simon Bruté de Rémur, First Bishop of Vincennes*. St. Meinrad: St. Meinrad Historical Essays. 1931. A large and well-documented work that developed out of a Ph.D. thesis; it is the most extensive life of Bruté in English, although not the most readable. Cf. Lemarié and Maynard (Nos. 510, 528).

474.   Gower, Joseph F., and Richard M. Leliaert, eds. *The Brownson-Hecker Correspondence*. Notre Dame: University of Notre Dame Press. 1979. The letters exchanged by the outstanding Catholic converts and apologists, Orestes A. Brownson and Isaac Hecker, between 1841 and 1872 are here provided with the necessary background and are fully annotated and indexed.

475.   Grant, Dorothy Fremont. *John England ... American Christopher*. Milwaukee: Bruce. 1949. This unscholarly treatment of selected aspects of the life of the first Bishop of Charleston adds nothing of value to Guilday's biography (No. 479).

476.   Gregorich, Joseph. *The Apostle of the Chippewas: The Life Story of the Most Rev. Frederick Baraga, the First Bishop of Marquette*. Chicago: Bishop Baraga Association. 1932. The best biography to date of the famous missionary who was also an accomplished student of Indian languages.

477.   Griffin, Martin I. J. *History of Rt. Rev. Michael Egan, First Bishop of Philadelphia*. Philadelphia: The Author. 1893. This work, which first appeared in succeeding issues of the *American Catholic Historical Researches*, is of value for its reprinting of documents, although defective in form and style.

478.   Guilday, Peter. *The Life and Times of John Carroll: Archbishop of Baltimore, 1735–1815*. 2 vols. New York: Encyclopedia Press. 1922. Reprint. (One vol.) Westminster, Md.: Newman. 1954. An extensive work which is especially valuable for the correspondence and documents it carries; because of numerous inaccuracies, however, it must be used with caution; now superseded in many particulars by Melville (No. 532).

479.   _____ . *The Life and Times of John England: First Bishop of Charleston, 1786–1842*. 2 vols. New York: America Press. 1927. Reprint. New York: Arno. 1969. Although his jurisdiction covered only North and South Carolina and Georgia, England's influence extended to the whole country; hence this heavily documented biography almost constitutes a history of the Church in the United States in the 1820's, 1830's, and early 1840's. In many ways this is the best of Guilday's many publications.

480.   Hanley, Thomas O'Brien, S.J., ed. *The John Carroll Papers*. Vol I: *1755–1791*; Vol. II: *1792–1806*; Vol. III: *1807–1815*. Notre Dame: University of Notre Dame Press. 1976. Commissioned by the American Catholic Historical Association, this comprehensive edition contains personal, official, and pastoral letters, sermons, comments, memoranda, and other writings of the first American bishop collected from depositories on both sides of the Atlantic. It suffers, however, from failure to use original manuscripts in some cases, from omission of other documents, and from inaccuracy in identifications and explanations. See the review by John J. Tierney in the *Catholic Historical Review*, LXIV (October, 1978), 660–670.

481.   Hassard, John R. G. *Life of the Most Reverend John Hughes: First Archbishop of New York*. New York: D. Appleton. 1866. Reprint. New York: Arno. 1969. Although very much out of date and written only

two years after Hughes' death, this volume remains the only real biography to date of the archbishop; notable for the correspondence printed either in part or *in extenso*. Hughes was the greatest leader of the Irish Catholics for a quarter-century, not only in New York State but in the entire country.

482.   Healy, Kathleen. *Frances Warde: American Founder of the Sisters of Mercy*. New York: Seabury. 1973. Based on extensive research in the United States, Ireland, and Rome, this biography reads almost like a chronicle of the establishment of twenty-seven foundations across the continent between 1843 and 1884.

483.   Hoffmann, Mathias M. *The Church Founders of the Northwest*. Milwaukee: Bruce. 1937. An able volume on the first Bishops of Dubuque and St. Paul and some of their contemporaries.

484.   Hogan, John J. *On the Mission in Missouri, 1857–1868*. Kansas City: J. A. Heilmann. 1892. Reprint. Glorietta, N. Mex.: Rio Grande. 1976. The memoirs of an Irish-born missionary who in 1868 became the first Bishop of St. Joseph and later (1880) of Kansas City; the account begins in 1857 and contains some interesting comments on the Civil War and its effects on the Church in Missouri.

485.   Holden, Vincent F., C.S.P. *The Early Years of Isaac Thomas Hecker, 1819–1844*. Washington, D.C.: Catholic University of America Press. 1939. Reprint. New York: AMS. 1974. An able study up to Hecker's conversion to Catholicism; done as a Ph.D. thesis, but now superseded by the author's more recent account of the Paulist founder (No. 486).

486.   _____ . *The Yankee Paul: Isaac Thomas Hecker*. Milwaukee: Bruce. 1958. The most recent scholarly treatment to date of the Paulist founder; carries the story to Hecker's return from Rome in 1858.

487.   Holman, Frederick V. *John McLoughlin: The Father of Oregon*. Cleveland: Arthur H. Clark. 1907. An able brief biography—about half the volume is given to the reproduction of documents—of the powerful factor of the Hudson's Bay Company who gave great assistance to the Church after his conversion in 1842.

488.   Horgan, Paul. *Lamy of Santa Fe: His Life and Times*. New York: Farrar, Straus and Giroux. 1975. Combining thorough research with literary skill and love for the Southwest, this distinguished writer has

produced the definitive biography of John Baptist Lamy, who from 1850, when he was appointed Vicar Apostolic of New Mexico, to 1885, when he resigned as Archbishop of Santa Fe, labored to revive and expand the Church among the Hispanic population and the new settlers. Awarded the Pulitzer Prize for History in 1976.

489.   Howlett, William J. *Life of Rev. Charles Nerinckx: Pioneer Missionary of Kentucky and Founder of the Sisters of Loretto at the Foot of the Cross.* 2nd ed. Techny, Ill.: Mission. 1940. The reprint of a popular biography that appeared originally in 1915.

490.   Hughes, Vincent R., O.P. *The Right Rev. Richard Luke Concanen, O.P.: First Bishop of New York, 1747–1810.* Fribourg, Switzerland: Studia Friburgensia. 1926. A Ph.D. thesis that is more pertinent to the church history of Ireland and England, since Concanen never reached the United States.

491.   Ives, L. Silliman. *The Trials of a Mind in Its Progress to Catholicism: A Letter to His Old Friends.* Boston: Patrick Donahoe. 1854. An account by the convert Protestant Episcopal Bishop of North Carolina written two years after his reception into the Church; more apologetical than autobiographical in character, although there are two brief chapters devoted to his conversion.

492.   Jacks, Leo V. *Claude Dubuis: Bishop of Galveston.* St. Louis: B. Herder. 1946. A superficial work that relies heavily on earlier French accounts of the second Bishop of Galveston.

493.   Jezernik, Maksimilijan. *Frederick Baraga: A Portrait of the First Bishop of Marquette Based on the Archives of the Congregatio de Propaganda Fide.* New York, Washington, D.C.: Studia Slovenica. 1968. Studying the missionary's life from the viewpoint of Rome but supplementing that documentation with other primary sources, Monsignor Jezernik does not repeat the complete treatment of the subject given by previous biographers, but rather concentrates on aspects on which he has brought new material to light.

494.   Johnson, Peter Leo. *Crosier on the Frontier: A Life of John Martin Henni.* Madison: State Historical Society of Wisconsin. 1959. A scholarly biography of Milwaukee's first bishop and archbishop who ruled the Church in Wisconsin from 1843 to 1881; especially good for questions related to the German Catholic immigrants.

495.   _____ . *Stuffed Saddlebags: The Life of Martin Kundig, Priest,*

1805–1879. Milwaukee: Bruce. 1942. The story of one of the outstanding German missionary priests of the Middle West told in a carefully documented account.

496.   Johnson, Robert C. *John McLoughlin: Patriarch of the Northwest*. Portland: Metropolitan. 1935. A popular biography that leans heavily on Holman (No. 487) and other earlier works.

497.   Kehoe, Lawrence. *Complete Works of the Most Reverend John Hughes: First Archbishop of New York*. 2 vols. New York: Catholic Publication House. 1865. Worthwhile source materials containing sermons, lectures, and some correspondence.

498.   Kelly, E. D., trans. *Correspondence of Rev. Louis Baroux, Missionary Apostolic of Michigan, to Rev. M. J. DeNeve, Superior of the American College at Louvain*. Ann Arbor: Ann Arbor Press. 1913. Reprint. Berrien Springs, Mich.: Hardscrabble Books. 1976. Baroux (1817—1897), who was a French member of the Congregation of Holy Cross, wrote this "History of the Pottawatomies" in 1862.

499.   Kennedy, Mary Benedicta, Sister, O.S.D. *Memoirs Historical and Edifying of a Missionary Apostolic*. Chicago: W. F. Hall. 1915. A translation made from a work originally published in 1844 for Italian readers by Samuel Mazzuchelli, O.P.; the narrative does not include material for the last twenty years of Mazzuchelli's life, 1844–1864. Now superseded by Armato (No. 426).

500.   Kennedy, Thomas. *Father Ryan: The Irish-American Poet-Priest of the Southern States*. Dublin: J. J. Lalor. n.d. A popular pamphlet on the Maryland-born priest who figured so prominently in the religious and literary history of the Confederacy; of some use in the absence of any real biography.

501.   King, Margaret Rives. *Memoirs of the Life of Mrs. Sarah Peter*. 2 vols. Cincinnati: R. Clarke. 1889. Written by an admiring daughter-in-law, these volumes incorporate a good deal of value to biographers of this remarkable convert laywoman by way of correspondence, diary entries, etc.

502.   Kohler, Mary Hortense, Sister. *Life and Work of Mother Benedicta Bauer*. Milwaukee: Bruce. 1937. The story of a Bavarian-born religious (1803–1865) who with a small group of companions came to this country in 1858 in response to the need for teaching sisters among the German immigrant colonies; documented from archival sources.

503.   Kowrach, Edward J. *Journal of a Catholic Bishop on the Oregon Trail: The Overland Crossing of the Rt. Rev. A. M. A. Blanchet, Bishop of Walla Walla, from Montreal to Oregon Territory, March 23, 1847 – January 23, 1851. Blackrobe Buries Whitmans*, by J. B. A. Brouillet. Fairfield, Wash.: Ye Galleon. 1978. In this folio-sized and richly designed volume the editor has provided a brief introduction to each of the two documents, extensive notes, and a bibliography. Cf. No. 101.

504.   Lambert, Bernard J. *Shepherd of the Wilderness: A Biography of Bishop Frederic Baraga*. L'Anse, Mich.: The Author. 1967. Although the narrative contains both repetitions and sketchy passages, some heroic adventures and unique experiences of the devoted missionary are grippingly recounted in this popular work.

505.   Lamers, William M. *The Edge of Glory: A Biography of General William S. Rosecrans, U.S.A.* New York: Harcourt, Brace and World. 1962. A documented life of a military officer who was a convert to Catholicism from his West Point days; he helped to bring his brother, Sylvester Rosecrans, first Bishop of Columbus, into the Church as well.

506.   Langan, Tom. *John Neumann: Harvester of Souls*. Huntington, Ind.: Our Sunday Visitor. 1976. This popular, undocumented, uncritical biography adds nothing to the work of Curley (No. 455).

507.   Lapati, Americo D. *Orestes A. Brownson*. New York: Twayne. 1965. This slender volume in Twayne's United States Authors series provides the best introduction to Brownson's life and thought, which are considered under the aspects of religion, social reform, political philosophy, and literary criticism.

508.   Laveille, E., S.J. *The Life of Father de Smet, S.J., 1801–1873*. Trans. Marian Lindsay. New York: P. J. Kenedy. 1915. A well-documented life of the promoter of the Jesuit missions among the western Indians; makes generous use of the correspondence in Chittenden-Richardson (No. 449).

509.   Lebreton, Dagmar Renshaw. *Chahta-Ima: The Life of Adrien-Emmanuel Rouquette*. Baton Rouge: Louisiana State University Press. 1947. A carefully documented and well-written biography of a missionary among the Indians who was likewise a writer and prominent literary figure in Louisiana (1813–1887).

510.   Lemarié, Charles. *Monseigneur Bruté de Rémur: Premier Evêque*

de Vincennes aux Etats-Unis, 1834–1839. Paris: Librairie C. Klincksieck. 1974. Based upon extensive research in both France and the United States (although some pertinent books have been overlooked), this biography brings to light valuable materials through long quotations from the primary sources and furnishes new insights regarding the highly intellectual, spiritual, and zealous churchman. This is the second volume of the author's trilogy, "Etudes sur les missionnaires bretons dans le Middle West Américain." Supersedes No. 473.

511. _____ . *Mgr. J.-B. David, 1761–1841.* "Etudes sur les missionnaires bretons dans le Middle West Américain (Contribution à l'histoire des origines du catholicisme aux Etats-Unis)," Vol. I: *Les origines religieuses du Kentucky.* Angers: The Author. 1973. This lengthy biography of the French Sulpician (who went as a missionary to Maryland in 1792 and on to Kentucky in 1811, founded the first seminary in the West and the Sisters of Charity of Nazareth, then became coadjutor and, for a brief time, ordinary Bishop of Bardstown) is based on some sources not used by Sister Columba Fox in her work on David (No. 466), which it supplements. Mainly intended for French readers, as the excessively numerous appendices (some only remotely related to the subject) suggest.

512. Lemcke, Peter Henry, O.S.B. *Life and Work of Prince Demetrius Augustine Gallitzin.* Trans. Joseph C. Plumpe. New York: Longmans, Green. 1940. A scholarly translation and edition of the biography of the Russian-born missionary in western Pennsylvania by one of his contemporaries.

513. Lewis, Walker. *Without Fear or Favor: A Biography of Chief Justice Roger Brooke Taney.* Boston: Houghton Mifflin. 1965. Though intended for the general reader and overloaded with anecdotes, this well-documented and well-written work by a corporation lawyer is the best available biography of the Catholic jurist. Sympathetic but objective, it puts the Dred Scott Decision in the context of Taney's characteristically humane concerns.

514. Lipscomb, Oscar Hugh. "The Administration of John Quinlan: Second Bishop of Mobile, 1859–1883." *Records* of the American Catholic Historical Society of Philadelphia, LXXVIII (March–December, 1967), 1–163. This well-documented M.A. thesis for the Catholic University of America is both an institutional history of the Church in Alabama and northwestern Florida during the Civil War and Reconstruction and a biography of the bishop.

515.   Lochemes, M. Frederick, Sister. *Robert Walsh: His Story*. New York: American Irish Historical Society. 1941. An able biography of the Catholic editor, writer, and diplomat, originally done as a Ph.D. thesis.

516.   Lyons, W. F. *Brigadier General Thomas Francis Meagher: His Political and Military Career with Selections from His Speeches and Writings*. New York: D. and J. Sadlier. 1870. An old work now superseded by Athearn (No. 427).

517.   McAllister, Anna Shannon. *Flame in the Wilderness: Life and Letters of Mother Angela Gillespie, C.S.C., 1824–1887*. Paterson, N.J.: St. Anthony Guild. 1944. A semipopular and well-written biography of the American foundress of the Sisters of the Holy Cross.

518.   ———— . *In Winter We Flourish: Life and Letters of Sarah Worthington King Peter, 1800–1877*. New York: Longmans, Green. 1939. An able documented work on the convert laywoman of Cincinnati who was largely responsible for the establishment of a number of women's religious communities in the United States.

519.   McArdle, Mary Aurelia, Sister. *California's Pioneer Sister of Mercy: Mother Mary Baptist Russell, 1829–1898*. Fresno: Academy Library Guild. 1954. A master's thesis on the Irish-born religious who founded the community in California in 1854.

520.   McCadden, Joseph and Helen. *Father Varela: Torch Bearer from Cuba*. New York: United States Catholic Historical Society. 1969. A scholarly life of the Reverend Felix Varela (1788–1853). Coming to New York as a political refugee from his native island in 1823, this scholar and statesman became prominent as an author, newspaper editor, and administrator of the diocese.

521.   McKee, Irving. *The Trial of Death: Letters of Benjamin Marie Petit*. Indianapolis: Indiana Historical Society. 1941. A translation and edition of twenty-seven letters of a missionary priest among the Potawatomi Indians of northern Indiana between April, 1836, and January, 1838, as well as a translation of his journal.

522.   Maes, Camillus P. *The Life of Rev. Charles Nerinckx*. Cincinnati: R. Clarke. 1880. A biography of the Belgian-born missionary of early Kentucky who founded the Sisters of Loretto in 1812; well done for so early a date, but since superseded by Howlett (No. 489).

523.   Magaret, Helene. *Father De Smet: Pioneer Priest of the Rockies.* New York: Farrar and Rinehart. 1940. Originally a Ph.D. thesis at the State University of Iowa; aside from a chronological table at the end, it is difficult to distinguish the book from a work of fiction.

524.   _____ . *Giant in the Wilderness: A Biography of Father Charles Nerinckx.* Milwaukee: Bruce. 1952. More a fictionalized account than a true biography, despite the subtitle, but more readable than the older works of Howlett and Maes (Nos. 489, 522).

525.   Marshall, Hugh, S.T. *Orestes Brownson and the American Republic: An Historical Perspective.* Washington, D.C.: Catholic University of America Press. 1971. This careful study, developed from a doctoral dissertation written at the Catholic University of America, places Brownson's political thought in the perspective of his whole intellectual evolution from the 1830's to the 1870's.

526.   Mast, M. Dolorita, Sister, S.S.N.D. *Always the Priest: The Life of Gabriel Richard, S.S.* Baltimore: Helicon. 1965. Intended for the general reader, this is a somewhat filiopietistic biography of the French Sulpician pastor in Detroit, who promoted not only religion and morality but also education, culture, and economic growth in that area from his arrival in 1798 to his death in 1832.

527.   Maynard, Theodore. *Orestes Brownson: Yankee, Radical, Catholic.* New York: Macmillan. 1943. An able study based on wide reading in the printed literature; probably the best of the author's biographies in American Catholic history; superseded by Ryan (No. 559).

528.   _____ . *The Reed and the Rock.* New York: Longmans, Green. 1942. A popular and somewhat impressionistic life of Simon Bruté, first Bishop of Vincennes; superseded by Lemarié (No. 510).

529.   Meagher, Walter J., S.J., ed. *"A Proper Bostonian, Priest, Jesuit": Diary of Fr. Joseph Coolidge Shaw, S.J., 1821–1851.* Boston: Privately printed. 1966. This diary of a member of a prominent family, convert to Catholicism, and diocesan priest who became a Jesuit novice one year before his death contains useful observations on religious conditions in Europe and America. A biographical appendix gives information on all persons mentioned in the text.

530.   Melville, Annabelle M. *Elizabeth Bayley Seton, 1744–1821.* New York: Charles Scribner's. 1951. Reprint. 1976. A scholarly

biography of the foundress of the Emmitsburg Sisters of Charity, the first native American sisterhood; originally done as a Ph.D. thesis.

531. _____ . *Jean Lefebvre de Cheverus, 1768–1836.* Milwaukee: Bruce. 1958. A first-class biography, scholarly and well written, of the first Bishop of Boston who died as Cardinal Archbishop of Bordeaux.

532. _____ . *John Carroll of Baltimore: Founder of the American Catholic Hierarchy.* New York: Charles Scribner's. 1955. A work of careful scholarship that corrects a number of errors in earlier biographies of Carroll, e.g., Guilday (No. 478); awarded the John Gilmary Shea Prize of the American Catholic Historical Association in 1955.

533. Messmer, Sebastian G., et al., eds. *The Works of the Right Reverend John England.* 7 vols. Cleveland: Arthur H. Clark. 1908. Sermons, lectures, and other writings of the first Bishop of Charleston. This edition is more critical than the earlier one by Reynolds (No. 555).

534. Miller, S. J. "Peter Richard Kenrick: Bishop and Archbishop of St. Louis, 1806–1896," *Records* of the American Catholic Historical Society of Philadelphia, LXXXIV (March, June, and September, 1973), 1–163. Although the main events of Kenrick's life are set down, this is not a complete biography but rather a scholarly investigation of his ecclesiology as he evolved and manifested it in his seminary studies, his writings, the governance of his diocese, and his conduct at the councils of Baltimore and the First Vatican Council.

535. Mondésir, Edouard de. *Souvenirs d'Edouard de Mondésir.* Baltimore: Johns Hopkins Press. 1942. A brief and sketchy memoir on American Catholicism by one of the original group of seminarians brought from France in 1791 by the Sulpicians; written in 1842 at the request of Etienne-Michel Faillon, S.S. (1800–1870), as part of a collection of materials for a biography of Jacques-André Emery (1732–1811), Sulpician superior-general; edited from a copy of the original manuscript in the Sulpician archives of Paris.

536. Moore, Guy W. *The Case of Mrs. Surratt: Her Controversial Trial and Execution for Conspiracy in the Lincoln Assassination.* Norman: University of Oklahoma Press. 1954. An able, documented, and convincing account of Mrs. Surratt's innocence.

537.   Mug, Mary Theodosia, Sister. *Journal and Letters of Mother Theodore Guérin*. St. Mary-of-the-Woods, Ind.: Sisters of Providence. 1942. An account of the foundation of the Sisters of Providence in Indiana, 1840–1856, told in original correspondence; a valuable collection of sources for Indiana Catholic history of the mid-century; supplements Brown (No. 871); Mother Theodore's cause for beatification has been introduced at the Holy See.

538.   Murphy, Grace. *Gallitzin's Letters: A Collection of the Polemical Works of the Very Reverend Prince Demetrius Augustine Gallitzin, 1770–1840*. Loretto, Pa.: Angelmodde. 1940. A reprinting of some of Gallitzin's apologetic works which grew out of controversies with Protestants, rather than a collection of his correspondence.

539.   Nichols, M. Leona. *The Mantle of Elias: The Story of Fathers Blanchet and Demers in Early Oregon*. Portland, Ore.: Binfords and Mort. 1941. Though it reads like a novel, this uncritical account of the Canadian priests who became Archbishop of Oregon City and Bishop of Vancouver Island is supported to some indefinable extent by uncited records; their roles in matters of importance to the national and universal Church are ignored.

540.   Nolan, Hugh J. *The Most Reverend Francis Patrick Kenrick: Third Bishop of Philadelphia, 1830–1851*. Washington, D.C.: Catholic University of America Press. 1948. A Ph.D. thesis that covers in a detailed way the career of Kenrick before his promotion to the See of Baltimore.

541.   Nugent, Helen Louise, Sister. *Sister Louise (Josephine Van der Schrieck), 1813–1886: American Foundress of the Sisters of Notre Dame of Namur*. Washington D.C.: Catholic University of America Press. 1931. A Ph.D. thesis on the Dutch-born religious who came to this country with her companions in October, 1840, to open in Cincinnati the first of a large number of American houses. While the work is obviously based on archival material (from which there is generous quoting), it makes no specific references to such material, although there is an essay on the sources.

542.   O'Brien, Joseph L. *John England, Bishop of Charleston: The Apostle to Democracy*. New York: Edward O'Toole. 1934. A popular work based in good measure on Guilday (No. 479).

543.   O'Daniel, Victor F., O.P. *An American Apostle: The Very Reverend Matthew Anthony O'Brien, O.P.* New York: Frederick Pustet.

1923. A life of the Irish-born friar (1804–1871) who served as provincial of the Dominicans in the United States. See also No. 546.

544. _____ . *The Father of the Church in Tennessee, Or the Life, Times, and Character of the Right Reverend Richard Pius Miles, O.P.* New York: Frederick Pustet. 1926. A life of the first Bishop of Nashville (1791—1860). See also No. 546.

545. _____ . *A Light of the Church in Kentucky, Or the Life, Labors, and Character of the Very Rev. Samuel Thomas Wilson, O.P.* New York: Frederick Pustet. 1932. A biography of the first American provincial of the Dominican friars (1761–1824). See also No. 546.

546. _____ . *The Right Rev. Edward Dominic Fenwick, O.P.: Founder of the Dominicans in the United States.* New York: Frederick Pustet. 1920. The life of the first Bishop of Cincinnati (1768–1832). The above four items are among the principal publications of the pioneer historian of the American Dominicans; all make ample use of archival materials not easily found elsewhere, but they suffer from a pro-Dominican bias that lessens their value to scholars.

547. Oetgen, Jerome. *An American Abbot: Boniface Wimmer, O.S.B., 1809–1887.* Latrobe, Pa.: Archabbey. 1976. This history of the founding of the first Benedictine monastery in the United States, St. Vincent's at Latrobe, Pennsylvania, in 1846 by monks from the Abbey of Metten in Bavaria, and of its growth and establishment of daughter houses in distant places is written with more attention to literary quality than to historical method.

548. O'Grady, John. *Levi Silliman Ives: Pioneer Leader in Catholic Charities.* New York: P. J. Kenedy. 1933. A popular biographical sketch of a convert social worker.

549. O'Hanlon, John. *Life and Scenery in Missouri: Reminiscences of a Missionary Priest.* Dublin: J. Duffy. 1890. The memoirs of an Irish-born missionary during the 1840's and 1850's; for a summary of its contents see Helena Concannen, "Canon John O'Hanlon (1821–1905): His Early Days in St. Louis," *Irish Ecclesiastical Record*, LXIX (January, 1947), 11–19.

550. O'Rourke, Timothy J. *Maryland Catholics on the Frontier: The Missouri and Texas Settlements.* Parsons, Kans.: Brefney. 1973. This large tome, reproducing a typescript by the photo-offset process, contains genealogical data on members of the families who migrated

to the Barrens in Perry County, Missouri, from the early 1800's on, and thence to Texas from the 1830's on.

551.   O'Shea, John J. *The Two Kenricks*. Philadelphia: J. J. McVey. 1904. A popular work superseded for Francis Kenrick's Philadelphia career by Nolan (No. 540) and for Peter Richard Kenrick by Miller (No. 534).

552.   Parisot, P. F., O.M.I. *The Reminiscences of a Texas Missionary*. San Antonio: Johnson Bros. 1899. The personal account of a French-born Oblate who came to this country in 1852 and was on the missions in the Southwest until the late 1880's.

553.   Perrichon, J. *Vie de Mgr. Dubuis, l'Apôtre de Texas*. Lyons: Librairie Vitte. 1900. While this is not a scientific work it is more reliable than Jacks (No. 492).

554.   Reardon, James Michael. *George Anthony Belcourt: Pioneer Catholic, Missionary of the Northwest, 1803–1874: His Life and Times*. St. Paul: North Central. 1955. A biography based on a considerable amount of unpublished correspondence in the diocesan archives of Quebec, Montreal, Dubuque, Fargo, etc.

555.   Reynolds, Ignatius Aloysius. *The Works of the Right Rev. John England: First Bishop of Charleston*. 5 vols. Baltimore: John Murphy. 1849. Reprint. New York: Arno. 1978. The writings are arranged under the following headings: dogmatic and polemical theology, history, miscellaneous, and discourses, pastoral letters, addresses, and orations. There is a general index to the entire collection. This edition contains some writings wrongly attributed to England. It is superseded by Messmer (No. 533).

556.   Rowe, Kenneth W. *Mathew Carey: A Study in American Economic Development*. Baltimore: Johns Hopkins Press. 1933. A Ph.D. thesis that analyzes the economic doctrines of the early Catholic publisher of Philadelphia; not a full-length biography.

557.   Rush, Alfred C., C.SS.R., trans. *The Autobiography of St. John Neumann, C.SS.R.: Fourth Bishop of Philadelphia*. Boston: St. Paul Editions. 1977. Written at the behest of the Redemptorist provincial when Neumann was appointed bishop in 1852, this "short account" covers the first forty-one years of his life. It is here rendered into idiomatic English and equipped with helpful notes.

558.   Ryan, Alvan S. *The Brownson Reader*. New York: P. J. Kenedy. 1955. A selection of excerpts from the works of Orestes A. Brownson on major topics such as education, politics, religion, etc.

559.   Ryan, Thomas R., C.PP.S. *Orestes A. Brownson: A Definitive Biography*. Huntington, Ind.: Our Sunday Visitor. 1976. This massive, thorough, orderly, and critical investigation of the life, thought, work, and character of a very controversial and complex man is a valuable contribution to American religious, intellectual, and political history.

560.   Salzbacher, Josef. *Meine Reise nach Nord-Amerika im Jahre 1842*. Vienna: Wimmer, Schmidt and Leo. 1845. Impressions of American Catholicism by an Austrian canon who visited the United States in the interests of the Leopoldine Foundation.

561.   Sargent, Daniel. *Mitri, Or the Story of Prince Demetrius Augustine Gallitzin, 1770–1840*. New York: Longmans, Green. 1945. A pleasantly written popular biography that incorporates some correspondence.

562.   Schauinger, J. Herman. *Cathedrals in the Wilderness*. Milwaukee: Bruce. 1952. A well-documented biography of Benedict J. Flaget, S.S., first Bishop of Bardstown.

563.   _____ . *Stephen T. Badin: Priest in the Wilderness*. Milwaukee: Bruce. 1956. A fully annotated life of the famous pioneer missionary of Kentucky and the Middle West.

564.   _____ . *William Gaston: Carolinian*. Milwaukee: Bruce. 1949. A brief life of the associate justice of the North Carolina supreme court; done originally as a Ph.D. thesis.

565.   Schlesinger, Arthur M., Jr. *Orestes A. Brownson: A Pilgrim's Progress*. Boston: Little, Brown. 1939. An able study of the Catholic publicist and controversialist.

566.   Shaw, Richard. *Dagger John: The Unquiet Life and Times of Archbishop John Hughes of New York*. New York: Paulist. 1977. This generally sympathetic, semipopular biography of the great ecclesiastical leader of the Irish-American Catholics in the middle decades of the nineteenth century is based largely on contemporary newspapers (especially the New York *Herald* edited by the aggressive James

Gordon Bennett) and insufficiently on manuscript sources and secondary literature; it emphasizes Hughes's public controversies and activities and neglects his quiet labors for the development of the Church in his (arch)diocese.

567.   Simpson, Lesley Byrd, ed. *The Letters of José Señán, O.F.M., Mission San Buenaventura, 1796–1823*. Trans. Paul D. Nathan. San Francisco: John Howell. 1962. These candid, vivid letters (nearly one hundred in number), written by a faithful Catalan missionary, reflect the decline of the California missions from their prosperous acme under Fermín de Lasuén to a state of neglect and peril.

568.   Skelton, Isabel. *The Life of Thomas D'Arcy McGee*. Gardenvale, Canada: Garden City. 1925. The first half of this large volume, embodying considerable correspondence, pertains to McGee's years in this country before his final departure for Canada in 1857; good for colonization and Irish nationalist movements of the mid-century.

569.   Spalding, John Lancaster. *The Life of the Most Reverend M.J. Spalding*. New York: Catholic Publication Society. 1873. For a book written by a nephew a year after the subject's death, this work is well done; incorporates considerable correspondence on the second Bishop of Louisville and seventh Archbishop of Baltimore; superseded by T. W. Spalding (No. 571).

570.   Spalding, Martin J. *Sketches of the Life, Times, and Character of the Rt. Rev. Benedict Joseph Flaget, First Bishop of Louisville*. Louisville: Webb and Levering. 1852. Reprint. New York: Arno. 1969. An important contemporary source for the history of early Catholic life in the new West, written two years after Flaget's death by his coadjutor and successor in the See of Louisville. Consecrated Bishop of Bardstown in 1810, this native of France was responsible at first for the whole Northwest Territory as well as Kentucky and Tennessee. Superseded by Schauinger (No. 562).

571.   Spalding, Thomas W. *Martin John Spalding: American Churchman*. Washington, D.C.: Catholic University of America Press in association with Consortium Press. 1973. This excellent biography of the prominent mid-nineteenth-century apologist, Bishop of Louisville, and Archbishop of Baltimore, is a revised doctoral dissertation from the Catholic University of America. Its author was awarded the John Gilmary Shea Prize. Supersedes J. L. Spalding (No. 569).

572. *Studia Neumanniana: Sancto Joanni Nepomuceno Neumann in solemni canonizatione obsequii fratrum munus.* Rome: Collegium S. Alfonsi de Urbe. 1977. This collection of seven articles by Giuseppe Orlandi (in Italian), André Sampers (in German), Alfred C. Rush (in English), and Nicola Ferrante (in Italian) on one report and various deposits of letters, on the death and burial, and on the processes of beatification and canonization of the Bishop of Philadelphia contains a wealth of information about the person and his diocese.

573.   Sveino, Per. *Orestes A. Brownson's Road to Catholicism.* Oslo: Universitetsforlaget/New York: Humanities. 1970. Studying in depth Brownson's religious and philosophical opinions up to 1844, the author demonstrates a basic consistency in his subject's intellectual development toward his conversion.

574.   Swisher, Carl Brent. *Roger B. Taney.* New York: Macmillan. 1935. This biography of the Maryland-born Catholic who became chief justice of the United States is still useful; cf. Lewis (No. 513).

575.   Sylvain, Robert, F.S.C. *La vie et l'oeuvre de Henry de Courcy, 1820–1861: Premier historien de l'église catholique aux Etats-Unis.* Quebec: Les Presses Universitaires Laval. 1955. A doctoral thesis at the Sorbonne on the man who, although he is not the first, is one of the earliest historians of the American Church.

576.   Szarnicki, Henry A. *Michael O'Connor, First Catholic Bishop of Pittsburgh, 1843–1860: A Story of the Catholic Pioneers of Pittsburgh and Western Pennsylvania.* Pittsburgh: Wolfson. 1975. Expanded from a doctoral dissertation submitted to the Catholic University of America, this thoroughly researched biography of an energetic, farsighted, and strong leader is also a history of his diocese in its infancy, of the beginnings of the religious orders he brought from Europe, and of local aspects of problems which troubled the whole Church in the United States such as nativism and the conflict between Irish and German Catholics.

577.   Terrell, John Upton. *Black Robe: The Life of Pierre-Jean de Smet: Missionary, Explorer, and Pioneer.* Garden City, N.Y.: Doubleday. 1964. This popular work lacks documentation, bibliography, and index, but in general it is factually accurate and sound in interpretation.

578.   Têtu, Henri. *Joseph-Octave Plessis: Journal des visites pastorales de*

1815 et 1816. Quebec: Imprimerie Franciscaine Missionaire. 1903. Chapters 6–7 and Appendix D of this work recount the story of the Bishop of Quebec's visits to the United States.

580.   Tourscher, Francis E., O.S.A., ed. *Diary and Visitation Record of the Rt. Rev. Francis Patrick Kenrick: Administrator and Bishop of Philadelphia, 1830–1851*. Lancaster, Pa.: Wickersham. 1916. A helpful source covering nineteen visitations, from Kenrick's nomination in February, 1830, to 1851.

581.   _____ , ed. *The Kenrick-Frenaye Correspondence, 1830–1862*. Lancaster, Pa.: Wickersham. 1920. A well-edited volume of letters with a good index; Frenaye's position as intimate friend and financial adviser to three bishops of Philadelphia gives it added importance; contains 283 letters on a wide variety of subjects, of which many are translations from Latin and French originals.

582.   Tyler, Samuel. *Memoir of Roger Brooke Taney*. 2nd rev. ed. Baltimore: John Murphy. 1876. Now superseded by Swisher and Lewis (Nos. 574, 513) as a biography, but still of value for correspondence and impressions of contemporaries on the Catholic jurist.

583.   Verwyst, Chrysostom, O.F.M. *Life and Labors of Rt. Rev. Frederic Baraga, First Bishop of Marquette*. Milwaukee: M. H. Wiltzius. 1900. Besides a life of Baraga, this volume also contains a series of sketches of earlier and contemporary missionaries of the Middle West; now superseded by Gregorich (No. 476).

584.   Wadhams, Juliana. *The Case of Cornelia Connelly*. New York: P. J. Kenedy. 1957. A thoroughly interesting and candid account of the foundress of the Sisters of the Holy Child Jesus (1809–1879), who was a Philadelphia-born convert to Catholicism. Cf. Bisgood (No. 433).

585.   Warner, Louis H. *Archbishop Lamy: An Epoch Maker*. Santa Fe: Santa Fe New Mexican. 1936. A purely popular account whose author says he has "not remotely attempted" to write for a scholarly audience; more a series of sketches of Lamy and the Southwest in his times than a real biography. It is superseded by Horgan (No. 488).

586.   Weber, Francis J. *A Biographical Sketch of Right Reverend Francisco Garcia Diego y Moreno: First Bishop of the Californias, 1785–1846*. Los Angeles: Borromeo Guild. 1961. This slender monograph, based for the most part on Bancroft and Engelhardt, gathers the salient facts on the establishment of the hierarchy in California.

587. _____ . *California's Reluctant Prelate: The Life and Times of Thaddeus Amat, C.M., 1811–1878*. Los Angeles: Dawson's Book Shop. 1964. A biography of the Spanish-born Vincentian who ruled the Diocese of Monterey-Los Angeles in the third quarter of the nineteenth century; done originally as a thesis for the master of arts degree (1961) at the Catholic University of America.

588. _____ . *Francis Mora: Last of the Catalans*. Los Angeles: Westernlore. 1967. This brief biography of Francisco Mora y Borrell (1827–1905), who served from 1878 to 1896 as Bishop of Monterey-Los Angeles, is carefully documented.

589. _____ . *Francisco Garcia Diego: California's Transition Bishop*. Los Angeles: Dawson's Book Shop. 1972. A slender but documented biography of the Mexican Franciscan who became first Bishop of the Two Californias (1840–1846) at a time of difficult change from missionary to parochial organization; it supersedes No. 586.

590. _____ . *Joseph Sadoc Alemany: Harbinger of a New Era*. Los Angeles: Dawson's Book Shop. 1973. With the aid of a recently discovered diary this brief sketch focuses on the years 1850–1853, when Alemany was Bishop of Monterey. An appendix relates the return of his remains from Spain to San Francisco in 1965.

591. _____ , trans. and ed. *The Writings of Francisco Garcia Diego y Moreno: Obispo de Ambas Californias*. Los Angeles: Dawson's Book Shop. 1976. Painstakingly collected and accurately translated, though not annotated with the desirable identifications and explanations, these 197 documents dating from the years 1820–1846, of the Mexican Franciscan missionary who became the first Bishop of the Californias in 1840, provide much information on the difficulties of the Church and its leader in that period of transition. A biographical essay gives historical background, but the glossary of names does not compensate for the lack of an index.

592. Williams, Margaret. *Second Sowing: The Life of Mary Aloysia Hardey*. New York: Sheed and Ward. 1942. An extensive work on a leading member of the Religious of the Sacred Heart; fictionalized in presentation, although the author maintains (p. 477) that the narrative is based upon documentary evidence.

593. Woodford, Frank B., and Albert Hyma. *Gabriel Richard: Frontier Ambassador*. Detroit: Wayne State University Press. 1958. A well-written and reliable biography of the French-born Sulpician who figures so prominently in the early history of Michigan.

594.   Yeager, M. Hildegarde, Sister, C.S.C. *The Life of James Roosevelt Bayley: First Bishop of Newark and Eighth Archbishop of Baltimore, 1814–1877.* Washington, D.C.: Catholic University of America Press. 1947. An able biography done as a Ph.D. thesis and based on extensive use of a large amount of archival material.

D. 1866–1900

595.   Ahern, Patrick Henry. *The Life of John J. Keane: Educator and Archbishop, 1839–1918.* Milwaukee: Bruce. 1954. A thorough and scholarly biography of one of the most important churchmen of the late nineteenth century; done originally as a Ph.D. thesis.

596.   Bell, Stephen. *Rebel Priest and Prophet: A Biography of Dr. Edward McGlynn.* New York: Devin-Adair. 1937. A popular life of a stormy petrel in the Archdiocese of New York during the Corrigan administration; the "rebel" apparently held more attraction for the author than the "priest"; not an objective or impartial study.

597.   Borden, Lucille Papin. *Francesca Cabrini: Without Staff or Script.* New York: Macmillan. 1945. A popular treatment of the foundress of the Missionary Sisters of the Sacred Heart, whose career in the United States was important for Italian immigrants. She was the first naturalized American citizen to be canonized (1946).

598.   Boucher, Arline, and John Tehan. *Prince of Democracy: James Cardinal Gibbons.* Garden City, N.Y.: Hanover. 1962. A popular biography.

599.   Brusher, Joseph S., S.J. *Consecrated Thunderbolt: Father Yorke of San Francisco.* Hawthorne, N.J.: Joseph F. Wagner. 1973. Evidencing intensive research, this overly sympathetic biography of Peter C. Yorke (1864–1925), who struggled with the A.P.A., advocated organized labor and political reform, published an influential weekly, and supported the independence movement in his native Ireland, is a contribution to the history of Irish Catholics in the Far West.

600.   Burton, Katherine. *No Shadow of Turning: The Life of James Kent Stone (Father Fidelis of the Cross).* New York: Longmans, Green. 1944. A popular account of a prominent convert from Episcopalianism which does not, however, replace the older work of Smith (No. 677).

601.   Callaghan, Emily A. *Memoirs and Writings of the Very Reverend James F. Callaghan.* Cincinnati: Robert Clarke. 1903. Sermons, lec-

tures, and newspaper articles (with a few letters) edited by the sister of a priest who served for a time as vicar-general of the Diocese of Little Rock, rector of the cathedral in Cincinnati, and for the years 1872–1881 editor of the *Catholic Telegraph;* useful materials for a biographer of Callaghan (1839–1899).

602. Callaghan, Nelson, J. *A Case for Due Process in the Church: Father Eugene O'Callaghan, American Pioneer of Dissent.* Staten Island, N.Y.: Alba. 1971. This brief and popular book is not a biography of the unscrupulous priest of the Diocese of Cleveland whom it extols as a hero but rather an attempt to find a champion of the rights of the clergy in the last third of the nineteenth century. The presentation is vitiated by a selective use of source materials and is filled with errors of fact and interpretation.

603. ———, ed. *The Diary of Richard L. Burtsell, Priest of New York: The Early Years, 1865–1868.* New York: Arno. 1978. The editor's sole contribution beyond the transcription is a twenty-seven-page preface, which is mainly a summary of Burtsell's life as revealed in his complete diary (up to his death in 1912). The entries for many days are omitted by the editor without explanation. No notes are provided, nor is there an index. The whole book is a reproduction of a typescript.

604. Carman, Harry J., Henry David, and Paul N. Guthrie. *The Path I Trod: The Autobiography of Terence V. Powderly.* New York: Columbia University Press. 1940. A posthumously published work of a prominent figure in the relations of the Catholic Church to the labor movement during the late nineteenth century.

605. *Character Glimpses of the Most Reverend William Henry Elder, Second Archbishop of Cincinnati.* New York: Frederick Pustet. 1911. This popular compilation is an appreciation, not a biography; but in the absence of any real life of this important prelate it is useful.

606. Cosgrove, John J. *Most Reverend John Lancaster Spalding, First Bishop of Peoria.* Mendota, Ill.: Wayside. 1960. A popular work by a retired pastor of the Diocese of Peoria; the chief value lies in the correspondence printed and the illustrations of the Spalding family; there are no footnotes, bibliography, or index. Cf. No. 679.

607. Curran, Robert Emmett. *Michael Augustine Corrigan and the Shaping of Conservative Catholicism in America, 1878–1902.* New York: Arno. 1978. This monograph, originally submitted as a doctoral

dissertation at Yale University in 1974 and subsequently revised but still presented here in typewritten form, is a work of solid scholarship that embodies the results of wide research. It is an objective treatment of the highly controversial Archbishop of New York and is a fresh contribution to the history of the many conflicts of the late nineteenth century.

608.   DeBaets, Maurice. *The Apostle of Alaska: The Life of the Most Reverend Charles John Seghers*. Trans. Sister Mary Mildred, S.S.A. Paterson: St. Anthony Guild. 1943. The French original of this work appeared in 1896; although it incorporates a considerable amount of data, it is not a really satisfactory biography of the second Archbishop of Oregon City, who was murdered in Alaska in 1886.

609.   De Mare, Marie. *G. P. A. Healy, American Artist: An Intimate Chronicle of the Nineteenth Century*. New York: David McKay. 1954. The first full-length biography of the portrait artist, written by his granddaughter; Healy's diaries and those of other members of the family have been used, although there is no documentation or bibliography.

610.   Di Donato, Pietro. *Immigrant Saint: The Life of Mother Cabrini*. New York: McGraw-Hill. 1960. A popular, uncritical biography of Frances Xavier Cabrini, who first came to the United States with six nuns in 1889.

611.   Dwyer, John T. *Condemned to the Mines: The Life of Eugene O'Connell, 1815–1891, Pioneer Bishop of Northern California and Nevada*. New York: Vantage. 1976. An amateur historian here presents a factual biography insofar as the limited sources permit, but he ignores his subject's attitudes toward questions of national and international significance.

612.   Egan, Maurice Francis. *Confessions of a Book-Lover*. Garden City, N.Y.: Doubleday, Page. 1922. Reminiscences of favorite reading from boyhood to old age by a prominent editor, professor of literature, and diplomat.

613.   ———— . *Recollections of a Happy Life*. New York: George H. Doran. 1924. The personal memoirs of Egan's varied career; chatty and often amusing comments on the Catholic leaders of the late nineteenth century, as well as on campus life at the University of Notre Dame and the Catholic University of America.

614.   Ellis, John Tracy. *John Lancaster Spalding, First Bishop of Peoria: American Educator.* Milwaukee: Bruce. 1962. This small monograph was the Gabriel Richard Lecture for 1961 of the National Catholic Educational Association.

615.   _____ . *The Life of James Cardinal Gibbons, Archbishop of Baltimore, 1834–1921.* 2 vols. Milwaukee: Bruce. 1952. A fully documented biography of a churchman whose life in a sense constituted almost a history of the American Church in the last quarter of the nineteenth and early twentieth centuries by reason of his leading role in events.

616.   _____ . *The Life of James Cardinal Gibbons.* Abridged by Francis L. Broderick. Milwaukee: Bruce. 1963.

617.   Farley, John Cardinal. *The Life of John Cardinal McCloskey, First Prince of the Church in America, 1810–1885.* New York: Longmans, Green. 1918. Hardly more than the public life of New York's second archbishop, although it has value for the correspondence carried in the text.

618.   Farrely, M. Natalena, Sister, S.S.J. *Thomas Francis Meehan, 1854–1942: A Memoir.* New York: United States Catholic Historical Society. 1944. This slender volume is in the nature of a popular appreciation and tribute rather than a critical study of Meehan's literary work and his efforts in behalf of American Catholic history.

619.   Flick, Ella Marie. *Beloved Crusader: Lawrence F. Flick, Physician.* Philadelphia. Dorrance. 1944. A biography of a Philadelphia doctor written by his daughter; Flick had a flair for history and served as president and counselor of both the American Catholic Historical Association and the American Catholic Historical Society of Philadelphia.

620.   Fogarty, Gerald P., S.J. *The Vatican and the Americanist Crisis: Denis J. O'Connell, American Agent in Rome, 1885–1903.* Rome: Università Gregoriana Editrice. 1974. This revised doctoral dissertation from Yale University presents from the vantage point of the rector of the North American College in Rome and representative of the liberal party of the American hierarchy to the Holy See, the familiar problems of the German question, the social question, the school question, the establishment of the Apostolic Delegation in the United States, and Americanism.

621.   Foley, Albert S., S.J. *Bishop Healy: Beloved Outcaste.* New York: Farrar, Straus and Young. 1954. A life of the second Bishop of Portland who was a mulatto; based upon original materials, although no documentation is supplied, nor is there a bibliography or index.

622.   Fox, Mary Harrita. *Peter E. Dietz: Labor Priest.* Notre Dame: University of Notre Dame Press. 1953. An able Ph.D. thesis on one of the leading figures in Catholic social action and reform in the late nineteenth and early twentieth centuries.

623.   Frawley, Mary Alphonsine, Sister, S.S.J. *Patrick Donahoe.* Washington, D.C.: Catholic University of America Press. 1946. A Ph.D. thesis that gives a thorough treatment of the owner and publisher of the Boston *Pilot;* contains about all that will ever be known about this key lay figure in New England Catholicism of the past century.

624.   Gaffey, James P. *Citizen of No Mean City: Archbishop Patrick Riordan of San Francisco, 1841–1914.* Wilmington, N.C.: Consortium. 1976. Combining thorough research with literary grace, this biography, originally undertaken as a doctoral dissertation in the Catholic University of America, constitutes one of the best works to date on Catholicism in the Far West from 1883 to World War I.

625.   Guilday, Peter. "John Gilmary Shea," *Historical Records and Studies,* XVII (July, 1926), 7–171. A commendable biographical study on the pioneer historian of American Catholicism; contains a large amount of correspondence and a bibliography of Shea's writings.

626.   Guy, Francis S. *Edmund Bailey O'Callaghan: A Study in American Historiography, 1797–1880.* Washington, D.C.: Catholic University of America Press. 1934. A Ph.D. thesis on a well-known editor of historical works; not a satisfactory life of O'Callaghan.

627.   Healy, George P. A. *Reminiscences of a Portrait Painter.* Chicago: A. C. McClurg. 1894. Memoirs of a ranking American artist of the past century, whose biography has been written by De Mare (No. 609).

628.   Hemesath, Caroline, Sister. *From Slave to Priest: A Biography of the Rev. Augustine Tolton, 1854–1897, First Afro-American Priest of the United States.* Chicago: Franciscan Herald Press. 1973. Lacking adequate source materials for a continuous narrative, the author has

supplied "imaginative recreations" to fill out the life of the Negro who was ordained in Rome and was pastor in Quincy and Chicago, Illinois.

629. Herbermann, Charles George. *Diary of a Visit to the United States of America in the Year 1883 by Charles Lord Russell of Killowen, Late Lord Chief Justice of England.* New York: United States Catholic Historical Society. 1910. The diary runs from August 14 to October 13, 1883, and is of interest for glimpses of American Catholicism as seen through the eyes of this foreign visitor.

630. _____ . *Forty Years in the United States of America, 1839– 1885, by the Late Rev. Augustus Thébaud, S.J.* New York: United States Catholic Historical Society. 1904. A memoir containing comments on Irish immigration and its results, rural and urban contrasts, schools and colleges, and general American religious conditions; Thébaud was born in France and came to the United States in 1838.

631. Howlett, William J. *Life of the Right Reverend Joseph P. Machebeuf.* Pueblo, Colo.: Franklin. 1908. A biography of a French-born missionary who served for seventeen years on the missions of New Mexico and who ruled the Church in Colorado, 1868–1889; carries a good deal of original correspondence.

632. Ireland, John. *The Church and Modern Society: Lectures and Addresses.* 2 vols. St. Paul: Pioneer. 1905. The thirty-one lectures and sermons contained in these volumes constitute a prime source for the life of the first Archbishop of St. Paul; several of the addresses made history in the American Church.

633. Jacks, Leo Vincent. *Mother Marianne of Molokai.* New York: Macmillan. 1935. This popular life of Marianne Kopp (or Cope, 1836–1918), the provincial of the Sisters of Saint Francis of Syracuse, New York, who led the first group of American sisters to the Hawaiian Islands to work among the lepers, contains some documentary material.

634. Judge, Charles J. *An American Missionary: A Record of the Work of Rev. William H. Judge, S.J.* Maryknoll: Catholic Foreign Mission Society of America. c. 1907. Letters of William Judge (1850–1899) who spent the last nine years of his life on the missions in Alaska; written to his Sulpician brother, who edited the volume.

635. Kelly, Margaret Jean, Sister. *The Career of Joseph Lane, Frontier*

Politician. Washington, D.C.: Catholic University of America Press. 1942. A Ph.D. thesis on the North Carolina-born politician who became governor of Oregon Territory (1848) and was converted to Catholicism in 1867.

636.   Kervick, Francis W. *Patrick Charles Keely, Architect: A Record of His Life and Work*. South Bend, Ind.: The Author. 1953. An illustrated brochure (70 pages) which reprints about a dozen of Keely's letters and gives a partial list of the cathedrals, parish churches, and other religious buildings which he designed; useful in lieu of a full-length study on the leading Catholic architect of the past century.

637.   Kirkfleet, Cornelius J., O.Praem. *The Life of Patrick Augustine Feehan, Bishop of Nashville, First Archbishop of Chicago, 1829–1902*. Chicago: Matre. 1922. One of the few works available on the Archdiocese of Chicago in the late nineteenth century, although not a definitive biography of the prelate, but rather an account of the external aspects of his administration.

639.   Kwitchin, Mary Augustine, Sister, O.S.F. *James Alphonsus McMaster: A Study in American Thought*. Washington, D.C.: Catholic University of America Press. 1949. An informative Ph.D. thesis on the colorful editor of the New York *Freeman's Journal* from 1848 to his death in 1886.

640.   Leclerc, Max. *Choses d'Amérique: Les crises économique et religieuse aux Etats-Unis*. Paris: Armand Colin et Cie. 1895. An account of a visit to this country (July–October, 1890) which spoke in tones of such enthusiasm and optimism about American Catholicism that it gave rise to resentment among conservative European Catholics looking for "Americanism"; crowned by the French Academy.

641.   Litz, Francis A. *Father Tabb: A Study of His Life and Works*. Baltimore: Johns Hopkins Press. 1923. This Ph.D. thesis is more an analysis of the convert-author's writings than a biography.

642.   _____ . *Letters—Grave and Gay and Other Prose of John Bannister Tabb*. Washington, D.C.: Catholic University of America Press. 1950. Contains 308 letters and notes of Tabb along with twenty-four letters written to him, of which only fifty were previously published; they run from May, 1873, the year after his conversion to Catholicism, to his death in 1909.

643. Loidl, Franz. *Erzbischof Friedrich Xaver Katzer: Edensee-Milwaukee, 1844–1903*. Vienna: Verlag Julius Lichtner. 1953. A seventy-page brochure on Milwaukee's third archbishop, based in the main on secondary sources.

644. Ludwig, M. Mileta, Sister, F.S.P.A. *Right-Hand Glove Uplifted: A Biography of Archbishop Michael Heiss*. New York: Pageant. 1968. This well-documented life of the Bavarian missionary who became the first Bishop of La Crosse in 1868 and Archbishop of Milwaukee in 1881 and died in 1890 sheds additional light not only on local religious conditions and affairs but also on issues of national importance.

645. McAllister, Anna Shannon. *Ellen Ewing, Wife of General Sherman*. New York: Benziger. 1936. This biography of a woman (1824–1888) who belonged to one of the most prominent Catholic families of the period has been "based upon family letters and records and withholds nothing material to its subject" (p. vii), according to the foreword written by P. Tecumseh Sherman, her son.

646. McCann, Mary Agnes, Sister. *Archbishop Purcell and the Archdiocese of Cincinnati*. Washington, D.C.: Catholic University of America Press. 1918. A slender Ph.D. thesis that makes some use of archival material, but is inadequate as a biography of Cincinnati's first archbishop.

647. McEniry, Blanche Marie, Sister. *Woman of Decision: The Life of Mother Mary Xavier Mehegan, Foundress of the Sisters of Charity of Saint Elizabeth*. New York: McMullen. 1953. A brief biography of a religious whose life (1825–1915) spanned the growth of her congregation.

648. McGloin, John B., S.J. *California's First Archbishop: The Life of Joseph Sadoc Alemany, O.P., First Archbishop of San Francisco, 1814–1888*. New York: Herder and Herder. 1966. A scholarly biography of the Catalan who developed the Catholic Church in much of California for over a generation.

649. _____ . *Eloquent Indian: The Life of James Bouchard, California Jesuit*. Stanford: Stanford University Press. 1949. Originally a Ph.D. thesis, this scholarly work makes good use of archival materials.

650. McGovern, James J. *The Life and Letters of Eliza Allen Starr*.

Chicago: Lakeside. 1905. The story of a literary figure who became a Catholic in 1854; good for the correspondence carried in the text.

651. _____ . *The Life and Writings of the Right Reverend John McMullen, First Bishop of Davenport, Iowa.* Chicago: Hoffmann. 1888. Although falling short of modern standards of biography in some particulars, this work has value for the numerous letters carried in the text.

652. McManamin, Francis G. *The American Years of John Boyle O'Reilly, 1870–1890.* New York: Arno. 1976. This doctoral dissertation, which was accepted by the Catholic University of America in 1959, treats the poet-patriot as spokesman for the Irish in Ireland and the United States, editor of *The Pilot* of Boston, a leader of the Irish Colonization Society, prominent literary figure, and critic of industrial society. A summary of this work was published by the Catholic University of America Press in 1959.

653. McSorley, Joseph, C.S.P. *Father Hecker and His Friends: Studies and Reminiscences.* St. Louis: B. Herder. 1952. A series of brief informative essays which are in part a memoir, since the author had known all but seven of the 252 Paulists to date of publication.

654. Maignen, Charles. *Father Hecker: Is He a Saint?* London: Burns and Oates. 1898. The English translation of a French work, *Etudes sur l'Américanisme: Le Père Hecker, est-il un saint?* (Rome: Desclée; Paris: V. Retaux. 1899), which added fuel to the fire of the Americanism controversy; called forth by Elliott (No. 463).

655. Malak, Henry M., T.O.S.F. *The Apostle of Mercy from Chicago.* Trans. Sister Mary Hugoline, O.S.F.K. London: Veritas. 1962. This pious biographical sketch of Josephine Dudzik (1860–1918), who, as Mother Mary Theresa, founded the Franciscan Sisters of Blessed Kunegunda in 1894, contains information on the condition of the Polish immigrants.

656. Malone, Sylvester L. *Dr. Edward McGlynn.* New York: Dr. McGlynn Monument Association. 1918. Reprint. New York: Arno. 1978. This compilation by a warm admirer of the controversial New York priest who died in 1900 contains a biographical sketch, the text of McGlynn's "Cross of the New Crusade" oration, excerpts from other speeches, tributes from friends and admirers; not a biography in the true sense.

657. _____ . *Memorial of the Golden Jubilee of the Rev. Sylvester Malone.* Brooklyn: The Author. 1895. A work similar to the above, on a Brooklyn priest prominent in movements for social reform and a more liberal approach to non-Catholics; Malone was Irish-born and came to the United States in 1839.

658. Maynard, Theodore. *Too Small a World: The Life of Mother Cabrini.* Milwaukee: Bruce. 1945. A readable popular biography of the Italian-born religious; useful for insights into the problems of the Italian immigrants in the late nineteenth century.

659. Miller, Leo F., Joseph C. Plumpe, Maurice A. Hofer, and George J. Undreiner. *Monsignor Joseph Jessing, 1836–1899: Founder of the Pontifical College Josephinum.* Columbus: Carroll. 1936. A well-documented symposium on a German-born priest who played a prominent role in the German immigrant settlements of Ohio; founder of the *Ohio Waisenfreund* in May, 1873, and of a seminary (September, 1888) for the education of priests to serve the German-American parishes.

660. Mooney, Joseph F. *Memorial of the Most Reverend Michael Augustine Corrigan, Third-Archbishop of New York.* New York: Cathedral Library Association. 1902. A compilation of tributes and appreciations with a brief biographical sketch; published on the occasion of the archbishop's death.

661. Moynihan, James A. *The Life of Archbishop John Ireland.* New York: Harper and Bros. 1953. Reprint. New York: Arno. 1976. The only biography of the first Archbishop of St. Paul who was one of the key figures in American Catholicism in the late nineteenth and early twentieth centuries; makes good use of the Ireland Papers, but has a rather strong bias in favor of the subject.

662. Pahorezki, M. Sevina, Sister. *The Social and Political Activities of William James Onahan.* Washington, D.C.: Catholic University of America Press. 1942. A Ph.D. thesis in sociology on a Chicago layman who played a prominent role in the colonization movement, the Catholic lay congresses of these years, and in the Catholic participation in the Columbian Exposition of 1893.

663. Patricia Jean, S.L., Sister. *Only One Heart: The Story of a Pioneer Nun in America.* Garden City, N.Y.: Doubleday. 1963. With its invented conversations and indistinguishable mixture of fact and

fancy, this affectionate life of Mother Praxedes (Susan Carty) of the Sisters of Loretto, who labored in Colorado, New Mexico, Missouri, and Texas from 1875 to 1933, is of no use to serious scholars.

664.   Powderly, Terence V. *Thirty Years of Labor, 1859–1889*. Columbus: Excelsior. 1890. The memoirs of a Catholic labor leader who later left the Church; Powderly was Grand Masterworkman of the Knights of Labor.

665.   Reilly, John T. *Collections and Recollections in the Life and Times of Cardinal Gibbons*. 10 vols. in 7. Martinsburg, W. Va., and McSherrystown, Pa.: The Author. 1890–1904. In spite of its title, this odd assortment of newspaper clippings, magazine articles, and correspondence on a wide variety of topics—often not even remotely relating to Gibbons—scarcely belongs to biographical writings; yet these bulky volumes compiled by a nonprofessional contain a considerable amount of material not easily found elsewhere; the editing shows little or no order or systematic arrangement.

666.   Richards, J. Havens, S.J. *A Loyal Life: A Biography of Henry Livingston Richards*. St. Louis: B. Herder. 1913. The story of a convert from the Protestant ministry who became prominent in Boston Catholic circles after his conversion in 1852; written by his son.

667.   Roche, James Jeffrey. *Life of John Boyle O'Reilly, Together with His Complete Poems and Speeches*. New York: Cassell. 1891. A biography by one of O'Reilly's close friends and associates on the staff of the Boston *Pilot*, written a year after his death; for more recent work see McManamin (No. 652).

668.   Rommel, Henri. *Thomas Bouquillon ... Notice Bio-Bibliographique*. Bruges: Louis de Plancke. 1903. An eighty-page booklet containing a biographical sketch, a bibliography of Bouquillon's writings, a French translation of the eulogy given by William J. Kerby (November 13, 1902), and an article by Thomas J. Shahan on Bouquillon from the *Catholic University Bulletin* of January, 1903; the closest thing available to a biography of the famous professor of moral theology in the Catholic University of America, who figured in the school controversy of the 1890's.

669.   Satolli, Francis Cardinal. *Loyalty to Church and State*. 2nd ed. Ed. J. R. Slattery. Baltimore: John Murphy. 1895. Reprint. New York: Arno. 1971. Sermons and addresses of the first apostolic delegate in the United States, delivered between 1889 and 1895 on such

subjects as education, temperance, the press, relations of Church and State, etc.

670.   Schofield, William G. *Seek for a Hero: The Story of John Boyle O'Reilly*. New York: P. J. Kenedy. 1956. A popular treatment by an editorial writer on the Boston *Traveler;* cf. McManamin (No. 652).

671.   Schroll, Agnes Claire, Sister, O.S.B. *The Social Thought of John Lancaster Spalding*. Washington, D.C.: Catholic University of America Press. 1944. A Ph.D. thesis in sociology that gives a good coverage of such topics as education, politics, religion, etc., as viewed by the first Bishop of Peoria.

672.   Segale, Blandina, Sister. *At the End of the Santa Fe Trail*. Milwaukee: Bruce. 1948. The amazing experiences of an Italian-born Sister of Charity of Cincinnati on the missions in New Mexico and Colorado in the 1870's and 1880's, told in the form of letters to her sister; excellent for insights into frontier conditions of the Church in the period.

673.   Seton, Robert. *Memories of Many Years, 1839–1922*. London: J. Long. 1923. The gossipy memoirs of a titular archbishop, the grandson of Mother Elizabeth Seton, who spent much time in Rome and was for some years stationed in New Jersey.

674.   Shearer, Donald, O.M.Cap. *Ignatius Cardinal Persico, O.M.Cap*. New York: Joseph F. Wagner. 1932. Originally an A.M. thesis, this slender work on the career of an Italian friar (1823–1895) who came to the United States in 1866 and was Bishop of Savannah, 1870–1872 is least satisfactory on Persico's time in this country.

675.   Sisters of Divine Providence. *Character Sketches of the Rt. Rev. C. P. Maes*. Baltimore: John Murphy. 1917. Brief essays and notes on the spiritual life of the Belgian-born third Bishop of Covington.

676.   Sisters of the Visitation. *Life and Characteristics of Right Reverend Alfred A. Curtis, Second Bishop of Wilmington*. New York: P. J. Kenedy. 1913. The only biography of a convert who was received into the Church by John Henry Newman in April, 1872, although it is entirely lacking in critical approach.

677.   Smith, Walter G., and Helen Grace Smith. *Fidelis of the Cross: James Kent Stone*. New York: G. P. Putnam's. 1926. The best life of the Episcopalian minister and educator (president of Hobart College)

who became a Catholic in 1869 and later won fame as a Passionist missionary.

678.   Stone, James Kent. *An Awakening and What Followed.* Notre Dame: Ave Maria. 1920. In part a spiritual autobiography of a prominent convert and a series of letters and reports on missionary experiences in Latin America.

679.   Sweeney, David Francis, O.F.M. *The Life of John Lancaster Spalding, First Bishop of Peoria, 1840–1916.* New York: Herder and Herder. 1965. A scholarly biography of the American hierarchy's outstanding intellectual.

680.   Synon, Mary. *Mother Emily of Sinsinawa: American Pioneer.* Milwaukee: Bruce. 1955. An informative semipopular life of the Irish-born woman who led the Dominican Sisters of Sinsinawa from 1867 to 1909; historians will be especially interested in Mother Emily's experiences in an Illinois coal-mining community and in the school controversy of the 1890's.

681.   Trudel, Marcel. *Chiniquy.* 2nd ed. Trois Rivières: Editions du Bien Public. 1955. A thoroughly documented life of the priest (1809–1899) who apostatized in the Diocese of Chicago in the 1850's and created a minor schism; Chiniquy was active for nearly a half century against the Catholic Church in the United States and his native Canada; for his writing see Nos. 1160, 1161.

682.   Walworth, Clarence A. *Reminiscences of Edgar P. Wadhams, First Bishop of Ogdensburg.* New York: Benziger. 1893. More than half of this volume is devoted to Wadhams' years as a Protestant; written by a fellow convert to Catholicism, a close friend and schoolmate at Chelsea Seminary, with numerous quotations from correspondence of the period; good for insights into the effects of the Oxford Movement in the United States.

683.   Weber, Francis J. *George Thomas Montgomery, California Churchman.* Los Angeles: Westernlore. 1966. This biographical sketch of the native American who was Bishop of Monterey-Los Angeles (1896–1902) and Coadjutor-Archbishop of San Francisco (1902–1907) is based to a large extent on primary sources.

684.   Weber, Ralph E. *Notre Dame's John Zahm: American Catholic Apologist and Educator.* Notre Dame: University of Notre Dame Press. 1961. A scholarly biography of a controversial figure of the late

nineteenth century in the conflict between religion and science; originally a Ph.D. dissertation at the University of Notre Dame.

685. Weibel, John Eugene. *Forty Years Missionary in Arkansas.* Trans. Sister M. Agnes Voth, O.S.B. St. Meinrad, Ind.: Abbey. 1968. First published in 1927, these memoirs of a self-sacrificing Swiss priest who began his missionary work in northeastern Arkansas in 1879 reveal not only his ingenuous character but also the pioneer conditions of the Catholic settlers.

686. Will, Allen Sinclair. *Life of Cardinal Gibbons, Archbishop of Baltimore.* 2 vols. New York: E. P. Dutton. 1922. A good popular biography written a year after Gibbons' death by a non-Catholic journalist who was a warm admirer; now superseded by Ellis (No. 615).

687. Zwierlein, Frederick J. *Letters of Archbishop Corrigan to Bishop McQuaid and Allied Documents.* Rochester: Art Print Shop. 1946. Further documents on the issues discussed *in extenso* in the work listed below; rather poorly edited.

688. _____. *The Life and Letters of Bishop McQuaid.* 3 vols. Rochester: Art Print Shop. 1925–1927. An extensive work that broke ground with the use of original sources for the period of the late nineteenth-century American Church; highly informative, although biased in favor of the subject.

E. 1900–1980

689. Abeloe, William N. *To the Top of the Mountain: The Life of Father Umberto Olivieri, "Padre of the Otomis."* Hicksville, N.Y.: Exposition. 1976. A popular biography of an Italian who was born in 1884, married, came to California in 1920, was divorced in 1929, became a professor at the University of Santa Clara, was ordained a priest in 1958, worked among Mexican Indians, and died in 1973.

690. Angell, Charles, S.A., and Charles LaFontaine, S.A. *Prophet of Reunion: The Life of Paul of Graymoor.* New York: Seabury. 1975. A popular, anecdotal biography of Lewis Thomas Wattson (1863–1940), the Episcopalian priest who founded the Society of the Atonement and was received into the Catholic Church in 1909. He was more successful in fund-raising and building for charitable purposes and in using the press and radio for evangelization than in his ecumenical endeavors.

691.   Ayscough, John [Francis Browning Drew Bickerstaffe-Drew]. *First Impressions of America*. London: John Long. 1921. A rather superficial travelogue, almost uniformly flattering, of the visit of a British army chaplain to this country in April–December, 1919; little by way of penetrating comment on American Catholic life.

692.   Barry, Colman J., O.S.B. *American Nuncio: Cardinal Aloisius Muench*. Collegeville, Minn.: Saint John's University Press. 1969. Utilizing both documents and interviews, Father Barry has written a sympathetic and reliable biography of Aloisius Muench (1889–1962), a native of Milwaukee who became Bishop of Fargo in 1935, American and papal representative in Germany in 1946, apostolic nuncio in Bonn in 1951, and cardinal in 1959. More attention is given to the Church in postwar Germany than in the United States.

693.   Blum, John M. *Joe Tumulty and the Wilson Era*. Boston: Houghton Mifflin. 1951. The only scholarly work yet done on the role played by President Wilson's Catholic secretary.

694.   Broderick, Francis L. *Right Reverend New Dealer: John A. Ryan*. New York: Macmillan. 1963. A concise, perceptive biography of John A. Ryan (1869–1945), a priest of the Archdiocese of St. Paul, who effectively promoted social justice as an author, publicist, lecturer, and professor at the Catholic University of America, director of the Social Action Department of the National Catholic Welfare Conference, and advisor to the Roosevelt administration.

695.   Buczek, Daniel S. *Immigrant Pastor: The Life of the Right Reverend Monsignor Lucyan Bójnowski of New Britain, Connecticut*. Waterbury: Association of Polish Priests in Connecticut. 1974. This well-researched biography of the Polish priest who from 1895 to 1957 built up the Parish of the Sacred Heart of Jesus with its many educational and social services and became the leader of the Polish clergy in New England, is a contribution to both ethnic and religious history.

696.   Buehrle, Marie Cecilia. *The Cardinal Stritch Story*. Milwaukee: Bruce. 1959. This popular, adulatory, superficial biography of Samuel Alphonsus Stritch (1887–1958) is based on extremely limited source materials.

697.   Burke, Ann Dempsey. *The Bishop Who Dared: A Biography of Bishop Michael Ryan Dempsey*. St. Petersburg, Fla.: Valkyrie. 1978.

His sister here gives a personal recollection of the Auxiliary Bishop of Chicago (1918–1974), who was an apostle to the black community in the inner city and director of the National Conference of Catholic Bishops' Campaign for Human Development.

698.   Burton, Katherine. *Mother Butler of Marymount*. New York: Longmans, Green. 1944. A popular biography of the superior of the Religious of the Sacred Heart of Mary and foundress of Marymount College (1860–1940).

699.   ———— . *Sorrow Built a Bridge*. New York: Longmans, Green. 1937. A popular work on Mother Alphonsa Hawthorne Lathrop, foundress of the Servants of Relief for Incurable Cancer.

700.   ———— . *The Golden Door: The Life of Katharine Drexel*. New York: P. J. Kenedy. 1957. Although it incorporates considerable archival material, this biography of the foundress of the Sisters of the Blessed Sacrament for Negro and Indian missions has many errors and leaves much to be desired by way of a life of this remarkable woman. It is now superseded by Duffy (No. 715).

701.   Cogley, John. *A Canterbury Tale: Experiences and Reflections; 1916–1976*. New York: Seabury. 1976. These memoirs of a liberal Catholic who was active in the Catholic Worker movement, an editor of *Commonweal*, and a correspondent at the Second Vatican Council were intended to justify his becoming an Episcopalian in 1973.

702.   Cronin, Bernard C. *Father Yorke and the Labor Movement in San Francisco, 1900–1910*. Washington, D.C.: Catholic University of America Press. 1944. A Ph.D. thesis in sociology on one phase of the life of the most famous priest of the Pacific Coast in the early twentieth century. For a complete biography see Brusher (No. 599).

703.   Crosby, Donald F., S.J. *God, Church, and Flag: Senator Joseph R. McCarthy and the Catholic Church, 1950–1957*. Chapel Hill: University of North Carolina Press. 1978. By analyzing the results of opinion polls and of elections and by studying the statements of clerical and lay leaders, the author shows that Catholics were divided among political lines in their reactions to the senator's goals and methods and were not radically different from other Americans in their views.

704.   Cunningham, James F., C.S.P. *American Pastor in Rome*.

Westminster, Md.: Newman. 1966. The memoirs of the Paulist who served twelve years as pastor of Santa Susanna, the American church, in Rome.

705.   Cutler, John Henry. *Cardinal Cushing of Boston*. New York: Hawthorn. 1970. A popular, anecdotal biography based largely on the recollections of those who knew the subject and written shortly before his death.

706.   Day, Dorothy. *From Union Square to Rome*. Silver Spring, Md.: Preservation. 1939. Reprint. New York: Arno. 1978. The autobiography of a social reformer, a convert from Communism, and cofounder of the Catholic Worker movement.

707.   _____ . *Loaves and Fishes*. New York: Harper and Row. 1963. A further memoir of the cofounder of the Catholic Worker movement.

708.   _____ . *The Long Loneliness: The Autobiography of Dorothy Day*. New York: Harper and Bros. 1952. A continuation of the autobiographical works of Dorothy Day.

709.   Deferrari, Roy Joseph. *A Layman in Catholic Education: His Life and Times*. Boston: St. Paul Editions. 1966. The candid autobiography of a professor and administrator who spent nearly half a century at the Catholic University of America, beginning in 1918. Cf. No. 991.

710.   Delany, Grace C. *The Life and Writings of the Right Reverend John Bernard Delany, Second Bishop of Manchester*. Lowell: Lawler. 1911. A popular memoir with excerpts from diaries and letters; the author states that "no attempt has been made at a formal biography."

711.   Delfeld, Paula. *The Indian Priest: Father Philip B. Gordon, 1885–1948*. Chicago: Franciscan Herald Press. 1977. A popular biography of the first American Indian priest, who belonged to the Diocese of Superior and worked boldly for his race.

712.   Dever, Joseph. *Cushing of Boston: A Candid Portrait*. Boston: Bruce Humphries. 1965. Because of its lack of serious research, of balanced judgments, and of precise presentation this personal portrait is worthless for historical purposes. It is journalistic in style, sycophantic in some places, and full of gossip, digressions, and preachments.

713. Devine, M. C., Sister. *The World's Cardinal*. Boston: Daughters of St. Paul. 1964. This first full-length biography of Richard James Cushing, Archbishop of Boston, undertaken during his lifetime presents many facts accurately but is one-sided, uncritical, eulogistic, and saccharine.

714. Donovan, John F., M.M. *A Priest Named Horse*. Huntington, Ind.: Our Sunday Visitor. 1977. A popular biography of Bernard F. Meyer (1891–1975) from Stuart, Iowa, who went to China as one of the first four Maryknoll missionaries in 1918 and labored there until 1950.

715. Duffy, Consuela Marie, Sister, S.B.S. *Katharine Drexel: A Biography*. Philadelphia: Peter Reilly. 1965. Paperback edition. Cornwells Heights, Pa.: Mother Katharine Drexel Guild. 1972. This well-documented and well-written life of Katharine Drexel (1858–1955), the Philadelphia heiress who founded the Sisters of the Blessed Sacrament for Indians and Colored People in 1891 and used her large fortune to support its missionary and educational work in twenty-one states, not only aids the cause of her beatification but also increases historical knowledge of racial conditions in the Catholic Church and in American society in the late nineteenth and early twentieth centuries.

716. Durkin, Joseph T., S.J. *General Sherman's Son: The Life of Thomas Ewing Sherman, S.J.* New York: Farrar, Straus and Cudahy. 1959. A documented, well-written, and candid account of the strange life of Thomas E. Sherman, S.J. (1856–1933).

717. Dye, Mary Elizabeth, Sister, O.S.U. *By Their Fruits: A Social Biography of Frederick Kenkel, Catholic Social Pioneer*. New York: Greenwich. 1961. A slight popular work of ninety pages with no footnotes, no index, but a brief bibliography.

718. Ecclesine, Margaret Wyvill. *A Touch of Radiance: Sister Honorat of the Bon Secours Sisters*. Milwaukee: Bruce. 1966. This popular biography of Alice Wyvill (1898–1961), the first American-born superior in the French congregation, a nurse, builder and administrator of hospitals and convalescent homes, and a woman of great sanctity, reads like a novel and makes no pretense of scholarship but contains many letters written by, to, or about her.

719. Emerson, Dorothy. *Among the Mescalero Apaches: The Story of Father Albert Braun, O.F.M.* Tucson: University of Arizona Press.

1973. A popular biography of a priest, ordained in 1915, who was a missionary to Indians in New Mexico, a chaplain during both World Wars, a prisoner of the Japanese, etc.

720. Fenton, John G. *Salt of the Earth: An Informal Portrait of Richard Cardinal Cushing.* New York: Coward-McCann. 1965. A popular biography written by a journalist five years before the cardinal's death.

721. Fine, Sidney. *Frank Murphy: The Detroit Years.* Ann Arbor: University of Michigan Press. 1975. *Frank Murphy: The New Deal Years.* Chicago: University of Chicago Press. 1979. When completed with a third volume, this will be the definitive biography of the Michigan Catholic statesman, but it contains little on his religious life.

722. [Flanagan], M. Raymond, O.C.S.O. *The Less Traveled Road: A Memoir of Dom Mary Frederic Dunne, O.C.S.O., First American Trappist Abbot.* Milwaukee: Bruce. 1953. A semipopular treatment of the Ohio-born monk who ruled the Abbey of Our Lady of Gethsemani in Kentucky from 1935 to his death in 1948.

723. [Fleming], Mary Celine, Sister, S.A. *A Woman of Unity.* Graymoor, Garrison, N.Y.: Franciscan Sisters of the Atonement. c. 1956. A sentimental biography of the foundress of the Franciscan Sisters of the Atonement, Mother Lurana White (1870–1935), written by the fourth mother general of the congregation.

724. Ford, George Barry. *A Degree of Difference.* New York: Farrar, Straus and Giroux. 1969. In these memoirs a liberal, opinionated priest (born in 1885) who was the energetic and enterprising pastor of Corpus Christi Church in New York for twenty-one years, popular counsellor to Catholic students at Columbia University, and active participant in many interdenominational and secular causes, justifies his disagreements with ecclesiastical authorities.

725. Fuchs, Lawrence H. *John F. Kennedy and American Catholicism.* New York: Meredith. 1967. More than half of the book deals with the author's conception of a basically Protestant "culture-religion" of America and with the reaction of American Catholics either as separatists or as forces of encounter from colonial times to 1960; the rest takes up Kennedy's campaign for president and his administration. The thesis of this Jewish admirer of the president is: "Because he was a Catholic, representing one sectarian religion thought to be

at odds with the culture-religion of Americanism, Kennedy, as a culture-hero, helped broaden the basis of consensus in American life by encouraging the forces of encounter within American Catholicism, and by opening the minds of non-Catholics to new opportunities for human communication, learning and growth in dialogue with Catholics" (p. 224).

726.   Gaffey, James P. *Francis Clement Kelley and the American Catholic Dream*. 2 vols. Bensenville, Ill.: Heritage Foundation. 1980. This scholarly biography of the founder of the Catholic Church Extension Society (who was also a military chaplain, negotiator in European and Mexican Church-State affairs, Bishop of Oklahoma, and author) is a significant contribution to the history of the Church in the first half of the twentieth century.

727.   Gallagher, Louis J., S.J. *Edmund A. Walsh, S.J.: A Biography*. New York: Benziger. 1962. This factual biography of the man who founded the School of Foreign Service at Georgetown University, was an agent of the Holy See, the Society of Jesus, and the American government in many countries, campaigned against international communism, and died in 1956, contains original materials but cites no sources.

728.   Gannon, David, S.A. *Father Paul of Graymoor*. New York: Macmillan. 1951. This semipopular biography of Father Paul James Francis (Lewis Thomas Wattson) (1863–1940), founder of the Society of the Atonement, although written with excessive filial piety, contains much primary source material. Cf. No. 690.

729.   Gannon, Robert I., S.J. *The Cardinal Spellman Story*. Garden City, N.Y.: Doubleday. 1962. Written five years before the death of Francis Spellman by a friend of long standing, this biography is neither complete, impartial, nor fully documented, but it is well organized, polished in style, and full of primary source material of permanent historical value such as extracts from diaries and letters which may never again be available.

730.   Gavin, Thomas F., S.J. *Champion of Youth: A Dynamic Story of a Dynamic Man, Daniel A. Lord, S.J.* Boston: St. Paul Editions. 1977. An intimate, candid biography of the priest (1888–1955) who promoted the Sodality of Our Lady, edited the *Queen's Work*, wrote countless books, pamphlets, and plays, organized the Summer Schools of Catholic Action, directed the Institute of Social Order, and became a popular preacher.

731.   Gibbons, James Cardinal. *A Retrospect of Fifty Years*. 2 vols. Baltimore: John Murphy. 1916. Reprint. New York: Arno. 1972. Volume I contains the memoirs of the cardinal's early years as a bishop, along with reprints of articles written from the Vatican Council; Volume II is mostly sermons preached on various occasions.

732.   Goldman, Eric F. *Charles J. Bonaparte, Patrician Reformer: His Earlier Career*. Baltimore: Johns Hopkins Press. 1943. An able Ph.D. thesis which carries Bonaparte up to his appointment as Theodore Roosevelt's attorney general in 1906.

733.   Goldstein, David. *Autobiography of a Campaigner for Christ*. Boston: Catholic Campaigners for Christ. 1936. The memoirs of a convert from Judaism (1870–1958) who became one of the best known and most widely traveled Catholic apologists and controversialists of the present century; entered the Church in 1905.

734.   Graham, Frank. *Al Smith, American*. New York: G. P. Putnam's. 1945. A popular illustrated appreciation rather than a biography; superseded by Handlin (No. 737).

735.   Grente, Georges. *Le beau voyage des cardinaux français aux Etats-Unis et au Canada*. Paris: Librairie Plon. 1927. A travelogue by the Bishop of Le Mans on his trip to this country in 1926 for the International Eucharistic Congress in Chicago; the first twelve chapters are devoted to observations on American Catholicism.

736.   Guidry, Mary Gabriella, Sister, S.S.F. *The Southern Negro Nun: An Autobiography*. New York: Exposition. 1974. This saccharine, uncritical account of the life of a missionary and teacher in British Honduras, Texas, and Louisiana (born in 1914) is of little value to historians.

737.   Handlin, Oscar. *Al Smith and His America*. Boston: Little, Brown. 1958. A sympathetic portrayal of Smith's political career; the best work to appear to date on the New York governor; belongs to the series Library of American Biography.

738.   Howard, J. Woodford, Jr. *Mr. Justice Murphy: A Political Biography*. Princeton: Princeton University Press. 1968. A well-researched but rather unsympathetic biography of the Catholic who was mayor of Detroit, governor-general and high commissioner of

the Philippines, governor of Michigan, attorney general of the United States, and associate justice of the Supreme Court; partially superseded by Fine (No. 721).

738a.   Huels, John M., O.S.M. *Father Keane, Servant of Mary*. Berwyn, Ill.: Servite. 1979. This brief biography of James R. Keane, a Servite who initiated and promoted the "Perpetual Novena" in honor of Our Sorrowful Mother in Chicago in 1937, spoke regularly on radio and later on television also, founded houses of his order in Ireland and Australia, and served in many other capacities up to his, death in 1975, is based on his correspondence but is more laudatory than critical.

739.   Hunton, George K. *All of Which I Saw, Part of Which I Was: The Autobiography of George K. Hunton, as told to Gary MacEoin*. Garden City, N.Y.: Doubleday. 1967. Hunton (1888–1967), a lifelong crusader for justice toward blacks, was cofounder of the Catholic Interracial Council of New York with John LaFarge, S.J., in 1934 and then served for nearly thirty years as its executive secretary. His recollections of relations with ecclesiastical and black leaders are clear, forthright, and modest. Unfortunately, there is no index.

740.   Kelley, Francis Clement. *The Bishop Jots It Down*. New York: Harper and Bros. 1939. The personal memoirs of the founder of the Catholic Church Extension Society who was second Bishop of Oklahoma City-Tulsa from 1924 to his death in 1948. For his biography see Gaffey (No. 726).

741.   Kennedy, Ambrose. *American Orator: Bourke Cochran, His Life and Politics*. Boston: Bruce Humphries. 1948. A popular account by an excongressman; McGurrin (No. 756) is a better work.

742.   _____ . *Quebec to New England: The Life of Monsignor Charles Dauray*. Boston: Bruce Humphries. 1948. A popular biography of a French-Canadian priest who came to the Diocese of Providence in 1872 and worked there until his death in 1931; of use for the French-Canadian immigrants in New England.

743.   Kinsman, Frederick J. *Salve Mater*. New York: Longmans, Green. 1920. The spiritual autobiography of the Protestant Episcopal Bishop of Delaware who became a Catholic in 1919.

744.   Kirwin, Harry W. *The Inevitable Success: A Biography of Herbert*

R. O'Conor. Westminster, Md.: Newman. 1962. A thoroughly documented life of a former governor of Maryland and United States senator.

745.   Klein Félix. *In the Land of the Strenuous Life.* Chicago: A. C. McClurg. 1905. A travelogue by a well-known professor of the Catholic Institute of Paris on his visit to the United States in 1903; Klein's admiration for American Catholicism was such as to cause him to be regarded with some suspicion by conservative Catholics among his fellow countrymen.

746.   Klinkhamer, Marie Carolyn, Sister, O.P. *Edward Douglas White: Chief Justice of the United States.* Washington, D.C.: Catholic University of America Press. 1943. An able Ph.D. theses on the Catholic jurist.

747.   Kotre, John N. *The Best of Times, the Worst of Times: Andrew Greeley and American Catholicism, 1950–1975.* Chicago: Nelson-Hall. 1978. A social psychologist uncritically presents a chronological review of the main theses of the priest-sociologist's writings ordered by major themes and adds Greeley's own refutation of criticisms.

748.   _____ . *Simple Gifts: The Lives of Pat and Patty Crowley.* Kansas City: Andrews and McMeel. 1979. This biography of Patrick Crowley (1911–1974) and his wife Patricia Caron (1913–   ), who were the principal founders and promoters of the Christian Family Movement and also members of Pope Paul VI's special study group on population and birth control, though based excessively on the author's interviews with the widow, contains much information on the contemporary history of the laity.

749.   La Farge, John, S.J. *The Manner Is Ordinary.* New York: Harcourt, Brace. 1954. Personal memoirs of a well-known Jesuit who was a member of a famous American family.

750.   _____ . *An American Amen: A Statement of Hope.* New York: Farrar, Straus and Cudahy. 1958. A continuation of the above.

751.   Lannie, Vincent P., ed. *On the Side of Truth: George N. Shuster: An Evaluation with Readings.* Notre Dame: University of Notre Dame Press. 1974. This volume contains an autobiographical sketch, a collection of Shuster's writings grouped under the headings of religion, politics, and education, and a select bibliography, but no index.

752.   Lunt, Richard D. *The High Ministry of Government: The Political Career of Frank Murphy.* Detroit: Wayne State University Press. 1965. An able account of a Catholic who served in a number of prominent posts such as governor of Michigan, high commissioner of the Philippines, attorney general of the United States, and associate justice of the Supreme Court in the generation after 1919; partially superseded by Fine (No. 721).

753.   McAuliffe, Harold J., S.J. *Father Tim.* Milwaukee: Bruce. 1944. A popular biography of Monsignor Timothy Dempsey, St. Louis pastor, noted for his "hotels" for homeless men, newsboys, and working girls established in a slum area of St. Louis between 1898 and 1906.

754.   McAvoy, Thomas T., C.S.C. *Father O'Hara of Notre Dame: The Cardinal-Archbishop of Philadelphia.* Notre Dame: University of Notre Dame Press. 1967. Written by a member of the same religious congregation with access to most of the pertinent sources, this lengthy and strictly chronological biography of John F. O'Hara (1888–1960), prefect of religion and president of the University of Notre Dame, auxiliary bishop and vicar-general to the military ordinary, Bishop of Buffalo, and Archbishop of Philadelphia, eschews direct criticism of its conservative, devout, idealistic subject but quotes unfavorable opinions expressed by others.

755.   McDevitt, Matthew, F.S.C. *Joseph McKenna, Associate Justice of the United States.* Washington, D.C.: Catholic University of America Press. 1946. A Ph.D. thesis on a California congressman who became McKinley's attorney general and a member of the Supreme Court from 1898 to 1925.

756.   McGurrin, James. *Bourke Cochran: A Free Lance in American Politics.* New York: Charles Scribner's. 1948. An able popular life of the New York congressman, orator, and Irish patriot.

757.   Madeleva, M., Sister, C.S.C. [Wolff]. *My First Seventy Years.* New York: Macmillan. 1959. A slender volume of memoirs by one of the best-known Catholic figures in the field of higher education for women; the author was president of Saint Mary's College, Notre Dame, for over a quarter-century.

758.   Marcus, Sheldon. *Father Coughlin: The Tumultuous Life of the Priest of the Little Flower.* Boston: Little, Brown. 1973. The only

significant new material used in this lively biography consists of two interviews that Father Coughlin granted the author in 1970, but it is used uncritically and inconsistently. Some information of human interest lacking in earlier studies is included here, but the definitive life cannot be written without access to the Radio Priest's own papers. See also Tull (No. 790).

759.   Marx, Paul, O.S.B. *Virgil Michel and the Liturgical Movement.* Collegeville, Minn.: Liturgical. 1957. A highly informative Ph.D. thesis in sociology on a key personality in twentieth-century American Catholicism.

760.   Maynard, Theodore. *A Fire Was Lighted: The Life of Rose Hawthorne Lathrop.* Milwaukee: Bruce. 1948. A popular biography of the convert daughter of Nathaniel Hawthorne who founded a religious community for the care of incurable cancer and who lived from 1851 to 1926.

761.   Menendez, Albert J. *John F. Kennedy: Catholic and Humanist.* Buffalo, N.Y.: Prometheus. 1978. This brief study of the President's religious commitment and its influence on his public policy and private conduct arrives at highly favorable conclusions.

762.   Merton, Thomas. *The Seven Storey Mountain.* New York: Harcourt, Brace. 1948. Autobiography of the young sophisticate and radical who became a Cistercian monk.

763.   _____ . *The Sign of Jonas.* New York: Harcourt, Brace. 1953. The diary and spiritual reminiscences of Father Louis, O.C.S.O., from December, 1946, to July, 1952.

764.   Miller, William D. *A Harsh and Dreadful Love: Dorothy Day and the Catholic Worker Movement.* New York: Liveright. 1973. Drawing upon the Catholic Worker papers and striving for meaning more than objectivity, the author has not written a biography of Dorothy Day (although he emphasizes her thought and action), but rather a study of the development of the Catholic Worker personalist philosophy to 1971.

765.   Murrett, John C. *Tar Heel Apostle: Thomas Frederick Price, Cofounder of Maryknoll.* New York: Longmans, Green. 1944. A popular treatment of the North Carolina missionary who in 1911 founded Maryknoll with James A. Walsh and who died in China in 1919.

766.   Noonan, Daniel P. *The Passion of Fulton Sheen.* New York: Dodd, Mead. 1972. An inept, superficial, and unreliable attempt at writing a life of the famous preacher and bishop has been made by a priest who served under him in the national office of the Society for the Propagation of the Faith.

767.   O'Connell, William, Cardinal. *Recollections of Seventy Years.* Boston: Houghton Mifflin. 1934. The highly personal memoirs of the second Archbishop of Boston who died in 1944.

768.   O'Hara, Constance. *Heaven Was Not Enough.* Philadelphia: J. B. Lippincott. 1955. Reminiscences of a woman who lost her faith in the 1920's and regained it twenty years later; contains interesting and amusing, if not always accurate, accounts of Philadelphia's Catholic community after 1911; the author was a grandniece of William O'Hara, Bishop of Scranton, 1868–1899.

769.   Owens, M. Lilliana, Sister, S.L. *Most Reverend Anthony J. Schuler, S.J., First Bishop of El Paso, and Some Catholic Activities of the Diocese, 1915–1942.* El Paso: Revista Católica Press. 1953. Although closely documented and supplied with an extensive bibliography, index, etc., this work suffers from the introduction of irrelevant material and the lack of a critical approach.

770.   Pelotte, Donald E., S.S.S. *John Courtney Murray: Theologian in Conflict.* New York: Paulist. 1976. This study attempts to be both a biography of the Jesuit professor at Woodstock College (1904–1967) and a critical analysis of his political, religious, philosophic thought, but lacks the depth necessary to do justice to the complex subject.

772.   Reardon, Maurice E. *Mosaic of a Bishop.* Cincinnati: St. Gregory's Seminary. 1957. A collection of sermons, addresses, and some of the writings of John T. McNicholas, O.P. (1877–1950), fourth Archbishop of Cincinnati; will be useful for a future biographer.

773.   Renner, Louis L., S.J., and Dorothy Jean Ray. *Pioneer Missionary to the Bering Strait Eskimos: Bellarmine Lafortune, S.J.* Portland, Oreg.: Binford and Mort. 1979. Based mainly on primary sources, this illustrated account of the Jesuit's work of evangelization practically amounts to a general history of the Church in northwestern Alaska from 1903 to 1947. Published for the Alaska Historical Commission.

774.   Ryan, John A. *Social Doctrine in Action: A Personal History.* New York: Harper and Bros. 1941. Memoirs of the leading Catholic figure in twentieth-century movements for social reform.

775.   Santen, Herman W. *Father Bishop, Founder of the Glenmary Home Missioners.* Milwaukee: Bruce. 1961. A slender, popular biography of William Howard Bishop (1885–1953), who founded societies of priests, brothers, and sisters.

776.   Sargent, Daniel. *All the Day Long.* New York: Longmans, Green. 1941. A popular life of Bishop James A. Walsh, cofounder of Maryknoll.

777.   Schneider, Nicholas. *The Life of John Cardinal Glennon, Archbishop of St. Louis.* Liguori, Mo.: Liguori. 1971. Rather than a biography properly so called, this small book is a series of undocumented vignettes on Glennon as archbishop, builder, preacher, churchman, citizen, leader, and cardinal, written by an admirer.

778.   Schneider, Nicholas A., comp. *Religious Views of President John F. Kennedy in His Own Words.* St. Louis: B. Herder. 1965. A collection of the Catholic president's remarks and addresses, proclamations and communiqués, answers to questions proposed at news conferences, excerpts from longer discourses, and an appendix containing some proclamations not found in the *Public Papers of the Presidents*—all reflecting his religious beliefs or illustrating the influence of religion on his thought—with a few brief explanatory notes by the compiler.

779.   Shaw, J. G. *Edwin Vincent O'Hara, American Prelate: A Biography.* New York: Farrar, Straus and Cudahy. 1957. A popular sketch of the third Bishop of Kansas City, an important figure in movements for social reform, rural life, and the liturgical revival, written a few months after his death.

780.   Sheerin, John B., C.S.P. *Never Look Back: The Career and Concerns of John J. Burke.* New York: Paulist. 1975. This brief, popular, uncritical biography of the influential Paulist priest and first general secretary of the National Catholic Welfare Conference who died in 1936 was written by a journalist who had access to previously closed papers but did insufficient general research. The book is weak in background, full of errors, and poorly composed; it also lacks an index.

781.   Shuster, George N. *The Ground I Walked On: Reflections of a*

College President. New York: Farrar, Straus and Cudahy. 1961. The Catholic author of these memoirs was president of Hunter College in New York from 1940 to 1960 and, during a leave of absence (1950–1951), land commissioner for Bavaria under the United States high commissioner for Germany.

782.   [Stoddard, John L.] *Rebuilding a Lost Faith, by an American Agnostic*. 4th ed. New York: P. J. Kenedy. 1924. A spiritual autobiography of the prominent lecturer who became a Catholic in 1922.

783.   Stokes, George Stewart. *Agnes Repplier, Lady of Letters*. Philadelphia: University of Pennsylvania Press. 1949. A biography done originally as a thesis; besides manuscript and published materials, the author employed information gleaned from a number of interviews with Miss Repplier.

784.   Storer, Maria Longworth. *In Memoriam: Bellamy Storer*. Boston: Merrymount. 1923. A revealing series of letters, covering the years 1899–1906, between the American ambassador to Austria-Hungary, President Theodore Roosevelt, and Archbishop Ireland, with the major portion pertaining to Ireland's prospects for a red hat.

785.   Sullivan, William Laurence. *Under Orders: The Autobiography of William Laurence Sullivan*. New York: Richard R. Smith. 1944. Reprint. Boston: Beacon. 1966. The memoirs of a former Paulist who left the Church in 1909, became a Unitarian minister in 1912, and married in 1913. Sullivan was an acknowledged modernist.

786.   Süssman, Cornelia, and Irving Süssman. *Thomas Merton: The Daring Young Man on the Flying Belltower*. New York: Macmillan. 1976. A brief, dramatized, undocumented biography of the convert, author, and Trappist monk (1915–1968).

787.   Taylor, D. Crane. *John L. Stoddard*. New York: P. J. Kenedy. 1935. A popular work that tries to estimate the influence of Stoddard as a lecturer and writer.

788.   Taylor, Myron C. *Wartime Correspondence between President Roosevelt and Pope Pius XII*. New York: Macmillan. 1947. Twenty-nine letters exchanged between the White House and the Vatican between December 23, 1939, and April 13, 1945, on the best means of bringing about an end to World War II; an introduction and brief explanatory notes by the president's personal representative at Vatican City.

789.   Tenison, Eva M. *Louise Imogen Guiney: Her Life and Works, 1861–1920*. London: Macmillan. 1923. The best available work on the distinguished Catholic essayist; told as far as possible "through her own words"; includes a descriptive bibliography of her writings that were published in book form.

790.   Tull, Charles J. *Father Coughlin and the New Deal*. Syracuse: Syracuse University Press. 1965. A heavily documented study with twenty-one pages of footnotes. Tull stated in his preface: "Despite the severe limitations imposed by the refusal of Father Coughlin and the Detroit Archdiocese to cooperate in any way, the purpose of this study is to probe thoroughly the controversial political career of the most colorful American Catholic priest of twentieth-century America" (p.ix).

791.   Twomey, Gerald, ed. *Thomas Merton: Prophet in the Belly of a Paradox*. New York: Paulist. 1978. The essays collected in this volume address many of the Trappist's social as well as monastic and cultural concerns, but are more laudatory than critical.

791a.   Vay de Vaya and Luskod, [Peter]. *The Inner Life of the United States*. New York: E. P. Dutton. 1908. The author, a Hungarian count and monsignor, describes his travels through the United States in 1905; contains interesting accounts of Hungarian immigrant colonies in Chicago, Cleveland, and other cities, with comments on the Church in various parts of the country.

792.   Vytell, Virginia Marie, Sister, C.J.C. *Praise the Lord You Nations*. Elmhurst, Pa.: N.p. 1976. Lithuania's historical and cultural development form a background for the life story of the Reverend Alphonsus Maria, C.P. (Julius Antanas Urbanavičius), missionary and founder of the Poor Sisters of Jesus Crucified and of the Sorrowful Mother. Father Alphonsus Maria was ordained a priest in Union City, New Jersey, in 1915 and died in 1949, but only the last part of this unscholarly, nationalistic, filiopietistic, and rambling book deals with his life.

793.   Walsh, James Edward. *Father McShane of Maryknoll: Missioner in South China*. New York: Lincoln MacVeagh, Dial. 1932. A popular, pietistic biography of Daniel L. McShane, who labored at Loting from 1919 till his death in 1927.

794.   Walsh, James Joseph. *Mother Alphonsa, Rose Hawthorne Lathrop*. New York: Macmillan. 1930. Written by a doctor, this earliest,

edifying biography of the writer, convert, and widow (1851–1926) who founded the Servants of Relief for Incurable Cancer to work among poor patients and affiliated the congregation with the Third Order of St. Dominic contains long excerpts from her own writings and from the community diary of her first associate, Mother Rose.

795.   Ward, Justine. *Thomas Edward Shields: Biologist, Psychologist, Educator.* New York: Charles Scribner's. 1947. A biography of a famous professor of the Catholic University of America by a personal friend and warm admirer.

796.   Warner, Emily Smith, with Daniel Hawthorne. *Happy Warrior: A Biography of My Father, Alfred E. Smith.* New York: Doubleday. 1956. A warm and intimate appreciation by Governor Smith's daughter.

797.   Waymann, Dorothy G. *Cardinal O'Connell of Boston.* New York: Farrar, Straus and Young. 1954. A documented, although somewhat chatty, biography of the second Archbishop of Boston by a convert journalist.

798.   Weber, Francis J. *John Joseph Cantwell: His Excellency of Los Angeles.* Hong Kong: Cathay. 1971. This well researched and well balanced biography of the Irish-born cleric who was bishop in southern California from 1917 to 1947 not only depicts the rapid institutional development of the diocese but also treats his ethnic, racial, and ecumenical concerns as well as his involvement in the nationally important Legion of Decency.

799.   _____ . *Thomas James Conaty: Pastor, Educator, Bishop.* Los Angeles: Westernlore. 1969. This biographical sketch of the priest from Massachusetts who was rector of the Catholic University of America from 1896 to 1903 and then Bishop of Monterey-Los Angeles until his death in 1915, illustrates the Irish-American ecclesiastical politics of the time.

800.   Wilken, Robert L., O.F.M. *Anselm Weber, O.F.M.: Missionary to the Navaho, 1898–1921.* Milwaukee: Bruce. 1955. A scholarly biography of an Indian missionary of the Southwest.

801.   Yzermans, Vincent A., ed. *Days of Hope and Promise: The Writings and Speeches of Paul J. Hallinan, Archbishop of Atlanta.* Collegeville, Minn.: Liturgical. 1973. Thirty-six pieces written between 1962 and 1968 dealing with various topics such as the Church, the

liturgy, peace, and Christian formation and leadership are reprinted, each with a prefatory paragraph giving the circumstances of composition or delivery. John Tracy Ellis has contributed a general introduction.

802. _____ . *The People I Love: A Biography of Luigi G. Ligutti.* Collegeville, Minn.: Liturgical. 1976. Written by an admiring journalist mainly on the basis of diaries, letters, and other papers supplied by Monsignor Ligutti, this popular life of the dynamic leader (active in many fields such as the National Catholic Rural Life Conference, international migration, Catholic missions, and the Food and Agriculture Organization) suffers from impreciseness in references to documentation, one-sidedness in the presentation of controversies, imbalance in the treatment of major topics, and lack of analysis and criticism of the subject's policies and actions.

803. Zwierlein, Frederick J. *Theodore Roosevelt and Catholics, 1882 – 1919.* St. Louis: The Reverend Victor T. Surew, Director of the Central Bureau of the Central Verein. 1956. While not strictly a biography, this volume treating Roosevelt's handling of Catholic problems and relationships, with special reference to the Philippines after the Spanish-American War, is classified under this heading by reason of its dependence upon the papers of Thomas A. Hendrick, Bishop of Cebu in the Philippines, 1903–1909.

V. RELIGIOUS COMMUNITIES

NO STUDENT of American Catholicism needs to be reminded of the role played by the religious orders and congregations in the history of the Church in this country. These communities have figured in practically every important undertaking of the Church since the days of the colonial missions. Varying greatly in dates of foundation, numbers, and the character of their work, some of these communities have already reached or are now approaching their sesquicentennial in the United States. Their history is a vital part of the American Catholic story. However, there have been relatively few volumes in the history of the religious communities that have met the canons of true scholarship. This is accountable in the main by several major causes: first, the task is often committed to a writer with no historical training; second, either the individual writer or his or her superiors suffers from a scruple concerning the revelation of untoward incidents in the community's past; and third, the reverse of the previous handicap permits a mistaken piety toward the Church or loyalty to one's community to dictate that deeds of ordinary character be portrayed in an exaggerated light. Recent years, however, have witnessed an improvement in some works in this category. To mention two, the volumes by Barry and Callahan (Nos. 811 and 873) listed below are examples of a mature and sensible approach to the unpleasant occurrences that have at one time or another beset the history of every religious community. In drawing up the following list two norms of selection have been used. An effort has been made, first, to represent the older and larger religious families within the American Church and, second, to include some of the better types of literature in this particular field. It should be emphasized, however, that the list contains a select sampling and is not meant to be complete.

A. GENERAL

804.   Code, Joseph B. *Great American Foundresses*. New York: Macmillan. 1929. Biographical sketches of sixteen foundresses of some of the leading communities of women in the United States.

805.   Dehey, Elinor Tong. *Religious Orders of Women in the United States*. Rev. ed. Hammond, Ind.: W. B. Conkey. 1930. Useful data on the foundation, development, and institutions of over 300 communities with a supplement, arranged by states, of their motherhouses, colleges, hospitals, etc., a glossary of terms, and photographs to accompany the text.

806.   Ewens, Mary, O.P. *The Role of the Nun in Nineteenth-Century America: Variations on the International Theme*. New York: Arno. 1978. In this doctoral dissertation accepted by the University of Minnesota in 1971 (and reproduced here from the original typescript), for each of the four periods into which the century is divided the formal role definitions of canon law, the roles sisters actually played, the problems posed by the American milieu, the interaction with society, and the roles seen in the contemporary literature are presented. The sociological concept of role is used to analyze historical and literary materials and popular ideas, and the interaction between religious women and the secular world is studied in terms of cultural conflicts between European and American values.

807.   Jolly, Ellen Ryan. *Nuns of the Battlefield*. Providence: Providence Visitor. 1927. Popular sketches of the work of twenty-one groups of sisters who acted as nurses during the Civil War.

B. MEN'S COMMUNITIES

808.   Angelus Gabriel, Brother, F.S.C. *The Christian Brothers in the United States, 1848–1948: A Century of Catholic Education*. New York: Declan X. McMullen. 1948. A centennial volume that furnishes a rich store of facts on one of the most important teaching communities of men; weak, however, in interpretation and on controversial matters.

809.   Assenmacher, Hugh, O.S.B. *A Place Called Subiaco: A History of the Benedictine Monks in Arkansas*. Little Rock: Rose. 1977. The first century of New Subiaco Abbey, along with its parochial missions (serving mainly German-speaking Catholics for many years), is recounted on the basis of primary sources which, regrettably, are not identified in notes. The book is illustrated with numerous photographs.

810.   Bacigalupo, Leonard, O.F.M. *The Franciscans and Italian Immigration in America*. Hicksville, N.Y.: Exposition. 1977. This brief history of the Custody, later the Province, of the Immaculate Con-

ception and its apostolate among Italians from 1901 to the present in New York, Massachusetts, Pennsylvania, and Canada includes a bibliographical essay.

811. Barry, Colman J., O.S.B. *Worship and Work: Saint John's Abbey and University, 1856–1956.* Collegeville, Minn.: St. John's Abbey. 1956. 2nd ed.: *1856–1980.* Collegeville: Liturgical. 1980. This centennial publication on the largest community of Benedictine monks in the world satisfies the most rigid demands of scholarship with extensive and informative notes, pleasing format, and copious illustrations. The new edition contains an epilogue on the developments of the subsequent quarter-century.

812. Battersby, William John [Brother Clair Stanislaus, F.S.C]. *The Christian Brothers in the United States, 1900–1925.* Winona, Minn.: St. Mary's College Press. 1967. This well-documented work is essentially a study of the Latin Question (whether or not the brothers were permitted by their statutes to teach the classical languages); the first half traces the controversy from its origins in 1853 to the negative decision of 1900, and the second half recounts the readjustments and developments in the Institute and its schools until the ban was lifted in 1923.

813. _____ . *The Christian Brothers in the United States, 1925– 1950.* Winona, Minn.: St. Mary's College Press. 1976. Continuing the preceding volume, the author not only sketches the internal life of the Institute as a whole but also chronicles the growth of existing institutions, the disappearance of some and the beginning of others, as well as the shift from primary to secondary education, through the "Golden Age" (1925–1930), the Depression, the war, and the postwar years; he also describes the brothers' missionary labors in the Philippines and Nicaragua, the operation of their winery in California, and their other activities.

814. Beckman, Peter, O.S.B. *Kansas Monks: A History of St. Benedict's Abbey.* Atchison, Kans.: Abbey Student Press. 1957. A scholarly and candid treatment of the Benedictines' first century in Kansas; amply illustrated.

815. Beirne, Kilian, Brother, C.S.C. *From Sea to Shining Sea: The Holy Cross Brothers in the United States.* Valatie, N.Y.: Holy Cross. 1966. In a simple, familiar style without a critical method or references to the sources employed, the author recounts the history of this religious congregation from 1841, when seven brothers arrived in

Indiana from France with Father Edward Sorin, to the present, when their teaching apostolate has spread across the continent.

816.   Bittle, Celestine N., O.M.Cap. *A Romance of Lady Poverty: The History of the Province of St. Joseph of the Capuchin Order in the United States.* Milwaukee: Bruce. 1933. A serious account of these friars from the time of their foundation in Wisconsin in 1856.

817.   Bluma, Dacian, O.F.M., comp., and Theophilus Chowaniec, O.F.M. *A History of the Province of the Assumption of the Blessed Virgin Mary.* Pulaski, Wis.: Franciscan Publishers. 1967. This documented and illustrated account begins with the erection of the friary in Pulaski by Franciscans from Poland in 1888, continues through the establishment of the province in 1939, and ends in 1966; it contains data on each friary, parish, educational institution, mission, and other apostolate belonging to the province.

818.   Byrne, John F., C.SS.R. *The Redemptorist Centenaries, 1732: Founding of the Congregation of the Most Holy Redeemer, 1832: Establishment in the United States.* Philadelphia: Dolphin. 1932. Aside from the first chapter (pp. 1-40), this large centennial book is devoted to a sectional development of the Redemptorists in this country; although a considerable amount of archival material has been used, the narrative is confined for the most part to the external history of the congregation, with very little critical approach.

819.   Callahan, Adalbert, O.F.M. *Medieval Francis in Modern America: The Story of Eighty Years, 1855–1935.* New York: Macmillan. 1936. A popular account, with some correspondence, of the friars' Province of the Most Holy Name embracing the states along the Atlantic Coast.

820.   Campbell, Thomas J., S.J. *Pioneer Priests of North America, 1642–1710.* 3 vols. New York: America Press. 1908–1911. Forty or more popular essays bearing on the labors of the principal Jesuit missionaries of the colonial period with a volume each devoted to the Iroquois (I), the Hurons (II), and the Algonquins (III).

821.   Catta, Etienne, and Tony Catta. *Basil Anthony Mary Moreau.* Trans. Edward L. Heston, C.S.C. 2 vols. Milwaukee: Bruce. 1955. Although this work is intended as a biography of the founder (1799–1873) of the Congregation of Holy Cross, it contains a detailed and documented treatment of the early struggles of the congregation in the United States, which began in October, 1841, under the leadership of Edward Sorin, C.S.C. (1814–1893).

822. Curley, Michael J., C.SS.R. *The Provincial Story: A History of the Baltimore Province of the Congregation of the Most Holy Redeemer.* Esopus, N.Y.: Mount Saint Alphonsus Bookstore. 1963. A thoroughly documented monograph which deals with the Redemptorists mainly in the eastern part of the United States.

823. Curran, Francis X., S.J. *The Return of the Jesuits: Chapters in the History of the Society of Jesus in Nineteenth-Century America.* Chicago: Loyola University Press. 1966. This collection of previously published articles, which are based on archival research and are marked by objective judgment, deals mainly with the educational, pastoral, and missionary work of foreign (French and German) Jesuits in the States of New York and Kentucky and in Canada.

824. [Flanagan], M. Raymond, O.C.S.O. *Burnt Out Incense.* New York: P. J. Kenedy. 1949. A popular treatment of the Trappists' first successful foundation in the United States, begun in Kentucky in 1848.

825. *The Friars Minor in the United States, with a Brief History of the Orders of St. Francis in General.* Chicago: Franciscan Herald Press. 1926. Brief sketches of the individual provinces and commissariats published in honor of the seventh centenary of St. Francis' death; illustrations and a directory of all the order's houses in this country at time of publication.

826. Garraghan, Gilbert J., S.J. *The Jesuits of the Middle United States.* 3 vols. New York: America Press. 1938. Reprint. New York: Arno. 1978. A work of real scholarship that brings to light a wealth of unpublished sources; more detailed for the period before 1860; treats the area from eastern Ohio to the Rocky Mountains.

827. Geiger, Maynard, O.F.M. *Biographical Dictionary of the Franciscans in Spanish Florida and Cuba, 1528–1841.* Paterson, N.J.: St. Anthony Guild. 1940. Annotated thumbnail sketches of some 750 friars who labored in the American Southeast and Cuba; includes useful lists of Franciscan missions in colonial Florida.

828. Habig, Marion A., O.F.M. *Heralds of the King: The Franciscans of the St. Louis-Chicago Province, 1858–1958.* Chicago: Franciscan Herald Press. 1958. An elaborate centennial volume replete with illustrations, lists of houses, bibliography, index, etc.; the most up-to-date account of the Friars Minor in the Middle West.

829. Herbermann, Charles G. *The Sulpicians in the United States.*

New York: Encyclopedia Press. 1916. In lieu of a much needed scholarly and up-to-date history of this society, this popular treatment still serves a useful purpose; superseded by Ruane (No. 855) for the period from 1791 to 1829.

830.   Hoffmann, Mathias M. *Arms and the Monk! The Trappist Saga in Mid-America.* Dubuque: William C. Brown. 1952. A history of the Abbey of Our Lady of New Melleray founded in 1849 near Dubuque; embodies considerable unpublished material, but there are neither references to sources nor an index.

831.   Hubert Gerard, Brother, F.S.C. *Mississippi Vista: The Brothers of the Christian Schools in the Mid-West, 1849–1949.* Winona, Minn.: St. Mary's College Press. 1948. This large and lavishly illustrated centennial volume contains historical sketches of the Christian Brothers' first mission and of all their institutions belonging to the St. Louis District, which embraces Illinois, Minnesota, Tennessee, and other states as well as Missouri.

832.   Hughes, Thomas, S.J. *History of the Society of Jesus in North America: Colonial and Federal.* 4 vols. New York: Longmans, Green. 1907–1917. These large volumes contain a vast amount of information, although they are poorly written and edited; two volumes are devoted to a narrative of the years 1580 to 1773, the other two to documents covering the period from 1605 to 1838.

833.   Isetti, Ronald Eugene, F.S.C. *Called to the Pacific: A History of the Christian Brothers of the San Francisco District, 1868–1944.* Moraga: St. Mary's College of California. 1979. This substantial and well-documented study is focused on the Latin Question, the outcome of which fundamentally changed the character and mission of the congregation on the West Coast.

834.   Iwicki, John, C.R. *The First One Hundred Years: A Study of the Apostolate of the Congregation of the Resurrection in the United States, 1866–1966.* Rome: N.p. 1966. This well-researched volume catalogues the labors of the Resurrectionist Fathers for the Poles in America—their parishes and other pastoral and missionary work, elementary and secondary schools, novitiates and seminary, newspapers, magazines, and other publications, and promotion of Catholic fraternal organizations.

835.   Janas, Edward T., C.R. *Dictionary of American Resurrectionists, 1865–1965.* Rome: N.p. 1967. Besides the dates and places of birth,

profession, ordination, and death or present assignment, these tabulated lists of deceased and living fathers and brothers contain extensive data on their labors in the United States.

836. Judy, Myron, O. Carm. *Carmel Came: A History of the American Carmelite Province of the Most Pure Heart of Mary, 1864–1900.* Downers Grove, Ill.: Aylesford Priory. 1964. This thoroughly documented study was originally carried in *The Sword* (XXIV [October, 1964], 3–156), a private publication of the Carmelite friars.

837. Kirkfleet, Cornelius J., O. Praem. *The White Canons of St. Norbert: A History of the Praemonstratensian Order in the British Isles and America.* West De Pere, Wis.: St. Norbert Abbey. 1943. Only the last section of this general work is devoted to this country, where the first foundation was made in Wisconsin in 1843.

838. Kleber, Albert, O.S.B. *History of St. Meinrad Archabbey, 1854–1954.* St. Meinrad, Ind.: A Grail Publication. 1954. A centennial work that makes ample use of unpublished materials; parts of the narrative are too polemical in tone, but on the whole it is a solid contribution of special importance for the German immigrant settlements in southern Indiana.

839. Knapke, Paul J., C.PP.S. *History of the American Province of the Society of the Precious Blood.* Vol. I: *Origins in Europe;* Vol II.: *Early Years in America, 1844–1859.* Carthagena, Ohio: Messenger Press. 1958, 1968. Volume I of this candid, critical, detailed, thoroughly documented and clearly organized study carries the narrative from the birth of the Swiss founder and first provincial in the United States, Francis de Sales Brunner, to his arrival with a few companions at Cincinnati on December 31, 1843. Volume II covers the first sixteen years in this country and ends with Father Brunner's death. It is a case study in the ecclesiastical history of the period.

840. Koren, Henry J., C.S.Sp. *Knaves or Knights? A History of the Spiritan Missionaries in Acadia and North America, 1732–1839.* Pittsburgh: Duquesne University Press. 1962. With some earlier brief exceptions, only the last chapter deals with the work of two members of the Congregation of the Holy Ghost in the United States, specifically in Maryland and the Virgin Islands, from 1794 to 1839.

841. Lapomarda, Vincent A., S.J. *The Jesuit Heritage in New England.* Worcester, Mass.: College of the Holy Cross. 1977. This

compilation of facts pertaining to persons, places, and topics related at least remotely to the Society of Jesus in each state of New England from the seventeenth century to the twentieth is presented with occasional repetition but with little interpretation. The appendices containing extensive lists may be useful for reference.

842.   Leutenegger, Benedict, trans. *The Zacatecan Missionaries in Texas, 1716 –1834: Excerpts from the Libros de los Decretos of the Missionary College of Zacatecas, 1707 –1828* with *A Biographical Dictionary* by Marion A. Habig. Austin: Texas Historical Commission. 1973. All references to the apostolic college's men in Texas have been excerpted from the books of minutes of the meetings of the guardian and his council and have been translated into English. The biographical sketches of 121 fathers and brothers include citations of sources.

843.   McGloin, John Bernard, S.J. *Jesuits by the Golden Gate: The Society of Jesus in San Francisco, 1849 –1969*. San Francisco: University of San Francisco Press. 1972. This commemorative history documents the work of the Jesuits centered on their Church of St. Ignatius and University of San Francisco, but glosses over internal and external controversies and fails to analyze the interaction of the religious and academic community with its urban milieu.

844.   Malone, Edward E., O.S.B. *Conception: A History of the First Century of the Conception Colony, 1858 –1958; A History of the First Century of Conception Abbey, 1873 –1973; A History of New Engelberg College, Conception College, and the Immaculate Conception Seminary, 1886 –1971*. Elkhorn, Nebr.: Michaeleen Press. 1971. Though marred by poor organization, needless repetitions, occasional digressions, and excessive quotation from sources, this folio-sized volume contains a large quantity of documented information on the foundations begun in Nebraska by monks from Engelberg Abbey in Switzerland.

845.   Merton, Thomas. *The Waters of Siloe*. New York: Harcourt, Brace. 1949. Well written, this general treatment of the Cistercians in the United States by a nonprofessional with an excellent sense of history contains chapters on the European background of the order, the nature of Cistercian life, a glossary of monastic terms, and a bibliography.

846.   Miller, Norbert H., O.M.Cap. *Pioneer Capuchin Missionaries in the United States, 1784 –1816*. New York: Joseph F. Wagner. 1932. Originally a thesis for the A.M. degree, this brief work is based for the most part on printed materials.

847. Mizera, Peter F. *Czech Benedictines in America, 1877–1901.* Lisle, Ill.: Center for Slav Culture, St. Procopius College. 1969. With abundant documentation the development is traced from the beginnings in Nebraska, through the founding of the priory in Chicago in 1885, to the opening of the college in Lisle; events of the twentieth century are treated with less detail.

848. Murphy, Joseph F., O.S.B. *Tenacious Monks: The Oklahoma Benedictines, 1875–1975: Indian Missionaries, Catholic Founders, Educators, Agriculturists.* Shawnee, Okla.: Benedictine Color Press, St. Gregory's Abbey. 1975. Though references to sources are sparse, this substantial history of Sacred Heart Mission, which became St. Gregory's Abbey, recounts both the internal tensions arising from the different European origins and monastic traditions of the members and their external difficulties on the frontier; it also traces their progress from Indian schools to a college.

849. Nevins, Albert J. *The Meaning of Maryknoll.* New York: McMullen. 1954. A popular and illustrated treatment of the first native American group of priests founded (in 1911) for the foreign missions.

850. O'Daniel, Victor F., O.P. *The Dominican Province of Saint Joseph: Historico-Biographical Studies.* New York: National Headquarters of the Holy Name Society. 1942. Mostly biographical in character, these twenty-four essays represent in part summaries of the author's previous biographies of American Dominicans, along with some new subjects; excellent control of the sources, although the value of the work is lessened by an uncritical attitude toward all that pertains to the order.

851. ———. *Dominicans in Early Florida.* New York: United States Catholic Historical Society. 1930. Brief biographical sketches of twenty or more friars of the early Spanish period.

852. Parkman, Francis. *The Jesuits in North America in the Seventeenth Century.* 2 vols. 33rd ed. Boston: Little, Brown. 1893. Although originally published in 1867, this work still makes the reading of history a high adventure; the style and overall conception help to make up in part for the lack of recent research and for the author's occasional misinterpretation of Catholic faith and practice.

853. Powers, George C., M.M. *The Maryknoll Movement.* New York: Catholic Foreign Mission Society. 1926. Originally an A.M. thesis, this work has been superseded by Nevins (No. 849).

854.   Rausch, Jerome W., O.S.C. *The Crosier Story: A History of the Crosier Fathers in the United States.* Onamia, Minn.: Crosier Press. 1960. A large and well-documented volume with numerous illustrations, index, etc., of a European community that came to this country in 1850 and began to work in Wisconsin.

855.   Ruane, Joseph W. *The Beginnings of the Society of St. Sulpice in the United States, 1791–1829.* Washington, D.C.: Catholic University of America Press. 1935. This Ph.D. thesis is characterized by an extensive use of unpublished materials and is especially useful for the beginnings of the educational institutions for men in the early Archdiocese of Baltimore.

856.   Schmitz, Joseph W., S.M. *The Society of Mary in Texas.* San Antonio: Naylor. 1951. Based largely on archival sources, this monograph traces the Marianists' history from their arrival in 1852 to date.

857.   Scollard, Robert J., C.S.B. *Dictionary of Basilian Biography: Lives of the Members of the Congregation of Priests of Saint Basil from Its Beginnings in 1822 to 1968.* Toronto: Basilian Press. 1969. Carefully compiled sketches of more than 300 Basilian fathers deceased before 1968, some of whom were born or labored in the United States.

858.   Skinner, Thomas L., C.SS.R. *The Redemptorists in the West.* St. Louis: Redemptorist Fathers. 1933. Although undocumented, this is a careful work based upon authentic records; bibliography and index; the area covered embraces the St. Louis Province of the congregation to the Pacific Coast.

859.   Tourscher, Francis E., O.S.A. *Old St. Augustine's with Some Records of the Work of the Austin Friars in the United States.* Philadelphia: Peter Reilly. 1937. The only general treatment—popular in character—of the Augustinians in this country; has thumbnail sketches of the early friars.

860.   Vogel, Claude, O.M.Cap. *Franciscan History of North America.* Washington, D.C.: Capuchin College. 1937. Papers read at the eighteenth annual meeting of the Franciscan Educational Conference, Santa Barbara, California, August 2–4, 1936; those of Lenhart, Lemay, and Geiger are of greater importance for source materials and areas of research.

861.   Walsh, James J. *The American Jesuits.* New York: Macmillan. 1934. Popular essays by a nonprofessional historian.

862. Wild, Joseph C., O.M.I. *Men of Hope: The Background and History of the Oblate Province of Our Lady of Hope (Eastern American Province).* Boston: Missionary Oblates of Mary Immaculate. 1967. This well-documented monograph narrates the foundations and missions of the Oblates in the northeastern United States from the middle of the nineteenth century on, the erection of the province in 1883, and the subsequent development to the early 1960's

863. *Woodstock Letters: A Record of Current Events and Historical Notes Connected with the Colleges and Missions of the Society of Jesus in North and South America.* Woodstock, Md.: Woodstock College. 1872–1969. These annual volumes contain a variety of materials, including correspondence, reminiscences, biographical sketches, and essays; a private publication intended for members of the order, but now available to outsiders.

864. *Wynne, John J., S.J. The Jesuit Martyrs of North America.* New York: Universal Knowledge Foundation. 1925. A series of brief sketches based on Thwaites (No. 420); superseded for Jogues and Brébeuf by Talbot (Nos. 417, 418).

865. Yuhaus, Cassian J., C.P. *Compelled to Speak: The Passionists in America, Origin and Apostolate.* Westminster, Md.: Newman. 1967. Originally written as a doctoral dissertation at the Pontifical Gregorian University, this well-documented monograph recounts both the foundation and expansion of the congregation in the United States, from the sending of the first Italian members in 1852 to the erection of the first province in 1863, and the development of its apostolate, especially the preaching of missions and retreats.

C. WOMEN'S COMMUNITIES

866. Ahles, Mary Assumpta, Sister, O.S.F. *In the Shadow of His Wings: A History of the Franciscan Sisters.* St. Paul, Minn.: North Central. 1977. Based on extensive research, this lengthy history of the Franciscan Sisterhood of Little Falls, Minnesota, recounts the founding of its first convent at Belle Prairie in 1872 by the enigmatic English convert, Mother Mary Ignatius (Elizabeth Hayes, 1823–1894), its early expansion (including the Negro apostolate in Georgia), its separation from the foundress in Rome in 1890 and reorganization as a diocesan institute, its establishment of hospitals, orphanages, schools, and missions (in South America) and its adaptation to the changed circumstances following the Second Vatican Council.

867.   Baska, Mary Regina, Sister, O.S.B. *The Benedictine Congrega-tion of Saint Scholastica: Its Foundation and Development, 1852–1930*. Washington, D.C.: Catholic University of America Press. 1935. A Ph.D. thesis that employs a considerable amount of archival mate-rial, on a congregation that immigrated from Bavaria to Pennsylvania and ultimately spread to New Jersey, Minnesota, Kansas, Alabama, and other states.

868.   Bernard, M., Mother. *The Story of the Sisters of Mercy in Missis-sippi, 1860–1930*. New York: P. J. Kenedy. 1931. A popular and illustrated volume with no references to sources, bibliography, or index.

869.   Boyle, Mary Electa, Sister. *Mother Seton's Sisters of Charity in Western Pennsylvania*. Greensburg: Seton Hill College. 1946. Al-though containing some hitherto unpublished material, there is no bibliography or index; not a scientific work.

870.   [Brosnahan], M. Eleanore, Sister, C.S.C. *On the King's High-way: A History of the Sisters of the Holy Cross of St. Mary of the Immaculate Conception, Notre Dame, Indiana*. New York: D. Appleton. 1931. The general historian's interest in this popular work by a nonprofessional will probably center on the lengthy chapter dealing with the Civil War; a number of documents reprinted; illustrations and an index.

871.   Brown, Mary Borromeo, Sister. *The History of the Sisters of Providence of Saint Mary-of-the-Woods*. Vol. I: *1806–1856*. New York: Benziger. 1949. This large and meticulously annotated work gives the French background of a community six of whose members came to Indiana in October, 1840, in response to the need for teachers in the frontier communities of the Diocese of Vincennes; contains a lengthy bibliography, appendices, numerous illustrations, and a good index. Continued by Logan (No. 902).

872.   Burton, Katherine. *Bells on Two Rivers: The History of the Sisters of the Visitation of Rock Island, Illinois*. Milwaukee: Bruce. 1965. The history of the community first at Maysville, Kentucky, on the Ohio River, and since 1899 at Rock Island on the Mississippi, along with the development of its school, Villa de Chantal, is presented in a popular fashion without references to sources or critical evaluations.

873.   Callahan, Mary Generosa, Sister, C.D.P. *The History of the Sisters of Divine Providence, San Antonio, Texas*. Milwaukee: Bruce.

1955. A thoroughly documented and candid story of a community that began its Texas history (1868) with a group of sisters from Alsace to serve the German missions; one of the best of recent works on American sisterhoods.

874. Callan, Louis, R.S.C.J. *The Society of the Sacred Heart in North America.* New York: Longmans, Green. 1937. A lengthy and documented history of a community whose American chapter opened with the arrival (1818) of Blessed Philippine Duchesne (1769–1852) and her companions from France; noteworthy for the Indian mission history of the West.

875. Clarissa, Mary, Mother, and Sister Mary Olivia. *With the Poverello: History of the Sisters of Saint Francis, Oldenburg, Indiana.* New York: P. J. Kenedy. 1948. An annotated treatment of a community that came from Germany in 1851; bibliography, notes, and an index.

876. Coogan, M. Jane, B.V.M *The Price of Our Heritage.* Vol. I: *1831–1869;* Vol. II: *1869–1920: History of the Sisters of Charity of the Blessed Virgin Mary.* Dubuque: Mount Carmel Press. 1975, 1978. The first of these extensively researched volumes, reproduced from a typescript, relates the founding of the congregation by Mary Frances Clarke and her companions in 1831, its ten years in Philadelphia (1833–1843), and its pioneering period in Iowa to the death of the priest superior, Terence J. Donaghoe; the second recounts the administrations of Mother Clarke and her first three successors.

877. Croghan, Mary Edmund, Sister, R.S.M. *Sisters of Mercy of Nebraska, 1864–1910.* Washington, D.C.: Catholic University of America Press. 1942. A Ph.D. thesis that employs some unpublished materials from the community's archives.

878. Currier, Charles Warren, C.SS.R. *Carmel in America: A Centennial History of the Discalced Carmelites in the United States.* Baltimore: John Murphy. 1890. A work—carefully prepared for so early a date—on the first group of contemplative nuns in this country; lengthy appendices with documents.

879. DeChantal, M., Sister, C.S.F.N. *Out of Nazareth: A Centenary of the Sisters of the Holy Family of Nazareth in the Service of the Church.* New York: Exposition. 1974. This detailed study relates the congregation's origins in Poland, its establishment in Chicago in 1885, its spread in the Americas, Europe, and Australia, and its work in

schools, hospitals, and orphanages but minimizes the internal contentions and external challenges which have contributed to its vigor and sense of identity.

880.   Dudine, M. Frederica, Sister, O.S.B. *The Castle on the Hill: Centennial History of the Convent of the Immaculate Conception, Ferdinand, Indiana, 1867–1967.* Milwaukee: Bruce. 1967. In the first part of this sizable work the regimes of the seven successive mothers superior of the convent are narrated, and in the second part sketches of its three daughterhouses, one college (St. Benedict), three high schools, and sixty elementary schools are presented. These Benedictine sisters worked mainly among German Catholics in Indiana.

881.   Duratschek, M. Claudia, Sister, O.S.B. *Under the Shadow of His Wings: History of Sacred Heart Convent of Benedictine Sisters, Yankton, South Dakota, 1880–1970.* Yankton, S. Dak.: Sacred Heart Convent. 1971. This slightly dramatized but factual account extends back to the community's origins in Switzerland in 1853 and includes its work in education on all levels, in hospitals, in Indian missions, and in foreign missions from Alaska to South America.

882.   Evans, Mary Ellen. *The Spirit Is Mercy: The Story of the Sisters of Mercy in the Archdiocese of Cincinnati, 1858–1958.* Westminster, Md.: Newman. 1959. A well-documented account with bibliography, illustrations, and index.

883.   Finck, Mary Helena, Sister. *The Congregation of the Sisters of Charity of the Incarnate Word of San Antonio, Texas: A Brief Account of Its Origin and Work.* Washington, D.C.: Catholic University of America Press. 1925. This slender Ph.D. thesis is not an adequate history of this community that has played an important part in the development of the Church in the Southwest.

884.   Francis Borgia, M., Sister, O.S.F. *He Sent Two: The Story of the Beginning of the School Sisters of St. Francis.* Milwaukee: Bruce. 1965. Based on archival materials and interviews but written in a simple, sentimental style, this book recounts the work of the foundress, Mother M. Alexia, and the cofoundress, Mother M. Alfons, who came from Germany to Wisconsin in 1873, and the subsequent expansion of the congregation's educational work to 1929.

885.   Gilmore, Julia, Sister, S.C.L. *We Came North: Centennial Story of the Sisters of Charity of Leavenworth.* St. Meinrad, Ind.: Abbey. 1961. A large and well-documented history of a community that branched

off from Nazareth, Kentucky; nine members reached Leavenworth in November, 1858, from a Nashville, Tennessee, house.

886. Hanousek, Mary Eunice, Sister. *A New Assisi: The First Hundred Years of the Sisters of St. Francis of Assisi, Milwaukee, Wisconsin, 1849–1949.* Milwaukee: Bruce. 1949. An illustrated centennial volume embodying some archival material.

887. Hart, Mary Francis Borgia, Sister, S.S.F. *Violets in the King's Garden: A History of the Sisters of the Holy Family of New Orleans.* N.p.: The Author. 1976. This chronicle of the congregation of colored women founded in 1852 is carefully compiled but is not the work of a professional historian.

888. Hayes, James M. *The Bon Secours Sisters in the United States.* Washington, D.C.: National Capital Press. 1931. A well-written—if uncritical—history of a community whose American chapter began with a small group who immigrated from Ireland to Baltimore in May, 1881; their work has been chiefly that of conducting hospitals and other charitable institutions.

889. Hegarty, Mary Loyola, Sister, C.C.V.I. *Serving with Gladness: The Origin and History of the Congregation of the Sisters of Charity of the Incarnate Word, Houston, Texas.* Houston: Bruce in cooperation with the Sisters of Charity of the Incarnate Word. 1967. This comprehensive centennial work recounts the background in France and Texas to the founding of the sisterhood by Bishop Claude M. Dubuis in 1866 to care for the sick and orphaned, and its subsequent development and expansion.

890. Herron, Mary Eulalia, Sister. *The Sisters of Mercy in the United States, 1843–1928.* New York: Macmillan. 1929. A general account treated by dioceses; not a scientific work; on these sisters in particular areas see the volumes by Bernard, Croghan, Evans, Holland, Lennon, McEntee, Roth, and Sabourin (Nos. 868, 877, 882, 891, 901, 910, 921, 922).

891. Holland, Mary Ildephonse, Sister. *Lengthened Shadows: A History of the Sisters of Mercy, Cedar Rapids, Iowa.* New York: Bookman. 1952. A semipopular work with lists of superiors, missions, etc.; superseded by Roth (No. 921).

892. Hurley, Helen Angela, Sister. *On Good Ground: The Story of the Sisters of St. Joseph in St. Paul.* Minneapolis: University of Minnesota

Press. 1951. A centennial volume that makes interesting reading, even if some of the interpretations are not always well balanced; semipopular in character, with reliance mainly on secondary sources and newspapers.

893.   *In the Early Days: Pages from the Annals of the Sisters of Charity of the Blessed Virgin Mary; St. Joseph's Convent, Mount Carmel, Dubuque, Iowa, 1833–1887.* St. Louis: B. Herder. 1912. A volume of correspondence relating to the first half-century of these sisters in this country.

894.   Johnston, S[ue] M[ildred Lee]. *Builders by the Sea: History of the Ursuline Community of Galveston, Texas.* New York: Exposition. 1971. This highly dramatized and meagerly documented account stretching from 1847 to the early twentieth century does scant justice to the nuns' contribution to education in East Texas.

895.   Kalinowski, Mary Theophane, Sister, C.S.S.F. *Felician Sisters in the West: The Origins and History of the Assumption of the Blessed Virgin Mary Province of Ponca City, Oklahoma.* Ponca City: Bruce in cooperation with the Felician Sisters of the Southwest U.S.A. 1967. Well researched in archives and newspapers, this is a brief account of the founding of the province in 1953 and of its work not only in Oklahoma but also in Texas, Missouri, Nebraska, and California during the first decade.

896.   Kavanagh, D[enis] J., S.J. *The Holy Family Sisters of San Francisco: A Sketch of Their First Fifty Years, 1872–1922.* San Francisco: Gilmartin. 1922. A jubilee volume that made some pretensions to incorporating reminiscences of the early sisters, etc. The community was founded in San Francisco.

897.   Keefe, St. Thomas Aquinas, Sister. *The Congregation of the Grey Nuns, 1737–1910.* Washington, D.C.: Catholic University of America Press. 1942. Although this Ph.D. thesis is largely devoted to the congregation's history in France and Canada, there is some material on its American missions.

898.   [Kelly], M. Rosalita, Sister, I.H.M. *No Greater Service: The History of the Congregation of the Sisters, Servants of the Immaculate Heart of Mary, Monroe, Michigan, 1845–1945.* Detroit: Marygrove College. 1948. This huge volume gives a well-documented account with illustrations, bibliography, and index; for the general historian of the Church it would have profited by less detail.

899. Kohler, Mary Hortense, Sister, O.P. *Rooted in Hope: The Story of the Dominican Sisters of Racine, Wisconsin.* Milwaukee: Bruce. 1962. This substantial history commemorating the centenary of the founding of the motherhouse of the Congregation of St. Catherine of Siena is a sequel to the same author's *Life and Work of Mother Benedicta Bauer* (No. 502). Material drawn from convent and parish archives, local histories, and reminiscences of sisters and alumnae illuminates the lives of early members and the schools and institutes the sisters conducted, especially in German communities in Wisconsin, Michigan, and Illinois from 1880 to 1962.

900. Lathrop, George Parsons, and Rose Hawthorne Lathrop. *A Story of Courage: Annals of the Georgetown Convent of the Visitation.* Boston: Houghton Mifflin. 1894. A well-written work on one of the most historic convents (1799) in the United States by a prominent author and his wife, both converted to Catholicism in 1891; based on archival materials, although there is neither citation of the sources nor a bibliography.

901. Lennon, Mary Isidore, Sister, R.S.M. *Milestones of Mercy: Story of the Sisters of Mercy in St. Louis, 1856–1956.* Milwaukee: Bruce. 1967. A centennial volume which would have been enhanced in value were it to have treated the impact upon the community of such matters as immigration, the cholera epidemics, and the Civil War.

902. Logan, Eugenia, Sister, S.P. *The History of the Sisters of Providence of Saint Mary-of-the-Woods, Indiana,* Vol. II *(1856–1894).* Terre Haute, Ind.: Moore-Langen Printing. 1978. This author continues the account begun by Sister Mary Borromeo Brown (No. 871), chronicling with a wealth of primary sources the events from the death of Mother Theodore Guerin and the tentative reorganization under Mother Mary Cecilia, through the establishment of schools and hospitals outside as well as inside Indiana, to the final Roman approbation of the rule and the recognition of the congregation as a pontifical institute.

903. Logue, Maria Kostka, Sister. *Sisters of St. Joseph of Philadelphia: A Century of Growth and Development, 1847–1947.* Westminster, Md.: Newman. 1950. A superior centennial history that gives a straightforward and fully documented treatment embodying a good deal of unpublished correspondence; illustrations, bibliography, and lists of missions.

904. Ludwig, M. Mileta, Sister. *A Chapter of Franciscan History: The*

Sisters of the Third Order of Saint Francis of Perpetual Adoration, 1849–1949. New York: Bookman. 1950. A documented account of the Bavarian religious who made their first American foundation in Wisconsin; well illustrated; a useful series of biographical sketches in an appendix as well as an essay on the sources.

905.   McCann, Mary Agnes, Sister. *The History of Mother Seton's Daughters: The Sisters of Charity of Cincinnati, Ohio, 1809–1923.* 3 vols. New York: Longmans, Green. 1917–1923. Based principally on sources in the community's archives, these large volumes give too detailed a treatment for the general reader.

906.   McCants, Dorothea Olga, Sister, trans. and ed. *They Came to Louisiana: Letters of a Catholic Mission, 1854–1882.* Baton Rouge: Louisiana State University Press. 1970. The 150 letters selected for publication describe the work of the Daughters of the Cross who came from France to establish schools in the central and northern parts of the state. They are sparsely annotated, but are provided with a brief introduction to each chronological section; many observations on the religious, cultural, social, economic, political, and military conditions of the period.

907.   McCarty, Mary Eva, Sister, O.P. *The Sinsinawa Dominicans: Outlines of Twentieth-Century Development, 1901–1949.* Sinsinawa, Wis.: St. Clara Convent. 1952. A carefully documented treatment of the recent history of a community founded in Wisconsin in 1847 by the Italian-born missionary, Samuel Mazzuchelli, O.P. (1806–1864).

908.   McDonald, M. Grace, Sister, O.S.B. *With Lamps Burning.* St. Joseph, Minn.: St. Benedict's Priory Press. 1957. A richly illustrated centennial volume on the Bavarian Benedictine Sisters who came to Minnesota in 1857; done largely from archival sources with commendable candor; maps, charts, and lists of the particular missions.

909.   McDowell, Catherine W., ed. *Letters from the Ursuline, 1852–1853.* San Antonio: Trinity University Press. 1977. This collection of letters written by Sisters Mary Patrick Joseph and Mary Augustine Joseph who left their convent in Waterford, Ireland, to start a mission in San Antonio gives their initial impressions of social and religious life in Texas.

910.   McEntee, Mary Veronica, Sister. *The Sisters of Mercy of Harrisburg, 1869–1939.* Philadelphia: Dolphin. 1939. A popular work with no reference to sources used.

911. McGill, Anna Blanche. *The Sisters of Charity of Nazareth, Kentucky*. New York: Encyclopedia Press. 1917. This centennial volume of one of the oldest (1812) sisterhoods in this country embodies considerable correspondence and a list of important dates, but there is no bibliography.

912. McGrath, M. Charles, Sister. *Yes Heard Round the World*. Paola, Kans.: Ursuline Sisters. 1978. This candid history of the Ursulines in Kansas focuses on the decision made in 1964 by the author, who was then superior, to experiment with reform of the habit, which attracted widespread attention and imitation by other religious congregations of women, and which led to further changes.

913. McNamee, Mary Dominica, Sister, S.N.D. of Namur. *Willamette Interlude*. Palo Alto: Pacific Books. 1959. The story of the coming of the first six Sisters of Notre Dame of Namur from Belgium to Oregon in 1844 (followed by the arrival of six more in August, 1847) and the community's early life in the Oregon Country; embodies considerable source materials from various ecclesiastical archives and has many pages of notes, bibliography, and index.

914. *Magnificat: A Centennial Record of the Congregation of the Sisters of Saint Felix (The Felician Sisters)*. Privately printed. 1955. This commemorative volume contains a historical sketch of the congregation, an account of its growth and development in Poland, the United States, and other countries of Europe and the Western Hemisphere, a description of its active apostolate, profiles of the founders and superiors general, and other information, as well as numerous illustrations.

915. Minogue, Anna Catherine. *Loretto: Annals of the Century*. New York: America Press. 1912. A popular illustrated work on the Sisters of Loretto who were founded in Kentucky in 1812.

916. _____. *Pages from a Hundred Years of Dominican History: The Story of the Congregation of Saint Catherine of Siena*. New York: Frederick Pustet. 1922. A popular work commemorating the centennial of another early Kentucky community founded in 1822.

917. Nolan, Charles E. *Bayou Carmel: The Sisters of Mount Carmel of Louisiana, 1833–1903*. Kenner, La.: The Author. 1977. This well-documented history of the initially French community which established schools in many towns in Louisiana originated as a doctoral dissertation at the Pontifical Gregorian University.

918.   *Not with Silver or Gold: A History of the Sisters of the Congregation of the Precious Blood, Salem Heights, Dayton, Ohio, 1834–1944.* Dayton: Sisters of Precious Blood. 1945. An anonymous account based for the most part on manuscript materials; these sisters came to Ohio from Switzerland in 1844 in response to a call for teachers for the children of German immigrant families.

919.   Owens, M. Lilliana, Sister, S.L. *Loretto in Missouri.* St. Louis: B. Herder. 1965. This history of the foundations of the Sisters of Loretto at the Foot of the Cross from 1823 to the middle of the twentieth century in the first state into which they expanded from Kentucky is also a contribution to the history of Catholic education.

920.   Palen, Imogene, Sister. *Fieldstones '76: The Story of the Founders of the Sisters of Saint Agnes.* [Oshkosh, Wis.:] Oshkosh Printers. 1976. This simple account of the Austrian priest Caspar Rehrl (1809–1881), who labored in Wisconsin and founded the Congregation of the Sisters of Saint Agnes of Fond du Lac in 1858, and of Mother Agnes (Anne Marie) Hazotte (1847–1905), who developed it, incorporates an abundance of primary sources.

921.   Roth, Mary Augustine, Sister, R.S.M. *Written in His Hands: The Sisters of Mercy of Cedar Rapids, Iowa, 1875–1975.* Cedar Rapids: Laurance Press. 1976. This schematic presentation of the leadership, organization, expansion, apostolate, formation, finances, constitutions, and membership of the congregation surpasses both in time covered and in scholarship the earlier work of Holland (No. 891).

922.   Sabourin, Justine, R.S.M. *The Amalgamation: A History of the Union of the Religious Sisters of Mercy of the United States of America.* St. Meinrad, Ind.: Abbey. c. 1976. This concatenation of long excerpts from letters with a connecting narrative chronicles the difficult process of uniting sixty independent motherhouses from 1927 to 1929.

923.   Savage, Mary Lucida, Sister. *The Congregation of Saint Joseph of Carondelet: A Brief Account of Its Origin and Its Work in the United States, 1650–1922.* Washington, D.C.: Catholic University of America Press. 1923. A Ph.D. thesis with the customary features, including lists of the congregation's houses in the United States.

924.   Semple, Henry C., S.J. *The Ursulines in New Orleans and Our Lady of Prompt Succor: A Record of Two Centuries, 1727–1925.* New York: P. J. Kenedy. 1925. A popular account of the first sisters to establish a convent (1727) in what was later to be the United States.

925. Sharkey, Mary Agnes, Sister. *The New Jersey Sisters of Charity*. 3 vols. New York: Longmans, Green. 1933. One of the most ambitious works of this kind; a detailed treatment based in part on archival sources and embracing the years 1859 to 1933; includes a good deal of biographical material on Mother Mary Xavier Mehegan (1824–1915), the foundress, as well as sketches of the individual missions of the community.

926. Thomas, M. Evangeline, Sister. *Footprints on the Frontier: A History of the Sisters of St. Joseph, Concordia, Kansas*. Westminster, Md.: Newman. 1948. A closely documented work on a congregation whose work in Kansas began with the arrival of six sisters from Rochester, New York, in June, 1883; shows the hand of the trained historian.

927. Walsh, Marie de Lourdes, Sister. *The Sisters of Charity of New York, 1809–1959*. 3 vols. New York: Fordham University Press. 1960. A handsome set of volumes with full references to sources, numerous illustrations, and index, which gives the story great amplitude on both education and charity levels.

928. Wand, Augustin C., S.J., and Sister M. Lilliana Owens, S.L., eds. *Documents: Nerinckx—Kentucky—Loretto, 1804–1851, in Archives Propaganda Fide, Rome*. St. Louis: Mary Loretto. 1972. This collection of documents (either originally written in English or translated into English) is poorly edited and lacks a historical introduction, adequate annotations, cross references, and index, but it illustrates the origins of religious orders on the frontier; deals with the long process of securing the Holy See's approbation of the Constitutions and Rules of the Sisters of Loretto.

VI. EDUCATION

THE LIST OF BOOKS under this heading is in no sense intended to be complete; it is meant merely to suggest some of the better works written in one of the most neglected areas of American Catholic history. In regard to the fairly numerous available items commemorating various anniversaries of institutions or of teaching communities, several in recent years have shown a marked improvement over the purely external and pietistic accounts which have in the past too often characterized these illustrated chronicles. Were it not for published doctoral theses, however, the scientific literature in this field would be barren indeed; and, as is to be expected, a number of the latter listed below are not free from the immaturity that is so frequently found in this category of published research. In addition to the following works on educational history it is suggested that the student consult certain items listed under "Men's Communities," e.g., Angelus Gabriel, Barry, and Beckman (Nos. 808, 811, 814).

A. GENERAL

929.   Bouquillon, Thomas. *Education: To Whom Does It Belong?* 2nd ed. Baltimore: John Murphy. 1892. A brochure that seeks to explain the respective rights to educate of parents, Church, and State; this work set off an acrimonious discussion among American Catholics in the 1890's on the State's relation to education.

930.   Bowler, Mary Mariella, Sister. *A History of Catholic Colleges for Women in the United States of America.* Washington, D.C.: Catholic University of America Press. 1933. A Ph.D. thesis in education that surveys the approximately seventy-five institutions founded between 1896 and 1932.

931.   Buetow, Harold A. *Of Singular Benefit: The Story of Catholic Education in the United States.* New York: Macmillan. 1970. This comprehensive survey, arranged topically within each of six chronological periods from the colonial missions to the 1960's, fo-

cuses on parochial schools. It sets its subject in the secular context, but does not provide new insights or interpretations. The only recent general treatment of American Catholic education, it supersedes Nos. 932, 933, and 934.

932.   Burns, James A., C.S.C. *The Catholic School System in the United States*. New York: Benziger Bros. 1908. *The Principles, Origin and Establishment of the Catholic School System in the United States*. 1912. Reprint. New York: Arno. 1969. This history of American Catholic education up to 1840 is now out of date because of subsequent publications.

933.   _____ . *The Growth and Development of the Catholic School System in the United States*. New York: Benziger Bros. 1912. Reprint. New York: Arno. 1969. This volume, covering the period from 1840 to 1910, is now obsolete.

934.   Burns, James A., C.S.C., and Bernard J. Kohlbrenner. *A History of Catholic Education in the United States*. New York: Benziger Bros. 1937. A condensation of Burns (Nos. 932, 933) brought down to date for textbook purposes; a considerable number of errors requires that it be used with some caution. See also No. 931.

935.   Cassidy, Francis P. *Catholic College Foundations and Development in the United States, 1677–1850*. Washington, D.C.: Catholic University of America Press. 1924. A Ph.D. thesis in education that sketches early Catholic efforts for higher education in this country.

936.   Conway, James, S.J. *The State Last: A Study of Doctor Bouquillon's Pamphlet*. New York: Frederick Pustet. 1892. One of a number of pamphlets written in answer to Bouquillon (No. 929); maintains that according to natural law—prescinding from the prerogatives of the Catholic Church—the right to educate belongs exclusively to the parent; the State is here cast solely in the role of a promoter and patron of education.

937.   Dunn, William Kailer. *What Happened to Religious Education? The Decline of Religious Teaching in the Public Elementary School, 1776–1861*. Baltimore: Johns Hopkins Press. 1958. A Ph.D. thesis in education that treats *inter alia* the Catholic involvement in the controversies over this issue before the Civil War. Although in the main it is based on printed sources, a considerable number of unpublished materials have been used, among them the Whitfield, Eccleston, and Kenrick Papers in the archives of the Archdiocese of Baltimore.

938.   Ellis, John Tracy. *American Catholics and the Intellectual Life*. Chicago: Heritage Foundation. 1956. An appeal for a reevaluation of Catholic efforts in view of the relatively poor showing in scholarship; this brochure appeared originally as an article in *Thought* (Autumn, 1955) and gave rise to a lively controversy.

939.   Erbacher, Sebastian A., O.F.M. *Catholic Higher Education for Men in the United States, 1850–1866*. Washington, D.C.: Catholic University of America Press. 1931. A Ph.D. thesis in education that continues Cassidy (No. 935); contains a list of these institutions.

940.   Evans, John Whitney. *The Newman Movement: Roman Catholics in American Higher Education, 1883–1971*. Notre Dame: University of Notre Dame Press. 1980. This work of thorough scholarship traces the troubled evolution of the pastoral care and religious education of Catholic students in secular colleges and universities from the beginnings to the development of "campus ministry."

941.   Gabel, Richard J. *Public Funds for Church and Private Schools*. Washington, D.C.: Catholic University of America Press. 1937. A highly detailed Ph.D thesis in education, with a bibliography of more than fifty pages.

942.   Gabert, Glen. *In Hoc Signo? A Brief History of Catholic Parochial Education in America*. Port Washington, N.Y.: Kennikat. 1973. This rapid survey, which studies the contents of "official documents" and their effects on the development of Catholic primary schools, contains some questionable interpretations and conclusions.

943.   [Galvin],Catharine Frances, Sister, S.S.J. *The Convent School of French Origin in the United States, 1727–1843*. Philadelphia: University of Pennsylvania Press. 1936. This doctoral dissertation traces separately the beginnings and evolution of the convent schools established by the Ursulines (New Orleans), Religious of the Sacred Heart (St. Charles, Missouri), Sisters of St. Joseph (Carondelet, Missouri), Sisters of Providence (St. Mary-of-the-Woods, Indiana), and Sisters of the Holy Cross (Notre Dame, Indiana), and studies collectively and comparatively their administration, curricula, and extra-curricular activities.

944.   Goebel, Edmund J. *A Study of Catholic Secondary Education during the Colonial Period up to the First Plenary Council of Baltimore, 1852*. Washington, D.C.: Catholic University of America Press. 1936. A Ph.D. thesis in education which presents a brief survey to

the middle of the nineteenth century; helpful lists of these schools by states are included.

945.   Holaind, René I., S.J. *The Parent First: An Answer to Dr. Bouquillon's Query.* New York: Benziger Bros. 1891. One of the more notable replies to No. 929; stresses the State's right to educate as deriving from the parents.

946.   Kaiser, M. Laurina, Sister, O.S.B. *The Development of the Concept and Function of the Catholic Elementary School in the American Parish.* Washington, D.C.: Catholic University of America Press. 1955. An analysis of the conciliar legislation and episcopal pronouncements of the hierarchy from 1790 to the present; a Ph.D. thesis in education.

947.   McDonald, Lloyd P., S.S. *The Seminary Movement in the United States: Projects, Foundations, and Early Developments, 1784–1833.* Washington, D.C.: Catholic University of America Press. 1927. A Ph.D. thesis in education which sketches briefly the institutions founded for the education of the clergy up to the Second Provincial Council of Baltimore.

948.   McCluskey, Neil G., S.J., ed. *Catholic Education in America: A Documentary History.* New York: Bureau of Publications, Teachers College, Columbia University. 1965. An introductory essay on "America and the Catholic School" precedes a collection of thirteen statements, given in full or in part, ranging in time from 1792 to 1950.

949.   McLaughlin, Raymond, Sister, O.S.B. *A History of State Legislation affecting Private Elementary and Secondary Schools in the United States, 1870–1945.* Washington, D.C.: Catholic University of America Press. 1946. A Ph.D. thesis in education; a lengthy appendix gives the constitutional provisions and state laws relating to these schools as they were in force in 1945.

950.   Meiring, Bernard Julius. *Educational Aspects of the Legislation of the Councils of Baltimore, 1829–1884.* New York: Arno. 1978. This Ph.D. dissertation, written in 1963 at the University of California, Berkeley (the typescript of which is here reproduced), is an analysis of the conciliar decrees in light of contemporary conditions of American society and the public schools, with some questionable interpretations.

951.   Morris, William S., S.S. *The Seminary Movement in the United*

States: Projects, Foundations, and Early Development, 1833–1866. Washington, D.C.: Catholic University of America Press. 1932. A Ph.D. thesis in education that continues McDonald (No. 947) to the Second Plenary Council of Baltimore.

952.   O'Dea, Thomas F. *American Catholic Dilemma: An Inquiry into the Intellectual Life.* New York: Sheed and Ward. 1958. A brief but challenging essay by a sociologist on the background and causes for the failure of American Catholics to show distinction in intellectual matters proportionate to their numbers.

953.   O'Neill, James M. *Religion and Education under the Constitution.* New York: Harper and Bros. 1949. A somewhat polemical analysis of the meaning of the First Amendment as applied to Church-State matters in education, with particular reference to the Everson and McCollum Cases; the author holds that the Supreme Court has substituted its own subjective interpretation of the amendment for the original meaning intended by the framers of the Bill of Rights.

954.   Power, Edward J. *Catholic Education in America: A History.* New York: Appleton-Century-Crofts. 1972. Divided into three periods (1786–1870, 1870–1940, 1940–1970), this thorough treatment of the dominant themes is supported by references to numerous published primary and secondary sources; the interpretation of persons, institutions, and events is judicious and impartial, except for the unduly harsh criticism of the bishops in the first period.

955.   _____ . *A History of Catholic Higher Education in the United States.* Milwaukee: Bruce. 1958. This earlier general work has certain weaknesses, e.g., regarding the relations of Catholic institutions to the accreditation movement and the last generation of these schools.

956.   Reilly, Daniel F., O.P. *The School Controversy, 1891–1893.* Washington, D.C.: Catholic University of America Press. 1943. Reprint. New York: Arno and the New York Times. 1969. A Ph.D. thesis that helped to open up a new field of investigation by the hitherto unpublished evidence brought to light; the author's leaning to Archbishop Ireland and the lack of fuller documentation for the side of Archbishop Corrigan detract somewhat from the balance of the treatment; appendices contain the texts of important documents.

957.   Steinberg, Stephen. *The Academic Melting Pot: Catholics and Jews in American Higher Education.* New York: McGraw-Hill. 1974. This work, originally a doctoral dissertation in sociology at the

University of California, Berkeley, based primarily on survey research but also historically informed, supports the hypothesis of difficulties in assimilation in explaining past Catholic deficiencies compared with Jewish achievement in the intellectual sphere.

B. REGIONAL STUDIES

958.   Bollig, Richard J., O.M.Cap. *History of Catholic Education in Kansas, 1836–1932*. Washington, D.C.: Catholic University of America Press. 1933. Records the development from early Indian schools to a system embracing 250 schools among a relatively poor and rural minority; a Ph.D. thesis in education. See No. 960.

959.   Connaughton, Edward A. *A History of Educational Legislation and Administration in the Archdiocese of Cincinnati*. Washington, D.C.: Catholic University of America Press. 1946. This Ph.D. thesis in education traces the history of Catholic schools in southern Ohio from 1825 to 1944 and analyzes the conciliar legislation that made the Province of Cincinnati one of the foremost in the country for its parochial schools. See No. 960.

960.   Connors, Edward M. *Church-State Relationships in Education in the State of New York*. Washington, D.C.: Catholic University of America Press. 1951. A Ph.D. thesis in education embracing the years 1825–1940; employs considerable archival material as well as printed sources; one of a series on Church-State relations in education in various states done by doctoral candidates of the Department of Education of the Catholic University of America; a continuation of Mahoney (No. 971). For others in the series, see Nos. 958, 959, 963–967, 969–974, 977.

961.   Donaghy, Thomas J., F.S.C. *Philadelphia's Finest: A History of Education in the Catholic Archdiocese, 1692–1970*. Philadelphia: American Catholic Historical Society. 1972. In spite of the author's obviously careful research, the scholarly value of this monograph is diminished by stylistic faults, factual inaccuracies, unsupported assertions, and certain ambiguities and omissions.

962.   Driscoll, Justin A. *With Faith and Vision: Schools of the Archdiocese of Dubuque, 1836–1966*. Dubuque: Bureau of Education, Archdiocese of Dubuque. 1967. A series of historical sketches of the elementary, private, interparochial high schools, superintendents of schools, and teaching communities.

963.   Gallagher, Marie Patrice, Sister. *The History of Catholic Elementary Education in the Diocese of Buffalo, 1847–1944.* Washington, D.C.: Catholic University of America Press. 1945. A survey of the parochial elementary schools from the establishment of the diocese; a Ph.D. thesis in education. See No. 960.

964.   Heffernan, Arthur J. *A History of Catholic Education in Connecticut.* Washington, D.C.: Catholic University of America Press. 1936. A Ph.D. thesis in education that surveys the century from c. 1835 to 1935; from printed sources only. See No. 960.

965.   Hurley, Mark J. *Church-State Relationships in Education in California.* Washington, D.C.: Catholic University of America Press. 1948. One of a series of Ph.D. theses in education on the subject of Church-State relations in various states. See No. 960.

966.   Jones, William H. *The History of Catholic Education in the State of Colorado.* Washington, D.C.: Catholic University of America Press. 1955. This large volume makes use of some archival materials; a Ph.D. thesis in education. See No. 960.

967.   Kucera, Daniel W., O.S.B. *Church-State Relationships in Education in Illinois.* Washington, D.C.: Catholic University of America Press. 1955. Another in the series of Ph.D. theses in education on Church-State relationships. See No. 960.

968.   Lannie, Vincent P. *Public Money and Parochial Education: Bishop Hughes, Governor Seward, and the New York School Controversy.* Cleveland: Press of Case Western Reserve University. 1968. This detailed account of the highly publicized efforts to obtain state aid for Catholic schools in New York in 1840–1842 through political action, and of the resulting Maclay Act, underplays the strong tradition of anti-Catholic bigotry and other nativist issues in the city.

969.   Leary, Mary Ancilla, Sister. *The History of Catholic Education in the Diocese of Albany.* Washington, D.C.: Catholic University of America Press. 1957. Based in part on archival materials, this Ph.D. thesis in education relates in detail—with numerous and elaborate tables and charts—a story that began in 1828. See No. 960.

970.   McCormick, Leo J. *Church-State Relationships in Education in Maryland.* Washington, D.C.: Catholic University of America Press. 1942. A Ph.D. thesis which belongs to the same series as Connors (No. 960) et al.

971.   Mahoney, Charles J. *The Relation of the State to Religious Education in Early New York, 1633–1825.* Washington, D.C.: Catholic University of America Press. 1941. A Ph.D. thesis in education based upon printed sources. Continued by Connors (No. 960).

972.   Mason, Mary Paul, Sister. *Church-State Relationships in Education in Connecticut, 1633–1953.* Washington, D.C.: Catholic University of America Press. 1953. See No. 960.

973.   Montay, Mary Innocenta, Sister. *The History of Catholic Secondary Education in the Archdiocese of Chicago.* Washington, D.C.: Catholic University of America Press. 1953. This large volume—a Ph.D. thesis in education—makes use of a considerable amount of unpublished material. See No. 960.

974.   North, William E. *Catholic Education in Southern California.* Washington, D.C.: Catholic University of America Press. 1936. The story is sketched from the educational features of the eighteenth-century missions to date; a Ph.D. thesis in education. See No. 960.

975.   Rouse, Michael Francis [Brother Bede, C.F.X.]. *A Study of the Development of Negro Education under Catholic Auspices in Maryland and the District of Columbia.* Baltimore: Johns Hopkins Press. 1935. A story that begins in 1818 and is developed in considerable detail, with convenient lists of the schools in question, samples of the curricula, etc.; a doctoral thesis in education.

976.   Sanders, James W. *The Education of an Urban Minority: Catholics in Chicago, 1833–1965.* New York: Oxford University Press. 1977. In this well-researched history of the world's largest Catholic school system under the administration of a single diocese the author, using a highly statistical and generally impersonal method, has focused his attention on the 1920's and on the archbishop of the interwar period, Cardinal George Mundelein; deals mainly with elementary schools but gives proportionate space to secondary schools; also traces the efforts of each nationality to establish ethnic parishes and schools.

977.   Sullivan, Mary Xaveria, Sister. *The History of Catholic Secondary Education in the Archdiocese of Boston.* Washington, D.C.: Catholic University of America Press. 1946. A Ph.D. thesis in education; some effort was made to find archival material, but for the most part the study is based on printed sources. See No. 960.

978.   Yeakel, Mary Agnes, Sister. *The Nineteenth Century Educational Contribution of the Sisters of Charity of Saint Vincent de Paul in Virginia.* Baltimore: Johns Hopkins Press. 1939. A thesis for the Ed.D. degree that traces the subject from 1833 to date; some hitherto unpublished sources are used.

C. INSTITUTIONS

979.   Ahern, Patrick H. *The Catholic University of America, 1887–1896: The Rectorship of John J. Keane.* Washington, D.C.: Catholic University of America Press. 1949. A candid and informative A.M. thesis done largely from archival sources. Continues Ellis (No. 998).

980.   Angelo, Mark V., O.F.M. *The History of St. Bonaventure University.* St. Bonaventure, N.Y.: Franciscan Institute. 1961. This doctoral dissertation, written at Fordham University, traces the development of the institution, opened as a college and seminary in 1859 at Allegany, New York, by Italian Franciscans, through its first century.

981.   Barry, Colman, J., O.S.B. *The Catholic University of America, 1903–1909: The Rectorship of Denis J. O'Connell.* Washington, D.C.: Catholic University of America Press. 1950. This A.M. thesis—a companion to Ahern and Hogan (Nos. 979, 1006)—makes a real contribution to the educational problems of the period by its thorough archival research and candid spirit.

982.   Battersby, William John [Brother Clair Stanislaus, F.S.C.]. *The Christian Brothers in Memphis: A Chronicle of One Hundred Years, 1871–1971.* Memphis: Christian Brothers College. 1971. This moderately documented and abundantly illustrated portrayal of Christian Brothers College refrains from critical evaluations.

983.   Brady, Charles A. *The First Hundred Years: Canisius College, 1870–1970.* Buffalo: Canisius College. 1969. As an institutional history this book lacks precise chronology, clear organization, essential information, references to sources, and an adequate index. The author indulges in wit and poetry and wanders into digressions, but ignores the larger issues of higher education.

984.   Brann, Henry A. *History of the American College.* New York: Benziger. 1910. A popular work now superseded by McNamara (No. 1016).

985. Cameron, Mary David, Sister. *The College of Notre Dame of Maryland, 1895–1945.* New York: Declan X. McMullen. 1947. A brief documented account of the first half-century of the oldest American Catholic college for women.

986. Casey, Mary Celestine, Sister, and Sister Mary Edmond Ferm. *Loretto in the Rockies.* Denver: Loretto Heights College. 1943. A popular account of a school that opened at its present site as an academy in 1891 and developed into a college for women in 1918.

987. Connelly, James F. *St. Charles Seminary, Philadelphia: A History of the Theological Seminary of Saint Charles Borromeo, Overbrook, Philadelphia, Pennsylvania, 1832–1979.* Philadelphia: St. Charles Seminary. 1979. This scholarly study covers every aspect of the topic and supersedes George E. O'Donnell's two volumes (No. 1024).

988. Covert, James T. *A Point of Pride: The University of Portland Story.* Portland: University of Portland Press. 1976. The history of the institution opened by the Congregation of Holy Cross in 1890 as Columbia College is related to contemporary social and political conditions in Oregon. The volume is large in format and abundantly illustrated.

989. Cunningham, Thomas W. *The Summit of a Century: The Centennial Story of Seton Hall University, 1856–1956.* South Orange, N.J.: Seton Hall University Press. 1956. An illustrated brochure of seven brief chapters, written by various members of the faculty and edited by one of the university's vice-presidents.

990. Daley, John M., S.J. *Georgetown University: Origin and Early Years.* Washington, D.C.: Georgetown University Press. 1957. Originally a Ph.D. thesis, this volume on the first half-century of the oldest Catholic college for men in the United States is a work of real scholarship; awarded the John Gilmary Shea Prize of the American Catholic Historical Association in 1958. Continued by Durkin (No. 995).

991. Deferrari, Roy J. *Memoirs of the Catholic University of America, 1918–1960.* Boston: St. Paul Editions. 1962. These forthright, topically arranged recollections of an energetic and progressive administrator are inevitably characterized by his subjective judgments of persons and programs.

992.   DeFrees, Madeline [Sister Mary Gilbert, S.N.J.M.]. *Later Thoughts from the Springs of Silence*. Indianapolis: Bobbs-Merrill. 1962. An informal memoir of Holy Names College, Spokane, Washington.

993.   Donaghy, Thomas J., F.S.C. *Conceived in Crisis: A History of LaSalle College*. Philadelphia: La Salle College. 1966. An "official" history with little critical approach.

994.   Durkin, Joseph T., S.J. *Georgetown University: First in the Nation's Capital*. Garden City, N.Y.: Doubleday. 1964. This slender, popular, illustrated volume commemorated the 175th anniversary of the university's founding.

995.   _____ . *Georgetown University: The Middle Years, 1840–1900*. Washington, D.C.: Georgetown University Press. 1963. A documented study which at times exaggerates the importance of men and movements in the institution's history. Continues Daley (No. 990).

996.   Dyer, Edward R., S.S. *Dunwoodie Letter*. Baltimore: Privately printed. 1906. This lengthy document, with English and French facing pages, is addressed to the Sulpicians in the United States to explain the withdrawal of five members of the Society of St. Sulpice, all of the faculty of St. Joseph's Seminary; with an appendix entitled, "A Statement of the Facts and Circumstances that Led to the With- drawal of Five of the Professors of Dunwoodie Seminary from the Society of St. Sulpice," signed by James F. Driscoll.

997.   Easby-Smith, James S. *Georgetown University in the District of Columbia, 1789–1907*. 2 vols. New York: Lewis. 1907. Now super- seded by Daley and Durkin (Nos. 990, 995) for the period up to 1900; Volume II useful for biographical sketches of faculty members and alumni.

998.   Ellis, John Tracy. *The Formative Years of the Catholic University of America*. Washington, D.C.: American Catholic Historical Associ- ation. 1946. This volume, done almost entirely from archival materi- als, places the institution in the American educational framework of the second half of the nineteenth century, and carries the story to the opening of the university in November, 1889; forms a series with the works of Ahern, Barry, and Hogan (Nos. 979, 981, 1006).

999.   Faherty, William B., S.J. *Better the Dream: Saint Louis— University and Community, 1818–1968*. St. Louis: St. Louis Univer-

sity. 1968. This sesquicentennial history of the institution founded by Bishop Louis Dubourg and taken over and reorganized by the Jesuits in 1829 is a scholarly, thorough, and well-written treatment.

1000. Gabriels, Henry. *Historical Sketch of St. Joseph's Provincial Seminary, Troy, New York.* New York: United States Catholic Historical Society. 1905. A brief popular account of the seminary that served the Province of New York from 1864 to 1896 by the second Bishop of Ogdensburg who, during the years 1864–1892, was first a professor and then president of the seminary; a biographical sketch of Gabriels and of the earlier New York seminaries by Charles G. Herbermann is included.

1001. *Golden Jubilee of St. Charles' College Near Ellicott City, Maryland, 1848–1898.* Baltimore: John Murphy. 1898. A similar volume to that for Saint Mary's Seminary, Baltimore (No. 1022), published in 1891.

1002. Hamilton, Raphael N., S.J. *The Story of Marquette University.* Milwaukee: Marquette University Press. 1953. An illustrated account of the external development of what is now the largest Catholic university in the country by one of its professors of history.

1003. Hammon, Walter, O.F.M. *The First Bonaventure Men: The Early History of St. Bonaventure University and the Allegany Franciscans.* St. Bonaventure: St. Bonaventure University. 1958. A series of essays on the school founded at Allegany in 1856 by a small group of Italian Franciscans; popular in character and superseded by Angelo (No. 980).

1004. Harney, Thomas E. *Canisius College: The First Nine Years, 1870–1879.* New York: Vantage. 1971. Based on published sources, written in a prosaic style, and filled with inconsequential minutiae and irrelevant digressions, this disproportionately long study of the beginnings of the college founded by Jesuits of the German Province in Buffalo can hardly be called a historical treatment.

1005. Hill, Walter H., S.J. *Historical Sketch of the St. Louis University.* St. Louis: Patrick Fox. 1879. Considering the early date, this is a fairly good work; it was written to commemorate the institution's golden jubilee, but is now superseded by Faherty (No. 999).

1006. Hogan, Peter E., S.S.J. *The Catholic University of America, 1896–1903: The Rectorship of Thomas J. Conaty.* Washington, D.C.: Catholic University of America Press. 1949. An A.M. thesis that gives a comparable treatment to Ahern and Barry (Nos. 979, 981) for the administration of the second rector.

1007.   Hope, Arthur J., C.S.C. *Notre Dame: One Hundred Years.* Notre Dame: University of Notre Dame Press. 1943. A semipopular centennial history that makes use of some archival material.

1008.   Howlett, William J. *Historical Tribute to St. Thomas Seminary at Poplar Neck, Near Bardstown, Kentucky.* St. Louis: B. Herder. 1906. A popular appreciation, with illustrations, of the first seminary established west of the Allegheny Mountains.

1009.   Johnson, Peter Leo. *Halcyon Days: Story of St. Francis Seminary, Milwaukee, 1856–1956.* Milwaukee: Bruce. 1956. A richly illustrated centennial volume based on a wide use of primary source materials by the seminary's professor of church history.

1010.   Keenan, Angela Elizabeth, Sister, S.N.D. of Namur. *Three against the Wind: The Founding of Trinity College, Washington, D.C.* Westminster, Md.: Christian Classics. 1973. The lives of Sisters Julia McGroarty, Mary Euphrasia Taylor, and Raphael Pike and their labors to lay the foundations and shape the pattern of this college for women from the late 1890's to the 1920's are sympathetically presented.

1011.   Kelly, Martin J., and James M. Kirwin. *History of Mt. St. Mary's Seminary of the West, Cincinnati, Ohio.* Cincinnati: Keating. 1894. A large illustrated volume covering the first sixty years, 1834–1894, of the major seminary of the Archdiocese of Cincinnati; popular in character.

1012.   Kenny, Michael, S.J. *Catholic Culture in Alabama: Centenary Story of Spring Hill College, 1830–1930.* New York: America Press. 1931. One of the very few books on Catholic education in the South, although not a scientific work; illustrated.

1013.   Lawler, Loretto R. *Full Circle: The Story of the National Catholic School of Social Service, 1918–1947.* Washington, D.C.: Catholic University of America Press. 1951. Beginning with the founding of a training school for Catholic women war workers in the District of Columbia, this history, based on primary sources but lacking footnotes, covers the entire existence of the school from its opening in 1921 to its merger with the School of Social Service of the Catholic University of America.

1014. Lukacs, John. *A Sketch of the History of Chestnut Hill College, 1924–1974*. Philadelphia: Chestnut Hill College. 1975. In this illustrated survey of the institution founded by the Sisters of Saint Joseph, a distinguished member of the faculty presents in microcosm the changes that occurred in Catholic higher education for women during that half-century.

1015. McKevitt, Gerald, S.J. *The University of Santa Clara: A History, 1851–1977*. Stanford: Stanford University Press. 1979. This well-documented and illustrated book traces the evolution of the first institution of higher learning in California from its founding as a college by Italian Jesuits, through its decline at the turn of the century, to its recent compromise between secular standards and Catholic values, in the context of contemporary Catholic higher education.

1016. McNamara, Robert F. *The American College in Rome, 1855–1955*. Rochester: Christopher. 1956. One of the best histories of an American Catholic educational institution; relates the story in minute detail and contains over 100 pages of highly informative footnotes and appendices, giving the text of the institution's charters and a full student register.

1017. McNamee, Mary Dominica, Sister, S.N.D. of Namur. *Light in the Valley: The Story of California's Catholic College of Notre Dame*. Berkeley: Howell-North. 1968. Continuing the account begun in her earlier work, *Willamette Interlude* (No. 913), the author relates with scholarly objectivity and literary grace the history both of the college, from its origins in the boarding school for girls opened at San Jose in 1851 to its relocation in Belmont in 1923, and of the California Province of the Sisters of Notre Dame.

1018. Meagher, Walter J., S.J., and William J. Grattan. *The Spires of Fenwick: A History of the College of the Holy Cross, 1843–1963*. New York: Vantage. 1966. This work received praise for its coverage of the facts, but was criticized for its failure to relate Holy Cross's story to general trends in American higher education.

1019. Medina Ascensio, Luis, S.J. *Historia del Seminario de Montezuma: Sus precedentes, Fundación, y Consolidación, 1910–1953*. Mexico City: Editorial Jus. 1962. The author treats first the persecution of the Church in Mexico and the two seminaries conducted consecutively in Castroville, Texas, between 1915 and 1930, and then the Seminary of Montezuma, which was opened in 1937 near Las Vegas,

New Mexico. The history traces the development of the idea of an interdiocesan seminary outside Mexico and illustrates the cooperation between the Mexican and North American hierarchies.

1020. _____ , ed. *Montezuma Intimo: Su escenario, su gente, su vida. Colección de artículos de distintos autores y épocas.* Mexico City: Editorial Jus. 1962. Various aspects of seminary life are vividly portrayed in these essays, memoirs, and poems.

1021. Melina, Mary M., and Edward F. X. McSweeny. *The Story of the Mountain: Mount Saint Mary's College and Seminary.* 2 vols. Emmitsburg, Md.: Weekly Chronicle. 1911. This oddly assorted work embodies a good deal of information, but it is poorly written and edited; there is need for an up-to-date history of this second oldest Catholic college for men in the United States.

1022. *Memorial Volume of the Centenary of St. Mary's Seminary of St. Sulpice.* Baltimore: John Murphy. 1891. Useful for lists of names of professors and students of the first Catholic seminary in the United States, but not a real history of the institution.

1023. Morrison, Betty L. *A History of Our Lady of Holy Cross College, New Orleans, Louisiana.* Gretna, La.: Her Publishing. 1977. This institutional history is traced back to the school which the Sisters Marianites of the Holy Cross opened on the premises of their orphanage in 1853 and is continued through the stages of an academy and a normal school, but it is mainly devoted to the period since 1938, when a four-year college program was begun.

1024. O'Donnell, George E. *St. Charles Borromeo Seminary, Overbrook.* 2 vols. Philadelphia: St. Charles Seminary. 1943–1953. *Saint Charles Seminary, Philadelphia.* Philadelphia: American Catholic Historical Society of Philadelphia. 1963. A series of popular essays on institutional development after 1832 with useful lists of alumni, but not adequate as a history of the major seminary of the Archdiocese of Philadelphia; Volume II contains lists of names and pictures of priests ordained between 1943 and 1953. It is superseded by Connelly (No. 987).

1025. Sauter, John D. *The American College of Louvain, 1857–1898.* Louvain: Publications Universitaires. 1959. A thoroughly documented account of the institution's first forty years, done as a dissertation for the doctorate in history at Louvain.

1026.   Scanlon, Arthur J. *St. Joseph's Seminary, Dunwoodie, New York, 1896–1921: With an Account of the Other Seminaries of New York.* New York: United States Catholic Historical Society. 1922. Scarcely more than a chronicle on the major seminary of the Archdiocese of New York and its predecessors.

1027.   Schlereth, Thomas J. *The University of Notre Dame: A Portrait of Its History and Campus.* Notre Dame: University of Notre Dame Press. 1976. This rather unique volume, a contribution to educational and social history, contains not only a narrative extending from 1842 to 1976 but also more than 430 photographs, reconstructed maps, lithographs, and architectural drawings, as well as appendices on special subjects.

1028.   Schoenberg, Wilfred P., S.J. *Gonzaga University: Seventy-five Years, 1887–1962.* Spokane: Gonzaga University. 1963. Written with humor and candor, this is a lengthy history of the institution founded by Father Joseph Cataldo, S.J.; it is well documented and presented against the background of contemporary social and economic conditions.

1029.   Sexton, John E., and Arthur J. Riley. *History of Saint John's Seminary, Brighton.* Boston: Roman Catholic Archbishop of Boston. 1945. One of the best histories of American Catholic seminaries; notable for its intelligent efforts at interpretation rather than the mere chronicling of facts.

1030.   Shea, John Gilmary. *Memorial of the First Centenary of Georgetown College, D.C., Comprising a History of Georgetown University.* New York: P. F. Collier. 1891. A useful volume in its day, but now superseded by Daley and Durkin (Nos. 990, 995).

1031.   Sister of Notre Dame. *An Historical Sketch of Trinity College, Washington, D.C., 1897–1925.* Washington, D.C.: Trinity College. 1925. This volume is largely a reprint of the silver jubilee story that appeared in the *Trinity College Record* in 1922, with the account brought down to 1925; it is a slender volume with no index; cf. Keenan (No. 1010).

1032.   Sullivan, Eleanore C. *Georgetown Visitation since 1799.* Privately printed. 1975. The history of this preparatory school for girls in Washington, D.C., is presented in the context of contemporary political and social conditions, in some instances with regrettable brevity; it is profusely illustrated.

1033.   Van der Heyden, J. *The Louvain American College, 1857 –1907*. Louvain: Fr. and R. Ceutrick. 1909. A semipopular treatment of the first half-century by one of its professors; although it embodies some correspondence, not a scientific work. It is superseded by Sauter (No. 1025).

1034.   White, James Addison. *The Founding of Cliff Haven: Early Years of the Catholic Summer School of America*. New York: United States Catholic Historical Society. 1950. A competent A.M. thesis that treats one of the few efforts made by American Catholics along the lines of Chautauqua.

VII. SPECIAL STUDIES

A. COLONIZATION

1035.   Henthorne, Mary Evangela, Sister, B.V.M. *The Irish Catholic Colonization Association of the United States: Its Origin and Development under the Leadership of the Rt. Rev. John Lancaster Spalding, Bishop of Peoria, President of the Association, 1879–1892.* Champaign, Ill.: Twin City. 1932. Part of a Ph.D. thesis on the colonization work of the first Bishop of Peoria done under the direction of the late Marcus L. Hansen.

1036.   Kelly, Mary Gilbert, Sister, O.P. *Catholic Immigrant Colonization Projects in the United States, 1815–1860.* New York: United States Catholic Historical Society. 1939. An able Ph.D. thesis, done, like the one above, under the direction of Hansen.

1037.   Shannon, James P. *Catholic Colonization on the Western Frontier.* New Haven: Yale University Press. 1957. Reprint. New York: Arno. 1976. A scholarly treatment of a somewhat neglected aspect of American Catholic history that concentrates on the Irish colonies in Minnesota; done originally as a Ph.D. thesis.

1038.   Spalding, John L. *The Religious Mission of the Irish People and Catholic Colonization.* New York: Catholic Publication Society. 1880. Reprint. New York: Arno. 1978. A popular work written by the president of the Irish Colonization Association with a view to promoting Catholic colonization in the West among urban Irish immigrants.

B. CONCILIAR AND LEGAL STUDIES

1039.   *Acta et Decreta Concilii Plenarii Baltimorensis Tertii: A.D. MDCCCLXXXIV.* Baltimore: John Murphy. 1886. Contains the general minutes, official documents, and decrees of the plenary council of November–December, 1884, as finally approved by the Holy See.

1040.   *Acta et Decreta Concilii Plenarii Baltimorensis Tertii in Ecclesia Metropolitana Baltimorensi Habiti a die IX. Novembris usque ad diem VII. Decembris A.D. MXCCCLXXXIV.* Baltimore: John Murphy. 1884. This edition of the 1884 council was printed for private circulation and includes the minutes of the private congregations. For the preliminary Latin documents, privately printed for the participants' use before the council opened, see John Tracy Ellis, *The Life of James Cardinal Gibbons* (No. 615), I, 210–211, n. 19–20; 231, n. 93; II, 656.

1041.   Barrett, John D., S.S. *A Comparative Study of the Councils of Baltimore and the Code of Canon Law.* Washington, D.C.: Catholic University of America Press. 1932. A thesis for the J.C.D. degree which shows how the universal code of 1918 affected the Baltimore legislation passed between 1829 and 1884; a number of other studies in this series from the university's School of Canon Law will be found helpful for legal aspects of the history of the American Church.

1042.   Casey, Thomas F. *The Sacred Congregation de Propaganda Fide and the Revision of the First Provincial Council of Baltimore, 1829–1830.* Rome: Apud Aedes Universitatis Gregorianae. 1957. The principal value of this doctoral thesis is the use that the author has made of hitherto unexploited documents in the archives of Propaganda, a number of which are reprinted in an appendix (pp. 172–226).

1043.   *Concilia Provincialia, Baltimori Habita ab anno 1829 usque ad annum 1849.* Baltimore: John Murphy. 1851. Contains the statutes of the first diocesan synod held in this country (1791), the regulations of the first meeting of the American bishops (1810), and the decrees of the seven provincial councils of Baltimore, 1829–1849.

1044.   *Concilii Plenarii Baltimorensis II., in Ecclesia Metropolitana Baltimorensi, ad Die VII. ad Diem XXI. Octobris, A.D. MDCCCLXVI., Habiti, et a Sede Apostolica Recogniti, Acta et Decreta.* Baltimore: John Murphy. 1868. Minutes, official documents, and decrees of the Second Plenary Council of October, 1866.

1045.   *Concilium Plenarium Totius Americae Septentrionalis Foederatae, Baltimori Habitum Anno 1852.* Baltimore: John Murphy. 1853. A similar volume to No. 1044 for the First Plenary Council of May, 1852; also includes the minutes and decrees of the Eighth (1855) and Ninth (1858) Provincial Councils of Baltimore.

1046.   Corecco, Eugenio. *La formazione della Chiesa Cattolica negli*

Stati Uniti d'America attraverso l'attività sinodale: con particolare riguardo al problema dell'amministrazione dei beni ecclesiastici. Brescia: Edizioni Morcelliana. 1970. Originally accepted as a doctoral dissertation in canon law at the University of Munich and subsequently embellished with new insights, this European view of the structure and legislation of the provincial and plenary councils in the United States places special emphasis on the trustee system and forms of incorporation of church property.

1047.   Curran, Francis X., S.J. *Catholics in Colonial Law.* Chicago: Loyola University Press. 1963. A compilation of laws and excerpts from laws of a penal nature against Catholics both in England and in America.

1048.   Dignan, Patrick J. *A History of the Legal Incorporation of Catholic Church Property in the United States, 1784–1932.* Washington, D.C.: Catholic University of America Press. 1933. Reprint. New York: AMS. 1974. A Ph.D. thesis that gives a thorough study of a highly important question in American Catholic history; summary of state laws on church property in Chapter VIII.

1049.   Guilday, Peter. *A History of the Councils of Baltimore, 1791–1884.* New York: Macmillan. 1932. Reprint. New York: Arno and the New York Times. 1969. The best general work on American canonical legislation, although containing a considerable number of errors; surveys the origins of the Church under foreign jurisdictions and affords insights into the Church's relations with its members as well as with those outside the fold. The councils dealt with education, discipline, politics, nativism, the place of the laity, immigration, and other important matters.

1050.   Hennesey, James, S.J. *The First Council of the Vatican: The American Experience.* New York: Herder and Herder. 1963. Developed from a doctoral dissertation written at the Catholic University of America and carefully documented from primary sources, this objective history of the participation of the American bishops from the time of their departure for Rome to that of their return to their dioceses interprets their attitudes toward, divisions over, and contributions to the conciliar debates and decrees, in the light of their predominantly pastoral concerns and unique national conditions.

1051.   Howe, Mark De Wolfe. *Cases on Church and State in the United States.* Cambridge, Mass.: Harvard University Press. 1952. Judicial decisions in which American courts have considered constitutional and other aspects of relationship between the churches and the civil government.

1052.   McGrath, John J., ed. *Church and State in American Law: Cases and Materials*. Milwaukee: Bruce. 1962. A collection of cases from state courts and the Supreme Court of the United States dealing with the internal affairs of the churches, private schools and charities, public schools, and freedom to proselytize and to act upon religious beliefs.

1053.   Mahoney, William. *Jura Sacerdotum Vindicata: The Rights of the Clergy Vindicated, or, A Plea for Canon Law in the United States, by a Roman Catholic Priest*. New York: James Sheehy. 1883. A volume by an unruly priest who was suspended by three different archbishops for disobedience and criticism of the hierarchy.

1054.   *The Memorial Volume: A History of the Third Plenary Council of Baltimore, November 9–December 7, 1884*. Baltimore: John Murphy. 1885. Of value solely for the external aspects of the council; includes texts of the sermons preached during the gathering.

1055.   Parsons, Wilfrid, S.J. *The First Freedom: Considerations on Church and State in the United States*. New York: Declan X. McMullen. 1948. A brief discussion of the First Amendment to the federal Constitution.

1056.   Tracy, Robert E. *American Bishop at the Vatican Council: Recollections and Projections*. New York: McGraw-Hill. c. 1966. 1967. In a personal, familiar style the first Bishop of Baton Rouge here tries to show the pastoral concerns of the Second Vatican Council and to clarify its aims and accomplishments for the average layman.

1057.   Yzermans, Vincent A., ed. *American Participation in the Second Vatican Council*. New York: Sheed and Ward. 1967. In this large volume, for each constitution, decree, and declaration issued by the council the editor gives a historical introduction, one or more "interventions" (in English) delivered orally by American fathers, and a commentary by an American expert.

1058.   Zollman, Carl. *American Church Law*. 2nd rev. ed. St. Paul: West Publishing. 1933. A good reference work for American law on such matters as ecclesiastical property, education, and religious societies, by a non-Catholic professor of law at Marquette University.

C. DOCTRINE, DISCIPLINE, AND DEVOTION

1059.   Brown, Francis F. *Priests in Council: A History of the National Federation of Priests' Councils.* Mission, Kans.: Andrews and McMeel. 1979. A priest-journalist who served as the Federation's director of public relations here reports the issues, mainly pertaining to social action, discussed at the annual conventions from 1968 (the founding) to 1978.

1060.   Callahan, Daniel. *The Mind of the Catholic Layman.* New York: Charles Scribner's. 1963. This broad survey of the role of the laity in the American Church from the 1770's to the present is based mainly on secondary sources, and is more notable for its attempts at interpretation and synthesis than for any original contribution to the factual record; it is conceived with special reference to the contemporary situation.

1061.   DeVito, Michael J. *The New York Review, 1905–1908.* New York: United States Catholic Historical Society. 1977. This doctoral dissertation from the Department of Theology of Fordham University is a critical study of the short-lived, scholarly journal which was published by St. Joseph's Seminary, Dunwoodie, Yonkers, and became involved in the Modernist controversy. It is of value in that it contains information not readily available elsewhere, but the factual inaccuracies, the misspelling and misuse of words, and the poor literary style detract from its worth. The volume is a reproduction of the typescript by the photo-offset process.

1062.   Dolan, Jay P. *Catholic Revivalism: The American Experience, 1830–1900.* Notre Dame: University of Notre Dame Press. 1978. A well-researched monograph on a theme hitherto largely unexplored. The author focuses mainly on the parish missions conducted by the Redemptorists, Jesuits, and Paulists.

1063.   Ellis, John Tracy, ed. *The Catholic Priest in the United States: Historical Investigations.* Collegeville, Minn.: St. John's University Press. 1971. Written by members of the Subcommittee on History of the Committee on Priestly Life and Ministry of the National Conference of Catholic Bishops as one of a series of studies in various disciplines, this volume contains essays by John Tracy Ellis ("The Formation of the American Priest: An Historical Perspective"), Robert Trisco ("Bishops and Their Priests in the United States"), Michael V. Gannon ("Before and After Modernism: The Intellectual Isolation of the American Priest"), John P. Marschall ("Diocesan and

Religious Clergy: The History of a Relationship, 1789–1969"), and David J. O'Brien ("The American Priest and Social Action").

1064.   Horka-Follick, Lorayne Ann. *Los Hermanos Penitentes: A Vestige of Medievalism in Southwestern United States.* Los Angeles: Westernlore. 1969. Although well-intentioned and widely researched, this assemblage of data on the origins, practices, political structure, economic position, social standing, artistic achievement, and relations with the clergy of the order which flourished in the second half of the nineteenth century fails to solve the mystery of the brotherhood because of inaccurate understanding, uncritical use, and illogical combination of the sources.

1065.   Klein, Félix. *Americanism: A Phantom Heresy.* Atchison, Kans.: Aquin Book Shop. 1951. An English translation of Volume IV of the memoirs (*Souvenirs* [Paris: Librairie Plon, 1948]) of one of the last living principals in the controversy over the alleged heresy in the Church of the United States; contains a foreword by James M. Gillis, C.S.P., the introduction of John Ireland to Walter Elliott's *Life of Father Hecker* (New York, 1891), and appendices (pp. 271–337) which reprint pertinent articles and documents on the controversy.

1066.   McAvoy, Thomas T., C.S.C. *The Great Crisis in American Catholic History, 1895–1900.* Chicago: Henry Regnery. 1957. Paperback edition. *The Americanist Heresy in Roman Catholicism, 1895–1900.* Notre Dame: University of Notre Dame Press. 1963. The most scholarly work to date on the Americanism controversy; awarded the John Gilmary Shea Prize of the American Catholic Historical Association in 1957.

1067.   McNamara, Robert F. *Catholic Sunday Preaching: The American Guidelines, 1791–1975.* Washington, D.C.: Word of God Institute. 1975. This brief review both of the legislation regarding Sunday preaching which was in force in the United States from colonial times to the Second Vatican Council and of the prevalent understanding and common practice of sermons, ends with some concrete suggestions for correcting the current imbalance of subject matter.

1068.   Mannix, Edward J. *The American Convert Movement.* New York: Devin-Adair. 1923. A popular work that is more of an effort at psychological analysis of the conversion to Catholicism of a group of prominent Americans between 1800 and 1920 than it is a history; appendices contain lists of autobiographies and dictionaries of American converts; not a scientific work.

1069. Micek, Adam A. *The Apologetics of Martin John Spalding*. Washington, D.C.: Catholic University of America Press. 1951. An S.T.D. thesis that deals with one of the leading Catholic apologists of the nineteenth century who became Coadjutor Bishop of Louisville in 1848 and died in 1872 as seventh Archbishop of Baltimore.

1070. Murnion, Philip J. *The Catholic Priest and the Changing Structure of Pastoral Ministry, New York, 1920–1970*. New York: Arno. 1978. This doctoral dissertation, accepted by Columbia University in 1972 and here reproduced from the original typescript, is an exercise in historical sociology which explores and compares the processes of recruitment and training for pastoral ministry, the viewpoints on central elements of church and ministry prevalent in the literature, and the performance of ministry in the 1920's and the 1960's.

1071. O'Brien, David J. *The Renewal of American Catholicism*. New York: Oxford University Press. 1972. This overlong, repetitious series of essays on contemporary issues by a liberal Catholic historian and activist is noteworthy mainly for its analysis of the interaction between religion and the world.

1072. Ong, Walter J., S.J. *American Catholic Crossroads*. New York: Macmillan. 1959. A stimulating series of brief essays which have their chief emphasis on the need for American Catholics to break isolationism and assume an active role in national life.

1073. *The Penitentes of New Mexico*. New York: Arno. 1976. This anthology contains three essays representing different points of view: In "The Passionists of the Southwest, or, The Holy Brotherhood" (1893), Alexander M. Darley, a Protestant minister, considered the fraternal Catholic society fanatical and excessive in its penitential practices; Alice C. Henderson viewed the group sympathetically but superficially in "Brothers of Light" (1937); Dorothy Woodward, in her previously unpublished dissertation, "The Penitentes of New Mexico" (1935), provided the most dispassionate and objective analysis of the society and its role in Hispano life.

1074. Stewart, James H. *American Catholic Leadership: A Decade of Turmoil, 1966–1976. A Sociological Analysis of the National Federation of Priests' Councils*. The Hague: Mouton Publishers. 1978. A model of organizational effectiveness is employed to analyze the changes of structure and goals as the Federation moved from a militant social movement for clerical rights within the Church to a more formal structure pressing for changes in the broader American and international society, shifting its emphasis from "interest" issues to "value" issues.

1075.   Weigle, Marta. *Brothers of Light, Brothers of Blood: The Penitentes of the Southwest.* Albuquerque: University of New Mexico Press. 1976. This scholarly investigation by an anthropologist traces the history of the lay brotherhood from the late eighteenth century to the twentieth, and describes its organization, customs, rituals, and legends; numerous historical documents are printed in appendices.

D. IMMIGRATION, ETHNIC, AND RACIAL HISTORY

1076.   Andrews, Theodore. *The Polish National Catholic Church in America and Poland.* London: S.P.C.K. 1953. A slender volume by a minister of the Protestant Episcopal Church done originally as a thesis for the doctorate in theology at the General Theological Seminary, New York. Although leaving much to be desired by way of interpretation and thoroughness of research, it is to date the only general account of the single serious schism from the ranks of the American Catholics.

1077.   Barry, Colman J., O.S.B. *The Catholic Church and German Americans.* Milwaukee: Bruce. 1953. A Ph.D. thesis that treats with thorough scholarship and objectivity the highly explosive nationalist differences between German and Irish Catholics of the United States in the past century.

1078.   Biever, Bruce Francis. *Religion, Culture, and Values: A Cross-Cultural Analysis of Motivational Factors in Native Irish and American Irish Catholicism.* New York: Arno. 1976. Applying the methodologies of social psychology and cultural anthropology and using the techniques of quantitative research, the Jesuit author attempts to define the distinctive opinions of Irish Catholics in Ireland and in the United States on such subjects as the Church's relations to politics, education, the social question, doctrinal communication, clerical-lay relations, and ritual, as they were manifested before the Second Vatican Council. This comparison of the influences of the Church on the two groups will be of value to future historians. This doctoral dissertation in American civilization was completed at the University of Pennsylvania in 1965 and is reproduced here in the original form by the photo-offset process.

1079.   Brown, Thomas N. *Irish-American Nationalism.* Philadelphia:

J. B. Lippincott. 1964. A paperback by a recognized expert on the history of the Irish in the United States.

1080.   Cada, Joseph. *Czech-American Catholics, 1850–1920*. Lisle, Ill.: Center for Slav Culture. 1964. Although this monograph is not documented, it is based on records found in parishes, missions, schools, and the Czech daily and periodical press; the immigrants' transfer of spiritual values to the United States and their cultural and educational efforts to adjust to a unique situation are emphasized.

1081.   Carthy, Mary Peter, Mother, O.S.U. *English Influences on Early American Catholicism*. Washington, D.C.: Catholic University of America Press. 1959. This doctoral dissertation in history reveals how the English Catholics helped to determine or modify the ideas of American Catholics in regard to ecclesiastical government and administration, liturgical and sacramental practice, education, and journalism from 1790 to 1852, with special emphasis on the periods of John Carroll and the Oxford Movement.

1082.   Dolan, Jay P. *The Immigrant Church: New York's Irish and German Catholics, 1815–1865*. Baltimore: Johns Hopkins University Press. 1975. Using two ethnic parishes in Lower Manhattan, this revised doctoral dissertation from the University of Chicago examines and compares the ordinary, faceless faithful of the two nationalities to determine their mobility and social status, the education of their children, their charitable activities, and parochial practices.

1083.   Domański, F., S.J., Z. Peszkowski, J. Swastek, and Sister M. Tullia, C.S.S.F., eds. *The Contribution of the Poles to the Growth of Catholicism in the United States*. [Sacrum Poloniae Millennium, Vol. VI.] Rome: N.p. 1959. This large tome contains an unsigned introduction and the following four contributions: J. M. A. Swastek, "The Formative Years of the Polish Seminary in the United States" (SS. Cyril and Methodius at Orchard Lake, Michigan); F. M. A. Bolek, "Catholic Priests of Polish Descent in the U.S. to 1957. A Tentative List" (arranged alphabetically); Z. M. A. Peszkowski, "List of Polish Catholic Parishes in the United States" (arranged by dioceses); and Sister Mary Tullia, C.S.S.F., "Polish American Sisterhoods..." (with each congregation's establishments and statistics).

1084.   Dyrud, Keith P., Michael Novak, and Rudolph J. Vecoli, eds. *The Other Catholics*. New York: Arno. 1978. The twelve articles in this anthology, either previously published, excerpted from doctoral dissertations, or expressly composed for this collection (but all reproduced from printed or typewritten originals by the photo-offset process), deal with the Czechs, Hungarians, Italians, Lithuanians, Poles, Rusins, Slovaks, Slovenes, and Syrians.

1085.   Foisy, J. Albert. *The Sentinellist Agitation in New England, 1925–1928.* Providence: Providence Visitor Press. 1930. A popular defense of episcopal authority in the brief nationalist rebellion of the 1920's among a minority of French-Canadian Catholics in the Diocese of Providence.

1086.   Gillard, John T., S.S.J. *The Catholic Church and the American Negro.* Baltimore: St. Joseph's Society Press. 1929. Reprint. New York: Johnson Reprint. 1968. A factual survey of the Church's relations to colored people in this country by a Josephite missionary.

1087.   _____ . *Colored Catholics in the United States.* Baltimore: Josephite Press. 1941. The same author here carries the story to the 1940's.

1088.   Greene, Victor. *For God and Country: The Rise of Polish and Lithuanian Ethnic Consciousness in America, 1860–1910.* Madison: State Historical Society of Wisconsin. 1975. Exaggerating the conflict between the "nationalists" and the "religionists" among the Poles of Chicago as a case study of a wider phenomenon, the author, in spite of wide research and ample documentation, and with numerous factual errors and gratuitous assertions, fails to prove his main contention that this tension developed the ethnic consciousness of the Polish immigrant masses.

1089.   Griffin, Joseph A. *The Contribution of Belgium to the Catholic Church in America, 1523–1857.* Washington, D.C.: Catholic University of America Press. 1932. Reprint. New York: AMS. 1974. The first three chapters of this Ph.D. thesis deal with Belgian missionaries during the colonial period; the story is brought down to the founding of the American College at Louvain.

1090.   Hamon, Edouard, S.J. *Les Canadiens-Français de la Nouvelle-Angleterre.* Quebec: N. S. Hardy. 1891. It is the author's intention to be neither *"un panégyriste ni un détracteur"*; the first part gives a historical sketch of the problem, with observations on the prospects for the retention of the immigrants' faith in the future, while the second section is a survey of individual French-Canadian parishes in

New England and New York; useful in view of the lack of studies of scholarly competence in this much neglected field of immigration history.

1091. Johnson, Nessa Theresa Baskerville. *A Special Pilgrimage: A History of Black Catholics in Richmond.* Richmond: Diocese of Richmond, Va.: 1978. Though lacking footnotes and bibliography and not well organized, this slender, abundantly illustrated volume, which covers more than a century and includes the work of religious congregations of men and women, is a contribution to the ecclesiastical and social history of the capital of Virginia.

1092. Linkh, Richard M. *American Catholicism and European Immigrants, 1900–1924.* Staten Island, N.Y.: Center for Migration Studies. 1975. Researched entirely in English-language sources and focused mainly on Poles and Italians, this study (in spite of inconsistencies, unwarranted generalizations, exaggerations, and omissions) is a useful introduction to the response of American Catholicism to the "new immigration." It surveys ways in which the Church helped the immigrants and ways in which Catholic immigrants helped themselves, and concludes that the Church was not a very active force for Americanization before World War I but with the advent of the war it did work efficiently to assimilate the immigrant.

1093. Maguire, Edward J., ed. *Reverend John O'Hanlon's "The Irish Emigrant's Guide for the United States": A Critical Edition with Introduction and Commentary.* New York: Arno. 1976. O'Hanlon, an Irish immigrant himself, wrote this manual in 1851, while he was serving as a priest in Saint Louis. The editor presents a brief summary of O'Hanlon's career, sets forth the causes of Irish emigration, describes the difficulties of crossing the Atlantic, traces the history of passenger acts in the United States Congress, and analyzes the impact of the Irish on religion and politics in America. The work was submitted as a doctoral dissertation to Saint Louis University in 1951.

1094. Rothan, Emmet H., O.F.M. *The German Catholic Immigrant in the United States, 1830–1860.* Washington, D.C.: Catholic University of America Press. 1946. A Ph.D. thesis based entirely on printed materials; while of some use as an introductory account, it does not contribute anything essentially new.

1095. Schiavo, Giovanni. *Italian-American History.* Vol. II: *The Italian Contribution to the Catholic Church in America.* New York: Vigo.

1949. Reprint. New York: Arno. 1975. This huge compilation of data taken from secondary sources is neither critical nor reliable. The first part recounts the labors of "pioneer priests" in all areas of what is now the United States from the sixteenth century on, and the second contains sketches of religious orders of men and women, and "parish histories" arranged by states.

1096.   Schrott, Lambert, O.S.B. *Pioneer German Catholics in the American Colonies, 1734–1784.* New York: United States Catholic Historical Society. 1933. A thesis for the A.M. degree based on printed sources; useful as an introduction to the subject.

1097.   Tomasi, Silvano M. *Piety and Power: The Role of the Italian Parishes in the New York Metropolitan Area, 1880–1930.* Staten Island, N.Y.: Center for Migration Studies. 1975. Though this abbreviated version of a doctoral dissertation done in sociology at Fordham University employs a dubious methodology, it is useful as a historical study of the ethnic parish as an agency aiding the immigrants both to preserve their old-world religion and to adjust to American urban life and culture.

E. INTERFAITH

1098.   Barrows, John Henry, ed. *The World's Parliament of Religions.* 2 vols. Chicago: Parliament. 1893. These volumes contain the texts of the papers read at the assembly in Chicago in 1893 by the representatives of all religions including the Catholics, e.g., Gibbons, Ireland, Walter Elliott, C.S.P., Robert Seton, and John J. Keane.

1099.   Bianchi, Eugene C. *John XXIII and American Protestants.* Washington, D.C.: Corpus Books. 1968. A heavily documented doctoral dissertation from Union Theological Seminary.

1100.   Curry, Lerond. *Protestant-Catholic Relations in America: World War I through Vatican II.* Lexington: University Press of Kentucky. 1972. This Protestant author offers a brief collation of materials drawn from books, journals, and newspapers interspersed with polite lectures to Catholics on the implications and dimensions of their positions; he has written not a history based on primary sources or marked by serious interpretation, but rather a book rendered worthless by insufficient research, superficial analysis, jejune prose, and judgments that are either false or simplistic or banal.

1101.   Herberg, Will. *Protestant-Catholic-Jew: An Essay in American*

Religious Sociology. Garden City, N.Y.: Doubleday. 1955. A penetrating analysis of religious thought in twentieth-century United States; offers many original insights.

1102.   Marty, Myron A. *Lutherans and Roman Catholicism: The Changing Conflict, 1917–1963*. Notre Dame: University of Notre Dame Press. 1968. This study of the opposition of the Lutheran Church–Missouri Synod to the Catholic Church in the United States, written by a member of the former, is arranged topically rather than chronologically and is mainly devoted to theological issues.

1103.   Scharper, Philip, ed. *American Catholics: A Protestant-Jewish View*. New York: Sheed and Ward. 1959. A series of six candid and critical essays, expressed with charity and urbanity, by Protestants and Jews on the Catholic community of the United States as they see it; weaknesses and strengths assessed from their respective viewpoints; an excellent introduction for those Catholics who would know what educated Americans not of the Catholic faith are thinking about them; a final brief essay by Gustave Weigel, S.J., written in appreciation of the foregoing.

1104.   Underwood, Kenneth Wilson. *Protestants and Catholics: Religious and Social Interaction in an Industrial Community*. Boston: Beacon. 1957. A doctoral thesis of the Yale Divinity School; although not professedly a work of history, it has value for historians, with its objective analysis of twentieth-century friction between Protestants and Catholics in the city of Holyoke, Massachusetts.

1105.   Walworth, Clarence W. *The Oxford Movement in America*. New York: United States Catholic Historical Society. 1974. This book, originally published in 1895 by one of the first Paulists, is the only work by a Catholic on the American phase of the Oxford Movement. The author's own place in the movement is analyzed in the new introduction by David J. O'Brien and commentary by James H. Smylie. Originally subtitled "Glimpses of Life in an Anglican Seminary."

F. INTERNATIONAL RELATIONS

1106.   Baisnée, Jules A. *France and the Establishment of the American Hierarchy: The Myth of French Interference, 1782–1784*. Baltimore: Johns Hopkins Press. 1934. A documentary refutation of an old fallacy concerning France's alleged interference in the appointment of the first American bishop; Chapter VI contains a critique of the accounts of six historians who had previously dealt with this subject.

1107.   Feiertag, Loretta Clare, Sister. *American Public Opinion on the Diplomatic Relations between the United States and the Papal States, 1847–1867.* Washington, D.C.: Catholic University of America Press. 1933. A Ph.D. thesis based upon a study of the diplomatic documents published by Stock (No. 1113) and the contemporary newspapers.

1108.   Feldblum, Esther Yolles. *The American Catholic Press and the Jewish State, 1917–1959.* New York: Ktav. 1977. This posthumous publication, based on the author's doctoral dissertation at Columbia University, is an objective analysis of the attitudes toward Zionism and Israel expressed in a number of newspapers, magazines, and periodicals from the Balfour Declaration to the Second Vatican Council.

1109.   Flynn, George Q. *Roosevelt and Romanism: Catholics and American Diplomacy, 1937–1945.* Westport, Conn.: Greenwood. 1976. On the basis of all available sources, the author studies the shift of American Catholics' attitude from isolationism to interventionism, their influence on Roosevelt's foreign policy during the Spanish Civil War, his appointment of Myron C. Taylor as his personal representative to Pope Pius XII, his efforts to win Catholic support for aid to the Soviet Union before Pearl Harbor, moral questions involved in World War II, and relations with the Holy See. He tends to give the benefit of any doubt to the president in cases of disagreement with Catholics.

1110.   Lallou, William J. *The Fifty Years of the Apostolic Delegation, Washington, D.C.: 1893–1943.* Paterson: St. Anthony Guild. 1943. A chronicle on the Apostolic Delegation with some biographical data on the first six delegates.

1111.   Laurent, Laval, O.F.M. *Québec et l'Eglise aux Etats-Unis sous Mgr. Briand et Mgr. Plessis.* Washington, D.C.: Catholic University of America Press. 1945. An S.T.D. thesis on American-Canadian Catholic relations during the administrations of Joseph-Olivier Briand (1766–1786) and Joseph-Octave Plessis (1808–1825) in the See of Quebec; makes generous use of manuscript sources in the Quebec archives.

1112.   Stock, Leo Francis. *Consular Relations between the United States and the Papal States, 1797–1870.* Washington, D.C.: American Catholic Historical Association. 1945.

1113. _____ . *United States Ministers to the Papal States: Instructions and Despatches, 1848–1868.* Washington, D.C.: American Catholic Historical Association. 1933. These two carefully edited volumes of documents from the archives of the Department of State provide ample coverage of official American-papal relations; each volume carries a lengthy and informative introduction.

1114. Weber, Francis J. *The United States Versus Mexico: The Final Settlement of the Pious Fund.* Los Angeles: Historical Society of Southern California. 1969. This history of the dispute reaching from the middle of the nineteenth century to 1967 was originally published in the *Southern California Quarterly* LI (June, 1969), 97–152, and here has a foreword by Earl Warren.

G. JOURNALISM AND PUBLISHING

1115. Baumgartner, Appolinaris W. *Catholic Journalism: A Study of Its Development in the United States, 1789–1930.* New York: Columbia University Press. 1931. A sketchy and poorly organized A.M. thesis; for newspapers up to 1840, Foik (No. 1118) is preferable.

1116. Belisle, Alexandre. *Histoire de la Presse Franco-Américaine.* Worcester: L'Opinion Publique. 1911. An old but useful item for French-Canadian immigration to this country; gives a history of their press from 1838 to 1911.

1117. Connaughton, M. Stanislaus, Sister, S.S.M. *The Editorial Opinion of the Catholic Telegraph of Cincinnati on Contemporary Affairs and Politics, 1871–1921.* Washington, D.C.: Catholic University of America Press. 1943. A Ph.D. thesis that offers capable coverage of an important half-century in the life of one of the oldest (founded in October, 1831) and best of American Catholic newspapers.

1118. Foik, Paul J., C.S.C. *Pioneer Catholic Journalism.* New York: United States Catholic Historical Society. 1930. The best general work for the Catholic newspapers and magazines published in the United States between the *Michigan Essay* (1809) and the launching of the New York *Freeman's Journal* (1840).

1119. Healey, Robert C. *A Catholic Book Chronicle: The Story of P. J. Kenedy and Sons, 1826–1951.* New York: P. J. Kenedy. 1951. A popular brochure on the first 125 years of the oldest Catholic publishing firm in the United States.

1120.   Hueston, Robert Francis. *The Catholic Press and Nativism, 1840–1860*. New York: Arno. 1976. Accepted by the University of Notre Dame in 1972, and based on English-language newspapers and *Brownson's Quarterly Review*, this doctoral dissertation deals with the role of the Irish Catholic immigrants in evoking Protestant hostility, and with the nature of the reactions of Catholic journalists. It is reproduced by the photo-offset process from the original type-script.

1121.   Reilly, Mary Lonan, Sister, O.S.F. *A History of the Catholic Press Association, 1911–1968*. Metuchen, N.J.: Scarecrow. 1971. Originally submitted as a doctoral dissertation at the University of Notre Dame, this clearly organized, if sometimes compressed, history of a complex and influential association reveals a wealth of data and treats professional questions as well as practical affairs.

1122.   Van Allen, Rodger. *The Commonweal and American Catholicism: The Magazine, the Movement, the Meaning*. Philadelphia: Fortress. 1974. This revision of a doctoral dissertation which was accepted by Temple University shows how the lay editors handled the most controversial religious and secular issues from 1924 to 1974. Impartial up to the Second Vatican Council, the treatment is thereafter biased in favor of the liberal causes espoused by the weekly.

H. LITERATURE

1123.   Messbarger, Paul R. *Fiction with a Parochial Purpose: Social Uses of American Catholic Literature, 1884–1900*. Brookline, Mass.: Boston University Press. 1971. By analyzing the lives and works of Catholic novelists, the author determines the dominant attitudes and assumptions of this religious subculture; he distinguishes "three faces" of Americanism as found in these writings and formulates a typology of behavioral variations extending to the present. Because of a dubious critical methodology, his hypotheses cannot be accepted without verification from other sources.

1124.   White, James A. *The Era of Good Intentions: A Survey of American Catholics' Writing between the Years 1880–1915*. New York: Arno. 1978. This analysis of novelists, poets, essayists, episcopal authors, and editors of journals, who used literary means to lead their fellow Americans and fellow Catholics to a better appreciation of religion, culture, and education, was submitted as a doctoral dissertation to the University of Notre Dame in 1957 and is here reproduced from the original typescript by the photo-offset process.

I. MISSIONS

1125. Bane, Martin J., S.M.A. *The Catholic Story of Liberia.* New York: Declan X. McMullen. 1950. A brief popular account of missionary endeavor in the American-founded Republic of Liberia and adjacent territories; special emphasis is placed on the work of Americans, both those who failed in the 1840's and the members of the American province of the Society of African Missions who began to have greater success in 1948.

1126. Blied, Benjamin J. *Austrian Aid to American Catholics, 1830– 1860.* Milwaukee: The Author. 1944. A careful monograph that makes good use of the *Berichte* of the Leopoldine Foundation of Vienna and other printed sources to tell the story of the assistance rendered by the Austrian immigrant aid society (founded in 1829) to Catholic missions in the United States.

1127. Corrigan, Raymond, S.J. *Die Kongregation de Propaganda Fide und ihre Tätigkeit in Nord-Amerika.* Munich: E. Joergen. 1928. A Ph.D. thesis useful for the early history of the Roman congregation under which the American Church was ruled until 1908.

1128. De Smet, P. J. *Western Missions and Missionaries: A Series of Letters.* New York: P. J. Kenedy. 1859. Reprint. Dublin: Irish University Press. 1972. Dated from 1844 to 1857, these fifty-two letters to the editor of the *Précis Historiques* in Brussels describe De Smet's travels to the Rocky Mountains, the Indian tribes that he visited, and the lives of ten Belgian and Jesuit missionaries in the United States.

1129. Donnelly, Joseph P., S.J., trans. *Wilderness Kingdom: Indian Life in the Rocky Mountains, 1840–1847; The Journals and Paintings of Nicolas Point, S.J.* New York: Holt, Rinehart and Winston. 1967. The memoirs in which the French missionary subsequently described the way of life of the Flatheads, Coeur d'Alenes, and Blackfeet in the present-day states of Montana and Idaho and chronicled the Christianizing labors of the Jesuits among them, lack adequate annotations as well as a critical introduction, basic bibliography, and index. This beautiful folio volume also contains 232 miniatures reproduced in full color and some fifty pen-and-ink sketches.

1130.   Hickey, Edward J. *The Society for the Propagation of the Faith: Its Foundation, Organization, and Success, 1822–1922*. Washington, D.C.: Catholic University of America Press. 1922. Reprint. New York: AMS. 1974. The history of a society that gave major assistance to the American Catholic missions in the nineteenth century; a Ph.D. thesis.

1131.   Kelley, Francis C., ed. *The First American Catholic Missionary Congress Held under the Auspices of the Catholic Church Extension Society of the United States of America, Containing Official Proceedings*. Chicago: J. S. Hyland. 1909. Reprint. New York: Arno. 1978. This large volume contains papers presented by clergymen and laymen on such topics as religious conditions in New Mexico and the Philippines, Indian and Negro missions, home missions in the cities, colonization, settlement work, immigration, and missions as a unifier. The congress, organized by Kelley and held in Chicago in 1908, marked an awakening of American Catholics to the obligation of promoting home and foreign missions.

1132.   Kelley, Francis C. *The Story of Extension*. Chicago: Extension. 1922. A popular account of the leading society for support of the home missions of the American Church, told by the man who founded it in 1905.

1133.   Latourette, Kenneth Scott. *The Great Century, A.D. 1800– A.D. 1914*. New York: Harper and Bros. 1941. Almost two-thirds of this able survey by an outstanding Protestant historian is devoted to Christianity's expansion in the United States with special reference to the Negroes and Indians; the fourth in a seven-volume work; excellent bibliography.

1134.   *Maryknoll Mission Letters*. New York: Field Afar. 1923–1946. These small volumes were issued to acquaint American Catholics with the problems of American missionaries in foreign lands. The first two volumes appeared in 1923 and 1927. The publication was resumed in 1942 as a semi-annual and was discontinued after the first issue of 1946.

1135.   *Our Negro and Indian Missions*. Washington, D.C.: Commission for the Catholic Missions among the Colored People and the Indians. 1925. This annual report of the secretary of the commission is a very useful item for checking the statistical growth in converts, churches, schools, etc., among the Catholic Negroes and Indians of the United States; between 1886 and 1925 the reports were issued from Baltimore and thereafter from the headquarters in Washington, D.C.

1136. Prucha, Francis Paul. *The Churches and the Indian Schools, 1888–1912*. Lincoln: University of Nebraska Press. 1979. This history of the Protestant attack upon federal support of Catholic mission schools and of the competition between the Catholic mission schools and the government Indian schools is thoroughly researched and attractively presented by a recognized authority on the subject.

1137. Rahill, Peter J. *The Catholic Indian Missions and Grant's Peace Policy, 1870–1884*. Washington, D.C.: Catholic University of America Press. 1953. A Ph.D. thesis on a complicated subject that makes use of a wide variety of unpublished materials.

1138. Roemer, Theodore, O.F.M.Cap. *Ten Decades of Alms*. St. Louis: B. Herder. 1942. A useful, if unimaginative, treatment of the support given by the French, Austrian, and Bavarian mission societies between 1822 and 1922 to the Catholic missions in this country; the discussion of the sources (pp. 263–273) is worthy of note; appendices on the dates of establishment of American dioceses and the statutes of the respective societies.

1139. ———— . *The Leopoldine Foundation and the Church in the United States, 1829–1839*. New York: United States Catholic Historical Society. 1933. An A.M. thesis that covers the first decade of the Austrian mission aid society. For a fuller treatment see Blied (No. 1126).

1140. ———— . *The Ludwig-Missionsverein and the Catholic Church in the United States, 1838–1918*. Washington, D.C.: Catholic University of America Press. 1933. Reprint. New York: AMS. 1974. This Ph.D. thesis makes ample use of unpublished correspondence in the society's Munich archives as well as the reports in its *Annalen* and other printed sources.

1141. Shea, John Gilmary. *History of the Catholic Missions among the Indian Tribes of the United States, 1529–1854*. New York: D. Dunigan. 1857. Reprint. New York: Arno. 1969. Also New York: AMS. 1973. In spite of its age this volume, by one of the best-informed writers of the past century on the Indian missions, still has value. The work of the Spanish and French missionaries, as well as of those in the English colonies and later in the United States, is here presented from the perspective and often in the words of the missionaries themselves. The tragic defeats as well as the notable successes of the missions are revealed in elaborate detail.

1142.   Thauren, Johannes, S.V.D. *Ein Gnadenstrom zur Neuen Welt and seine Quelle: Die Leopoldinen Stiftung zur Unterstützung der amerikanischen Missionen.* Vienna-Mölding: Missionsdruckerei St. Gabriel. 1940. Based upon the *Berichte* of the Austrian missionary aid society; valuable chiefly for the essays devoted to seven missionaries who worked among the German-speaking Catholics of the United States and the list of references from the *Berichte* to individual American dioceses.

J. NATIONAL AFFAIRS

1143.   Blied, Benjamin J. *Catholics and the Civil War.* Milwaukee: The Author. 1945. Although somewhat fragmentary, these ten brief essays—based upon printed sources—present a cross section of opinion and action which reveals the Catholic antipathy toward abolition and the attitudes of both northern and southern Catholics toward the slavery issue and the war.

1144.   _____ . *Catholic Aspects of the War for Independence, the War of 1812, the War with Mexico, the War with Spain.* Milwaukee: The Author. 1949. A handy brochure containing four brief essays based largely on secondary sources.

1145.   Burns, Robert Ignatius, S.J. *The Jesuits and the Indian Wars of the Northwest.* New Haven: Yale University Press. 1966. With a wealth of documentary material drawn from numerous manuscript depositories, and with a fullness of presentation, Father Burns portrays the efforts of the few missionaries scattered through the vast wilderness of the Oregon country from Fort Benton, Montana, to Puget Sound to preserve peace between the Indians and the whites and to promote interracial justice from 1840 to 1880.

1146.   Dohen, Dorothy. *Nationalism and American Catholicism.* New York: Sheed and Ward. 1967. A perceptive monograph by a sociologist of Fordham University that highlights the "patriotism" of Catholics as seen through the following six prelates: John Carroll, John Hughes, John England, John Ireland, John Lancaster Spalding, and James Gibbons.

1147.   Doyle, David Noel. *Irish-Americans, Native Rights, and National Empires: The Structure, Attitudes, and Division of the Catholic*

Minority in the Decade of Expansion, 1890–1901. New York: Arno. 1976. Studying the reactions of the American Irish and American Catholics to the issues posed by United States foreign policy (especially the Chilean, Samoan, Hawaiian, Cuban, Venezuelan, and Armenian concerns of 1890–1897, the Spanish-American War, and the conquest of the Philippines), the author contends that the Irish middle class formed Catholic opinion in opposition to the "New Imperialism" of the Western powers, although some clerics wished to take advantage of the government's protection revitalizing the Church in Cuba and the Philippines. The work was presented as a doctoral dissertation at the University of Iowa in 1976.

1148. Flynn, George Q. *American Catholics and the Roosevelt Presidency, 1932–1936.* Lexington: University of Kentucky Press. 1968. Resting upon abundant source material, this well-balanced book emphasizes certain topics such as Catholic support of the New Deal, finance and agriculture, the National Recovery Administration, labor and social security, diplomatic recognition of the Soviet Union, the persecution of the Church in Mexico, and the campaign of 1936 involving Father Charles E. Coughlin. The author's thesis is that during this administration Catholics were finally brought fully into the mainstream of American political life.

1149. Griffin, Martin I. J. *Catholics and the American Revolution.* 3 vols. Ridley Park, Pa.: The Author. 1907–1911. Not a connected history but rather a huge collection of disparate articles, some long (such as the biographies of John Barry, Casimir Pulaski, and Thaddeus Kosciuszko) and most short, containing much documentary material without any attempt at analysis.

1150. McEniry, Blanche Marie, Sister. *American Catholics in the War with Mexico.* Washington, D.C.: Catholic University of America Press. 1937. A Ph.D. thesis that includes a chapter on the controversial case of the San Patricio Battalion; based for the most part on printed sources.

1151. McNeal, Patricia F. *The American Catholic Peace Movement, 1928–1972.* New York: Arno. 1978. This doctoral dissertation, submitted to Temple University in 1974 (and here reproduced from the original typescript), traces the thought and action of American Catholic organizations and individuals concerned about war and pacifism from the founding of the Catholic Association for International Peace to the protests against the war in Vietnam, with an uncritical treatment of Daniel and Philip Berrigan.

1152.   Meconis, Charles A. *With Clumsy Grace: The American Catholic Left, 1961–1975*. New York: Seabury. 1979. On the basis of written materials and individual interviews, the antiwar movement of the radical clergy and laity is sympathetically related by one of those personally involved.

1153.   Metzger, Charles H., S.J. *Catholics and the American Revolution*. Chicago: Loyola University Press. 1962. A thorough and scholarly work that makes use of all available sources in print as well as some manuscript sources.

1154.   Reuter, Frank T. *Catholic Influence on American Colonial Policies, 1898–1904*. Austin: University of Texas Press. 1967. This brief, dispassionate account of American Catholic opinion regarding the Church-State problems created by the United States' occupation of Cuba, Puerto Rico, Guam, and the Philippines after the Spanish-American War, and of the efforts of the bishops to obtain from the government a favorable solution, is marred by insufficient research and consequently by inadequate interpretation.

1155.   Williams, Michael. *American Catholics in the War*. New York: Macmillan. 1921. A rather superficial account of the contribution made to the nation during World War I by the National Catholic War Council; introductory chapters on the role of American Catholics in the history of the nation.

1156.   Zahn, Gordon C. *Another Part of the War: The Camp Simon Story*. Amherst: University of Massachusetts Press. 1979. This account, written by a sociologist and pacifist, of the unsuccessful camp for Catholic conscientious objectors located near Warner, New Hampshire, and operated by the Catholic Worker movement in 1942–1943, suffers from defects of methodology and lack of objectivity.

K. NATIVISM

Only a sampling of books on the Ku Klux Klan is given here; for a complete listing see William H. Fisher, *The Invisible Empire: A Bibliography of the Ku Klux Klan* (Metuchen, N.J.: Scarecrow. 1980.).

1157.   Alexander, Charles C. *The Ku Klux Klan in the Southwest*. Lexington: University of Kentucky Press. 1965. This monograph deals with Texas, Louisiana, Oklahoma, and Arkansas during the 1920's.

1158. Billington, Ray Allen. *The Protestant Crusade, 1800–1860: A Study of the Origins of American Nativism.* New York: Macmillan. 1938. Reprint. New York: Rinehart. 1952. A work of genuine scholarship which describes the development of the anti-Catholic, antiforeign movement in the United States up to the decline of the Know-Nothings.

1159. Chalmers, David M. *Hooded Americanism: The First Century of the Ku Klux Klan, 1865–1965.* Garden City, N.Y.: Doubleday. 1965. A journalistic account with few footnotes, yet of value for the Klan's role in politics.

1160. Chiniquy, Charles P. T. *Fifty Years in the Church of Rome.* 43rd ed. Chicago: Craig and Barlow. 1886. See next entry.

1161. _____ . *Forty Years in the Church of Christ.* Chicago: Fleming H. Revell. 1900. Two highly personal volumes by a Canadian-born apostate priest who brought on a schism among some of the French-Canadians of the Diocese of Chicago in the 1850's, and continued to belabor the Catholic Church until his death forty years later; Chiniquy's books furnished material for the propaganda of groups like the A.P.A. in the late nineteenth century.

1162. Crowley, Jeremiah J. *Romanism: A Menace to the Nation.* 2nd ed. Cincinnati: The Author. 1912. A vitriolic tract by an apostate priest of the Archdiocese of Chicago which includes an earlier work, *The Parochial School: A Curse to the Church, a Menace to the Nation* (2nd ed. Chicago: The Author. 1905); according to the author, he left the Church "voluntarily" in 1908 (p.9); like those of Chiniquy, the works of Crowley were widely distributed by anti-Catholic groups.

1163. Desmond, Humphrey J. *The A.P.A. Movement.* Washington, D.C.: New Century. 1912. A slight account by a Catholic journalist; now superseded by Kinzer (No. 1171).

1164. Feldberg, Michael. *The Philadelphia Riots of 1844: A Study of Ethnic Conflict.* Westport, Conn.: Greenwood. 1975. Originally a doctoral dissertation at the University of Rochester, this broad investigation traces the roots of the hostility between the Irish Catholics and the nativists more to cultural, occupational, social, and political differences than to purely religious bigotry or economic rivalry.

1165. Fell, Marie Léonore, Sister. *The Foundations of Nativism in American Textbooks, 1783–1860.* Washington, D.C.: Catholic Univer-

sity of America Press. 1941. A Ph.D. thesis that analyzes the leading
school readers, histories, and geographies of the period with a view
to determining the influence they had in creating anti-Catholic and
antiforeign attitudes.

1166.   Geniesse, J. B. *Pour aider à la solution de questions qui s'agitent
aux Etats-Unis et au Canada.* Rome: Privately printed. 1912. A private
memoir of 246 printed pages dealing with the schools, the lay participation in church affairs, and the language problem.

1167.   Gohmann, Mary de Lourdes, Sister. *Political Nativism in
Tennessee to 1860.* Washington, D.C.: Catholic University of America
Press. 1938. One of a series of Ph.D. theses done under the direction
of the late Richard J. Purcell on nativism in various states. See also
Nos. 1173, 1174, 1175, 1179, 1186.

1168.   Higham, John. *Strangers in the Land, Patterns of American
Nativism, 1860–1925.* New Brunswick: Rutgers University Press.
1955. This scholarly volume contains the best accounts now in print
of the A.P.A. and first Ku Klux Klan; notable for the originality and
richness of detail with which these movements are given their proper
setting.

1169.   Jackson, Kenneth T. *The Ku Klux Klan in the City, 1915–1930.*
New York: Oxford University Press. 1967. The author shows that
the roots of the Klan in the 1920's are to be found in the growing
urban centers of all sections of the country and not merely in the
declining rural towns as was previously supposed, and that the city
chapters provided the leadership, resources, and essential dynamics
of the movement. After studying selected cities in the North, South,
and West, he concludes that at least half of the members resided in
metropolitan areas, where they belonged mainly to the lower middle
class and to conservative, nonritualistic Protestant denominations
such as the Baptist, Methodist, or Christian churches.

1170.   Kinsman, Frederick J. *Americanism and Catholicism.* New
York: Longmans, Green. 1924. A series of popular essays written by
a convert from the Protestant Episcopal Church to interpret Catholicism for non-Catholics and to show its compatibility with the national ethos.

1171.   Kinzer, Donald L. *An Episode in Anti-Catholicism: The American Protective Association.* Seattle: University of Washington Press.
1964. This heavily documented monograph renders Desmond (No.

1163) obsolete. Relatively few of the A.P.A.'s records have remained, but Kinzer covers its press thoroughly. It was originally a doctoral dissertation done at the University of Washington.

1172.   Lichtman, Allan J. *Prejudice and the Old Politics: The Presidential Election of 1928*. Chapel Hill: University of North Carolina Press. 1979. Using sophisticated methods of quantitative analysis, the author shows that the major source of conflict in the contest between Alfred E. Smith and Herbert Hoover was the ethnocentric defensiveness of Protestants, rather than their perception of differing from Catholics over social and cultural issues.

1173.   McConville, Mary St. Patrick, Sister. *Political Nativism in the State of Maryland, 1830–1860*. Washington, D.C.: Catholic University of America Press. 1928. See No. 1167.

1174.   McGann, Agnes Geraldine, Sister. *Nativism in Kentucky to 1860*. Washington, D.C.: Catholic University of America Press. 1944. See No. 1167.

1175.   McGrath, Paul of the Cross, Sister. *Political Nativism in Texas, 1825–1860*. Washington, D.C.: Catholic University of America Press. 1930. See No. 1167.

1176.   Marshall, Charles C. *The Roman Catholic Church in the Modern State*. New York: Dodd, Mead. 1928. A study by a Protestant lawyer that grew out of the exchange of letters between the author and Governor Alfred E. Smith in the *Atlantic Monthly* (April and May, 1927); the most serious challenge offered to Smith on the score of his religious faith during the presidential campaign of 1928.

1177.   Moore, Edmund A. *A Catholic Runs for President: The Campaign of 1928*. New York: Ronald. 1956. Reprint. Gloucester, Mass.: Peter Smith. 1968. An objective study that provides a full account of Alfred E. Smith's presidential candidacy.

1178.   Myers, Gustavus. *History of Bigotry in the United States*. New York: Random House. 1943. Ed. and rev. Henry M. Christman. New York: Capricorn. 1960. Although many categories of victims of religious, political, and racial intolerance, especially the Jews, are included, Catholics are given a large share of the extensive treatment. The new edition omits four chapters dealing chiefly with European history in a very general sense, and adds three covering the years 1942–1960.

1179.   Noonan, Carroll J., S.S. *Nativism in Connecticut, 1829–1860.*
Washington, D.C.: Catholic University of America Press. 1938. See
No. 1167.

1180.   Randel, William Peirce. *The Ku Klux Klan: A Century of
Infamy.* Philadelphia: Chilton. 1965. Of the 262 pages of text of this
volume, 182 are devoted to the first Klan, not the revived organization of 1915; there are bibliographical notes for each chapter, but no
footnotes; although religious groups like Methodists and Presbyte-
rians are mentioned in the index, Catholics are not, and there is but a
single reference to Alfred E. Smith.

1181.   Ray, Mary Augustina, Sister, B.V.M. *American Opinion of
Roman Catholicism in the Eighteenth Century.* New York: Columbia
University Press. 1936. Reprint. New York: Octagon. 1974. A
superior Ph.D. thesis that does for the eighteenth century what
Billington (No. 1158) and Higham (No. 1168) have done for later
periods; for a comparable study of the entire colonial period (but
confined to New England), cf. Riley (No. 232).

1182.   Schmeckebier, Lawrence F. *History of the Know-Nothing Party
in Maryland.* Baltimore: Johns Hopkins Press. 1899. A slender and
dated Ph.D. thesis based entirely on printed sources.

1183.   Scisco, Louis Dow. *Political Nativism in New York State.* New
York: Columbia University Press. 1901. A Ph.D. thesis based largely
on newspapers.

1184.   Silva, Ruth C. *Rum, Religion, and Votes: 1928 Reexamined.*
University Park: Pennsylvania State University Press. 1962. This
slender monograph maintains by means of statistical analysis that
Smith was defeated not by his religion and prohibition stand, but
rather because it was a Republican year and his membership in the
Democratic party proved his greatest liability.

1185.   Sylvain, Robert. *Alessandro Gavazzi, 1809–1899: Clerc,
Garibaldien, Prédicant des Deux Mondes.* 2 vols. Quebec: Centre
Pédagogique. 1962. A biography of an ex-Barnabite priest who
played a leading role in the anti-Catholic movement of the 1850's and
after.

1186.   Thomas, M. Evangeline, Sister. *Nativism in the Old Northwest, 1850–1860.* Washington, D.C.: Catholic University of America
Press. 1936. A Ph.D. thesis belonging to the series cited above (No.

1167); embraces the States of Ohio, Indiana, Illinois, Michigan, and Wisconsin; based chiefly on printed sources, although some use is made of manuscript materials.

1187. Williams, Michael. *The Shadow of the Pope.* New York: McGraw-Hill. 1932. A defense of American Catholicism against the attacks of the first Ku Klux Klan; not a scientific work.

L. SOCIAL STUDIES

In addition to the items listed below attention is called to a number of biographical works which constitute studies in the social thought of individual American Catholics, e.g., Kwitchin, Pahorezki, Schroll, and Cronin (Nos. 639, 662, 671, 702).

1188. Abell, Aaron I., ed. *American Catholic Thought on Social Questions.* Indianapolis: Bobbs-Merrill. 1968. This posthumously published anthology of thirty-nine substantial documents dating from the 1850's to the 1960's, each with its own introduction in addition to the general introduction, bibliography, and index, is especially useful for teaching and ready reference.

1189. Abell, Aaron I. *American Catholicism and Social Action: A Search for Social Justice, 1865–1950.* Garden City, N.Y.: Hanover. 1960. Paperback edition. Notre Dame: University of Notre Dame Press. 1963. A well-documented account by a specialist in American social history; an essay on the sources and an adequate index.

1190. Amberg, Mary Agnes. *Madonna Center: Pioneer Catholic Social Settlement.* Chicago: Loyola University Press. 1976. Written between 1940 and 1942 and based largely on personal recollections and newspaper clippings, this chronicle of a social settlement founded for the Italians in Chicago in 1898 makes no pretense at scholarship.

1191. Betten, Neil. *Catholic Activism and the Industrial Worker.* Gainesville: University Presses of Florida. 1976. On the basis of considerable research in both periodicals and manuscripts, the author studies not only the influence of Catholic radicalism on the labor movement but also the impact of bishops, priests, laymen, and organizations on unionism from 1920 to the late 1940's.

1192. Bland, Joan, Sister, S.N.D. *Hibernian Crusade: The Story of the Catholic Total Abstinence Union of America.* Washington, D.C.: Catholic University of America Press. 1951. A Ph.D. thesis that handles an important phase of nineteenth-century Catholic reform effort in an imaginative and competent manner.

1193.   Brokhage, Joseph D. *Francis Patrick Kenrick's Opinion on Slavery*. Washington, D.C.: Catholic University of America Press. 1955. After an introductory survey of the teaching of Catholic theologians on the morality of slavery, this S.T.D. thesis concentrates on the works of the leading American Catholic theologian of the 1840's and 1850's; the author concludes that Kenrick's views, based largely on European traditionalists, were of little help in solving the problem of slavery in this country.

1194.   Brophy, Mary Liguori, Sister. *The Social Thought of the German Roman Catholic Central Verein*. Washington, D.C.: Catholic University of America Press. 1941. A Ph.D. thesis in sociology that analyzes the social thought of one of the most progressive groups among nineteenth-century American Catholics; includes a chapter on the organization's history from 1855 to World War I.

1195.   Browne, Henry J. *The Catholic Church and the Knights of Labor*. Washington, D.C.: Catholic University of America Press. 1949. Reprint. New York: Arno. 1976. Based upon unpublished materials in both the Powderly Papers and ecclesiastical archives, this Ph.D. thesis is an intensive study that concentrates on the relations of the Church to the American labor movement during the critical 1880's.

1196.   Caravaglios, Maria Genoino. *The American Catholic Church and the Negro Problem in the XVIII-XIX Centuries*. Rome: The Author. 1974. Employing a dubious methodology, lacking clear organization, containing much extraneous material, misunderstanding the mentality of nineteenth-century American Catholics, and viewing isolated incidents or documents without proper perspective, this Italian doctoral dissertation adds little to knowledge of the subject. The long appendix consists of Roman documents, some translated into English, most from the 1860's.

1197.   Cornell, Thomas C., and James H. Forest, eds. *A Penny a Copy: Readings from the Catholic Worker*. New York: Macmillan. 1968. The editors have collected editorials and articles spanning the years 1933–1966 and illustrating the movement's social concerns, but they have not provided introductions, annotations, explanations, or even an index.

1198.   Cross, Robert D. *The Emergence of Liberal Catholicism in*

America. Cambridge, Mass.: Harvard University Press. 1958. Quadrangle paperback edition: 1968. Originally a Ph.D. thesis, this able monograph shows a thorough coverage of the printed literature on American Catholicism from c. 1880 to c. 1900; the interpretations and judgments are on the whole remarkably sound for a non-Catholic author; the final chapter on the Church in the twentieth century is the weakest part of the book. In the "second printing" factual and typographical errors have been corrected.

1199. Donohoe, Joan Marie, Sister, S.N.D. *The Irish Catholic Benevolent Union*. Washington, D.C.: Catholic University of America Press. 1953. A Ph.D. thesis that studies the impact of this first national organization of English-speaking American Catholic laymen on the social and political life of their coreligionists from 1869 to 1893; special emphasis is given to questions relating to the schools, immigration, and colonization.

1200. Gavin, Donald P. *The National Conference of Catholic Charities, 1910–1960*. Milwaukee: Bruce Press. 1962. This organizational history is well-planned and well-proportioned but it is sketched without the detail and documentation a critical study would require, controversies among the members are hardly treated, and much of the concomitant development in social work and welfare services is omitted or barely mentioned.

1201. Gleason, Philip. *The Conservative Reformers: German-American Catholics and the Social Order*. Notre Dame: University of Notre Dame Press. 1968. This masterly study of the assimilation and Americanization of a particular immigrant group, in terms of its conception and promotion of social reform, focuses on the German Catholic Central-Verein and its organ, the *Central-Blatt and Social Justice*, under the leadership of Frederick P. Kenkel in the first three decades of the twentieth century.

1202. Gudelunas, William A., Jr., and William G. Shade. *Before the Molly Maguires: The Emergence of the Ethno-Religious Factor in the Politics of the Lower Anthracite Region, 1844–1872*. New York: Arno. 1976. In this refinement of the doctoral dissertation that Gudelunas presented at Lehigh University in 1972, the authors argue that ethnic and religious loyalties outweighed economic and social concerns in determining voting patterns in Schuylkill County, Pennsylvania, as Irish Catholics and German Lutherans consistently supported the Democratic Party, which held power for most of the period without greatly improving its constituents' standard of living.

1203.   McColgan, Daniel T. *A Century of Charity: The First One Hundred Years of the Society of St. Vincent de Paul in the United States.* 2 vols. Milwaukee: Bruce. 1951. One of the few works of a thorough character in the history of organized charity among the American Catholics.

1204.   Macdonald, Fergus. *The Catholic Church and the Secret Societies in the United States.* New York: United States Catholic Historical Society. 1946. A careful A.M. thesis that carries the story down to the end of the nineteenth century; based upon archival sources.

1205.   McQuade, Vincent A., O.S.A. *The American Catholic Attitude on Child Labor since 1891: A Study of the Formation and Development of a Catholic Attitude on a Specific Social Question.* Washington, D.C.: Catholic University of America Press. 1938. This Ph.D. dissertation in sociology, based chiefly on Catholic periodical literature, was occasioned by the proposed amendment to the federal Constitution on which Catholics disagreed among themselves.

1206.   Mueller, Franz H. *Kirche und Industrialisierung: Sozialer Katholizismus in den Vereinigten Staaten und in Deutschland bis zu Pius XII.* Osnabrück: Verlag A. Fromm. 1971. This slightly shortened and revised (but not brought up to date in bibliography) version of the same author's essay in *The Challenge of Mater et Magistra* (ed. Joseph N. Moody and Justus George Lawler, 1963) provides a useful comparison between German and American Catholic social thought.

1207.   Nuesse, Celestine J. *The Social Thought of American Catholics, 1634–1829.* Washington, D.C.: Catholic University of America Press. 1945. A superior Ph.D. thesis in sociology; one of the few competent monographs in the field of American Catholic intellectual history.

1208.   O'Brien, David J. *American Catholics and Social Reform: The New Deal Years.* New York: Oxford University Press. 1968. Based on their published writings, this revised doctoral dissertation from the University of Rochester studies with discernment the manner in which American Catholics in the 1930's interpreted and applied the social teachings of the Church to the problems created by the Great Depression, devoting particular attention to communism, organized labor, John A. Ryan and the Social Action Department of the National Catholic Welfare Conference, Father Charles Coughlin, and the Catholic Worker movement.

1209.   O'Dea, Thomas F. *The Catholic Crisis.* Boston: Beacon. 1968. A sociologist's analysis of the causes of the crisis within the Church of the United States in the 1960's.

1210.   O'Grady, John. *Catholic Charities in the United States: History and Problems.* Washington, D.C.: National Conference of Catholic Charities. 1930. Reprint. New York: Arno. 1971. A semipopular work with bibliography and index by the secretary of the NCCC; now somewhat out of date, but the only general treatment of the subject.

1211.   Rice, Madeleine Hooke. *American Catholic Opinion in the Slavery Controversy.* New York: Columbia University Press. 1944. By a careful coverage of available sources—mostly in print—and a judicious and well-balanced interpretation, this Ph.D. thesis gives about as satisfactory a general account of the subject as we shall have until more archival sources are brought to light.

1212.   Roohan, James Edmund. *American Catholics and the Social Question, 1865–1900.* New York: Arno. 1976. This dissertation on the gradual development of the church leaders' consciousness of the need for change in the economic system and of their involvement in the labor strife of the period was accepted by Yale University in 1952, and is here reproduced from the original typescript. It is based largely on printed sources and has long since been superseded by more detailed studies on many particular topics.

1213.   Shanahan, Robert J., S.J. *The History of the Catholic Hospital Association, 1915–1965: Fifty Years of Progress.* St. Louis: Catholic Hospital Association. 1965. This substantial study, the first half of which was written as a doctoral dissertation in history at Saint Louis University, deals not only with the organizational development of the association but also with related topics such as nursing service and education, hospital standardization and administration, federal legislation and religious problems, and relations with other national Catholic bodies. It lacks references to secondary sources, a bibliography, and an index.

1214.   Ward, Leo R., C.S.C., ed. *The American Apostolate: American Catholics in the Twentieth Century.* Westminster, Md.: Newman. 1952. A symposium of eighteen essays of a popular or semipopular nature by as many authors on a wide variety of subjects, including social action, the press, the liturgy, organized charity, rural life, art, apologetic methods, and the N.C.W.C.

1215.   Witte, Raymond Philip, S.M. *Twenty-five Years of Crusading: A History of the National Catholic Rural Life Conference.* Des Moines: National Catholic Rural Life Conference. 1948. Based on official records, publications, and the written and oral testimony of contemporaries, this account of the origins, activities, and achievements of the organization is more triumphalistic than critical.

1216.   Yzermans, Vincent A. *With Courage and Hope: The Catholic Aid Association, 1878–1978.* St. Paul, Minn.: Catholic Aid Association. 1978. This brief centennial history traces the development of a German Catholic fraternal society into an effective instrument for the promotion of social justice and of educational, missionary, and charitable undertakings in Minnesota and the Dakotas.

VIII. PERIODICALS

OF THE TWENTY-SIX PERIODICALS listed below, only thirteen are strictly historical in character, and of these nine have long since ceased publication. These figures tell their own story concerning the fate of historical journals among American Catholics. In addition to those listed, attention is called to the periodicals published by various state historical societies wherein material may often be found that is useful to American Catholic history. In this sense the student will also wish to consult the leading journals of a wider scope such as the *American Historical Review*, the *Hispanic American Historical Review*, and the *Journal of American History*.

1217. *Acta et Dicta*, St. Paul, July, 1907–July, 1910; July, 1915–July, 1918; October, 1933–October, 1935. An annual volume dealing with the history of the Church in the Province of St. Paul; discontinued after 1935.

1218. *American Catholic Historical Researches*, Philadelphia, 1884–1913. This publication began originally under the editorship of Andrew A. Lambing (1842–1918) and continued through the issue of April, 1884, as *Historical Researches in Western Pennsylvania*, serving as an organ of the Ohio Valley Catholic Historical Society; in July, 1885, the name changed to *Catholic Historical Researches*, which continued through the issue of October, 1886; with the January, 1887 number, it came under the editorship of Martin I. J. Griffin (1842–1911) and remained a more or less private enterprise until his death; a new series was begun in 1905, and in 1913 the publication was merged with the *Records* (No. 1236); a general index published in 1916 covers Volumes I–XXIX (July, 1884–July, 1912); chiefly of value for the reprinting of documents not easily found elsewhere; unsystematic in its earlier years, and materials on the Church in Pennsylvania predominate throughout.

1219. *American Catholic Quarterly Review*, Philadelphia, 1876–1924. Earlier volumes have importance for articles by prominent Catholics which are now primary sources on these men, e.g., James A. Corcoran (1820–1889), the editor and a leading theologian; Patrick N. Lynch (1817–1882), third Bishop of Charleston; John Gilmary Shea (1824–1892), the church historian, etc.; articles are popular or semipopular in character and on a variety of subjects; valuable for the lines of American Catholic thought on current questions; it came to an end with Volume XLIX (April, 1924); there is a general index for Volumes I–XXV (January, 1876–October, 1900).

1220. *American Ecclesiastical Review*, Philadelphia, 1889–1944; Washington, D.C., 1944–1975. A monthly journal for the clergy, containing some historical articles, reprints of papal documents, and discussion of theological questions; two volumes per year; now discontinued; principally of use to historians as a medium for tracing theological thought among American Catholic writers; general indices published for Volumes I–C (1889–1931), and Volumes CI–CXXX (1939–1954).

1221. *The Americas*, Washington, D.C.: 1944– . This scholarly quarterly of the Academy of American Franciscan History is devoted to the history of the western hemisphere; of value to historians of American Catholicism for occasional articles, documents, and reviews on the colonial history of the Spanish borderlands.

1222. *Ave Maria*, Notre Dame, 1865–1968. A popular weekly (later biweekly) magazine of use for the history of devotional practices among American Catholics and for occasional historical contributions embodying materials from the manuscript collections of the University of Notre Dame; now discontinued.

1223. *Brownson's Quarterly*, New York, 1844–1875. This journal— suspended during 1865–1872—is especially good for the literature on controversial questions then before the American Catholic community; of prime importance for Orestes Brownson (1803–1876), the editor, who often wrote most of a single issue.

1224. *Catholic Historical Review*, Washington, D.C., 1915– . The first six volumes of this quarterly (1915–1920) were devoted exclusively to the history of the Church in the United States, the ones since then to the universal Church; a general index covering Volumes I–XX (1915–1935), compiled by Harold J. Bolton, was published in 1938; another general index, covering Volumes XXI–L (1935–1965), compiled by Edward J. Heiss, was published in 1969; the *Review* is the best historical journal published under American Catholic auspices.

1225. *Catholic Univeristy Bulletin*, Washington, D.C., 1895–1928. In its early years this quarterly contained many learned articles on various subjects; good for the historian of intellectual trends among American Catholics; absorbed in April, 1898, by the *Catholic University Chronicle* and continued to 1928 in thirty-four volumes; a general index published for Volumes I–XIII (1895–1907); resumed publication in November, 1932, but in an entirely altered form as a magazine of general circulation to acquaint readers with developments at the Catholic University of America.

1226. *Catholic World*, New York, 1865– . The first issue of this monthly magazine appeared in April, 1865, with the convert John R. G. Hassard (1836–1888) as editor and under the general supervision of Isaac T. Hecker, C.S.P. (1819–1888), founder of the Paulist Fathers; earlier volumes are especially useful to historians for contributions of leading American Catholics and for the thought patterns of the period.

1227. *Globe Review*, Philadelphia, October, 1889–Winter, 1905. This lively magazine, edited by a convert, William Henry Thorne (1839–1907), appeared ordinarily about four times a year through its fourteen volumes; Thorne was violently hostile to the so-called liberals and Americanists among the Catholics of the late nineteenth century.

1228. *Historical Bulletin*, St. Louis, 1922–1957. A quarterly for teachers and students of history edited by the Jesuits of St. Louis University; contained brief revisionist articles from time to time and annual listing of publications in American Catholic history; absorbed by *Manuscripta* in February, 1957, in its thirty-fifth volume.

1229. *Historical Records and Studies*, New York, 1899–1964. An annual volume published by the United States Catholic Historical Society; contents both popular and scholarly, and in later years it contained some good research articles; an index for Volumes I–X (January, 1899–January, 1917) appears in the issue of December, 1917 (XI, 141–171).

1230. *Homiletic and Pastoral Review*, New York, 1899– . A monthly magazine intended principally for the clergy; of use to historians as indicating trends in theological controversies; name changed from *Homiletic Monthly and Catechist* in the issue of October, 1920.

1231.   *Illinois Catholic Historical Review*, Chicago, 1918–1929. In this quarterly, articles and source materials on the colonial era predominated, with emphasis on the Middle West; the journal passed into the hands of Loyola University, Chicago, with the issue of July, 1929, and was renamed *Mid-America* (No. 1234).

1232.   *Iowa Catholic Historical Review*, Dubuque, 1930–1936. Nine issues of this slender publication appeared at irregular intervals between January, 1930, and February, 1936; suspended since that date.

1233.   *Maine Catholic Historical Magazine*, Waterville, 1913–1916. This publication, containing for the most part popular articles, began as a monthly and continued as such up to July, 1916, when it became a quarterly; ceased publication soon thereafter.

1234.   *Mid-America*, Chicago, 1929– . A quarterly published at Loyola University and in the early decades devoted principally to the Middle West; in recent years most of the articles have dealt with American secular history and very few with religious history.

1235.   *New York Review: A Journal of the Ancient Faith and Modern Thought*, New York, 1905–1908. Edited at St. Joseph's Seminary, Dunwoodie, this quarterly was one of the most learned reviews ever undertaken under American Catholic auspices; of interest to historians for the handling of current theological questions; suspended with the issue of July, 1908, and generally regarded as one of the casualties of the Modernist movement; see DeVito (No. 1061).

1236.   *Records of the American Catholic Historical Society of Philadelphia*, Philadelphia, 1887– . The earlier issues of this quarterly contain many worthwhile articles and are especially valuable for the publication of source materials; a general index was published for Volumes I–XXXI covering the years 1886–1920; for some years the articles were more popular in style and were restricted more closely to Philadelphia Catholic history; in recent years the articles have ranged over the entire country and even beyond its borders; lately it has in effect become an annual.

1237.   *Review of Politics*, Notre Dame, 1939– . Although the principal concern of this able quarterly is political science, it carries from time to time articles and reviews of value to historians of the American Church.

1238. *Sacred Heart Review*, East Cambridge, Mass., 1888–1918. A weekly founded and edited by John O'Brien (1838–1917), pastor of Sacred Heart Church; attracted some leading contributors and was vigorous and forthright in style; for many years it was one of the most widely read and frequently quoted Catholic organs in the country.

1239. *St. Louis Catholic Historical Review*, St. Louis: 1918–1923. This quarterly was a valuable medium for the publication of important source materials; discontinued after the issue of July, 1923.

1240. *Social Justice Review*, St. Louis, 1908– . This monthly magazine, first called *Central-Blatt and Social Justice*, is the official organ of the Catholic Central-Verein and is of value for indicating the social thought of American Catholics of German extraction.

1241. *Theological Studies*, Woodstock, Md., 1940– . A learned quarterly edited as a cooperative enterprise by the Jesuit theological faculties of the United States; excellent for American Catholic theological opinion, as well as for occasional articles and reviews in the history of the Church of this country. Now published in Washington, D.C.

1242. *United States Catholic Historical Magazine*, New York, 1887–1892. The official quarterly of the United States Catholic Historical Society of New York until the death of John Gilmary Shea in 1892; contained notes, brief and uncritical articles; chiefly of value for the documents printed; each volume had its own index; lapsed after Volume IV and was succeeded in 1899 by the society's *Historical Records and Studies* (No. 1229).

IX. HISTORICAL SOCIETIES

1243. Academy of American Franciscan History, founded in April, 1944, at Washington, D.C., by the provinces of the Friars Minor in the United States. Official organ is *The Americas* (No. 1221), a quarterly that began publication in July, 1944. The Academy also publishes a "Documentary Series," a "Monograph Series," a "Bibliographical Series," "Franciscan Historical Classics," "Miscellaneous," and a calendar of American documents in the Propaganda Fide Archives (No. 17).

1244. American Catholic Historical Association, founded in December, 1919, at Cleveland, by Peter Guilday, et al. Official organ is the *Catholic Historical Review* (No. 1224). The association holds an annual three-day meeting in Christmas week of each year at the same time and place as the annual meetings of the American Historical Association and other national historical societies. It also holds a meeting each spring at some Catholic university or college. Besides the quarterly journal, the association has published three volumes of papers read at annual meetings and two volumes of documents (Nos. 1112, 1113), and has sponsored the collection and editing of the papers of John Carroll (1735–1815), first Archbishop of Baltimore, as a project affiliated with the National Historical Publications Commission (No. 480). In 1944 the Association instituted the annual John Gilmary Shea Prize for a volume on the history of the Catholic Church, broadly considered, awarded in those years when the committee feels a work worthy of the prize has been published. It also awards the Howard R. Marraro Prize annually for a work on Italian history or Italo-American history or relations. A Committee on the History of American Catholicism has been active for several years.

1245. American Catholic Historical Society of Philadelphia, founded in July, 1884. The chief publication has been the *Records* (No. 1236). The society holds meetings at irregular intervals at its Philadelphia headquarters; the extensive newspaper collection, archives, and library of the society are housed at St. Charles Seminary, Overbrook, Philadelphia.

1246. Catholic Historical Society of Indiana, founded in October, 1926, at Indianapolis. Only one small *Bulletin* was ever published; the society has remained largely inactive.

1247. Catholic Historical Society of St. Louis, founded in February, 1917, at St. Louis. Published the *St. Louis Catholic Historical Review* (No. 1239) from October, 1918, to July, 1923, when the society's activities ended.

1248. Catholic Historical Society of St. Paul, founded in April, 1905, at St. Paul. Published an annual volume entitled *Acta et Dicta* (No. 1217) between 1907–1918 with a gap for 1911–1914; the society was dormant from 1918 to 1933, was then reorganized and the *Acta et Dicta* revived, but it again became inactive after 1935.

1249. Catholic Historical Society of Wisconsin, founded in April, 1959, at Ashland. Likewise failed to survive.

1250. Illinois Catholic Historical Society, founded in February, 1918, at Chicago. Published a quarterly journal, the *Illinois Catholic Historical Review* (No. 1231) from 1918 to 1929, after which the society ceased to function.

1251. Iowa Catholic Historical Society, founded in March, 1928, at Dubuque. Its first publication, *Collections* (Dubuque, 1929), was begun in 1929 with a booklet, "The Catholic Sponsors of Iowa," by Mathias M. Hoffman, and was discontinued after the second number, "Saint Peter's Parish, Keokuk, Iowa." In 1930 the first issue of the *Iowa Catholic Historical Review* appeared, and continued at irregular intervals until 1936 when it ceased publication.

1252. Kansas Catholic Historical Society, founded in 1930, at Atchison. Headquarters of the society are at St. Benedict's College, where a collection of materials for Kansas Catholic history was assembled; no publications to date; for a general description of the society's collection see Beckman (No. 108), p. 158.

1253. Long Island Catholic Historical Society, founded in February, 1892, by Marc F. Vallette and George E. O'Hara. In 1894 the name was changed to the Brooklyn Catholic Historical Society, which published one volume of *Records* in 1901; the society failed to meet after that date.

1254. Maine Catholic Historical Society, founded in 1913, at Portland. Published the *Maine Catholic Historical Magazine* (No. 1233), first as a monthly and later as a quarterly; discontinued entirely c. 1929.

1255.   New England Catholic Historical Society, founded in June, 1900, at Boston, by William Byrne. Eight brief brochures under the title of *Publications* appeared up to 1908, after which the society disbanded.

1256.   Ohio Valley Catholic Historical Society, founded in February, 1884, at Pittsburgh, by Andrew A. Lambing. In July, 1884, Lambing began publication of the *Historical Researches in Western Pennsylvania* under the society's auspices; for the sequel to this publication see *American Catholic Historical Researches* (No. 1218). The activities of this group were later carried on under the name of the Catholic Historical Society of Western Pennsylvania.

1257.   Texas Catholic Historical Society, founded in 1926, at Austin, by Paul J. Foik, C.S.C. Established as an auxiliary to the Texas Knights of Columbus Historical Commission, which had been founded in May, 1923, with headquarters at St. Edward's University; met semiannually for many years and published quarterly *Preliminary Studies*; the commission originally set up to sponsor the writing of the Catholic history of Texas by Castañeda (No. 123). After a dormant period, it was revived in 1976.

1258.   United States Catholic Historical Society, founded in December, 1884, at New York, by John Gilmary Shea, et al. Published *Proceedings* (1885–1887) and then the *United States Catholic Historical Magazine* (1887–1892) (No. 1242); from 1893 to 1897 the society was dormant; in 1899 it began publishing an annual volume, *Historical Records and Studies*, discontinued after 1964 (No. 1229); since 1903 the society has published thirty-five volumes in its monograph series; a meeting held normally on an evening in November of each year.

NOTE: Most of the societies listed above held quarterly, semiannual, or annual meetings during their active years, where papers on various phases of the Catholic history of their respective areas were read. On the useful function that can be performed by groups of this kind, see the views of a non-Catholic scholar, Waldo G. Leland, "Concerning Catholic Historical Societies," *Catholic Historical Review*, II (January, 1917), 386–399.

Index

THE NUMBERS indicated refer to the numbered entries of the bibliography. The material is indexed by author, title, and subject.

Copyedited by Cecelia A. Albert and Grace Holsinger
Composed in VIP Janson by McAdams Type of Santa Barbara
Printed and bound by BookCrafters of Chelsea, Michigan
Designed by Tom Reeg

Date Due